NEVER TELL ANYONE YOU'RE JEWISH

D1388513

In memory of my parents, Artur and Jadwiga

NEVER TELL ANYONE YOU'RE JEWISH

My Family, the Holocaust and the Aftermath

MARIA CHAMBERLAIN

VALLENTINE MITCHELL
LONDON • CHICAGO

First published in 2022 by Vallentine Mitchell

Catalyst House,
720 Centennial Court,
Centennial Park, Elstree WD6 3SY, UK

814 N. Franklin Street,
Chicago, Illinois,
60610 USA

www.vmbooks.com

British Library Cataloguing in Publication Data:
An entry can be found on request

ISBN 978 1 80371 014 3 (Paper)
ISBN 978 1 80371 015 0 (Ebook)
ISBN 978 1 80371 016 7 (Kindle)

Library of Congress Cataloging in Publication Data:
An entry can be found on request

Contents

Acknowledgements

I always knew that this book had to be written, but the process took several years with numerous lengthy stops and starts. I am indebted to my family and many friends for their interest and encouragement to start, but more importantly to finish the project. My son Martin was the first to read chunks of the initial draft and I am indebted to him for applying his judicial hatchet to over-wordy passages, while believing that the task was doable and worth doing. My husband, David, provided instantaneous comment when I read the text aloud to him as it was being written. My teenage grandchildren, Amy, Evie and Freddie listened spell-bound, while I told them a few dumbed-down versions of the stories. Amy, who was nine when my mother died, distilled some of the 'story fragments' into her dresses (see page 225).

In the earlier stages of the writing, I was grateful for the advice of the 'Stranger than Fiction' group of non-fiction authors, who met monthly in a central Edinburgh pub. 'Put more of yourself' into the book was the general advice they offered. I thank Professor Jonathan Silverton for introducing me to them.

I have many friends to thank for encouragement and editorial help. I would like to single out a few. Kirstie Taylor, the daughter of my father's friend, Bill Taylor, was the most amazing editor (it had to be in hard copy as she does not 'do' computers). Kirstie, who has known my family since her birth and called my father 'Uncle Arthur', had been brought up on my family's Holocaust stories. Her help with tone and logic was therefore invaluable. I am particularly indebted to my friend Marcia Rodriguez who during a socially distanced walk at the beginning of the first lockdown encouraged me dig out the files from the back of the hard drive. 'If not now, when?', she said, 'You will never again have so much time.' Gillean Somerville-Arjat read the chapters as they were completed, and her valuable comments and encouragements made me go on until a structure began to take shape.

I am grateful to Olenka Frenkiel for making available to me her father's unpublished memoirs, and to Professor Melissa Aronczyk, the grand-daughter of my father's death-march companion, Bernard Aronczyk, for the valuable bundle of post-war correspondence between them.

While our son Martin, husband David, and friends Kirstie, Marcia and Gillean have each read most of the text, other friends were sent parts of the manuscript for factual checking and comment. Valerie, John and Daniel McClean were sent the bits about looted Nazi art; Dr Henry Noltie commented on the chapter about Jakub; my childhood friend, Adam Rutkowski, replied to the chapter 'After the War' with several photographs which I had not seen; my cousin, Igor Opoczyński, corrected the chapter about Aleksander Bieberstein; my friend Ewa Kalina provided interesting vignettes about my Uncle Ludwik and Aunt Jasia; Professor Paul Broda, Sue Lieberman, Grazyna Cydzik and Ewa Sharwood-Smith read and commented on the Prologue.

In the process of the research, I sought the advice of several Holocaust historians. I thank the genealogist, Geoffrey Weisgard, who enthusiastically provided me with lots of excellent starter references. I am particularly grateful to Professor Trevor Royle, who through lockdown read most of my manuscript and offered the much-needed encouragement. I also thank Professor Dan Stone of the Royal Holloway, who commented on the sub-chapter on the death marches, Professor Evgeny Finkel of John Hopkins University who answered questions on matters pertaining to the Kraków *Judenrat*, and Martyna Grądzka of the Warsaw Ghetto Museum for information about the Kraków orphanages.

I am hugely grateful to my friend, Dr Chris Jeffree, for re-photographing most of the images to maximise their resolution. I thank Andy Quinn of Emma Quinn Design for his map of the death march route (page 84) and redrawing the map of Belzec (page 162) so that it is acceptable in greyscale.

Other friends and relatives contributed their expertise and interest. I am grateful to my friends Dr Patricia and Professor Angus Macdonald for their sharp logic and visual sense, Katherine Steinhardt and Kate Miller of kate-miller.com. for artistic input, my Polish cousin Lucjan Wroński and his son Jan for archival material and unobtainable books, and my Israeli cousin Talia Mor for precious family photographs. I thank Ewa Sharwood-Smith for translating some tricky Polish passages and to Grażyna Bielecka for transcribing illegible Polish handwritten letters into perfectly legible ones, a task that she undertook through lockdown and claims to have enjoyed.

I am grateful to the United States Holocaust Memorial Museum and also Yad Vashem for allowing me free access to their image collection and for sending me high resolution versions of those that I selected, and to Chris Webb, author and historian, for several images from his private archive.

The team at Vallentine Mitchell have been a pleasure to work with. I thank Toby Harris for his instant email replies, my editor Lisa Hyde and designer Jenni Tinson for their forbearance while I change my mind, and I thank the mysterious 'reader' who gave the work a thumbs-up while noticing a dearth of umlauts.

Lastly, I would like to thank my husband David for his emotional support throughout.

Prologue

'Memory is no use to the remembered, only to those who remember. We build ourselves with memory and console ourselves with memory.'
Laurent Binet[1]

'At last, we are finally free', said my mother, 'but you must never, ever tell anyone you are Jewish'. I leaned over the rail of the cross-channel ferry that was bringing us to England. In the churning waters, a piece of detached seaweed danced, turned, and then floated past. I remember feeling like that seaweed – infinitesimal, uprooted, adrift. And how Jewish were we? Not very, to my mind, though somehow Hitler must have known we were. I blinked away the tears and cheered myself up by thinking of the three things I had been looking forward to: seeing my uncle, eating a banana and watching television. When I left Poland the day before, my best friend, Joanna, had wrapped her hands round my neck and asked me to send her a doll with eyes that opened and closed. I determined to go shopping right away and started to compose a letter to her about our journey and about the England I had not yet seen.

My parents, Artur and Jadwiga, have now died, but they gave me permission to 'tell', while at the same time reminding me that they preferred to be remembered for their achievements, not by their Holocaust experiences. They buried themselves in their world of work, first in Kraków, and later in Edinburgh. Both were scientists. My father was a geneticist, instrumental in uncovering the effect of Thalidomide on embryo development. He gained modest success in his field, becoming an honorary citizen of the state of Tennessee and a Fellow of the Royal Society of Edinburgh. My mother was a clinical chemist, who worked on the role of cholesterol in heart disease.

When I was growing up my parents were not yet part of history, they were just two exasperating, difficult, domineering people, totally incompatible with each other and not entirely comfortable in my world. When I was an adult, I pursued the usual adult goals of work and motherhood and was too wrapped up in the present to look to the past.

Now the time has come to probe, too late to ask questions, but not too early to be able to make use of the rich resources available in hard copy and online. It is only now that interesting connections between people and events can be discovered. The research I have undertaken over the last few years has been an obsessive, harrowing, spiritual journey back into a toxic world, with 'the restless dead asserting their claims', as Hilary Mantel put it: 'they have something to tell us, something we need to understand'.

My parents rarely spoke of the torments they have suffered, and neither left any substantial published testimony. They talked about these things from time to time, when something triggered a memory, but sparingly because deep revelations upset their physical health and peace of mind. Yet now I cherish each vignette as I try to reconstruct their world. When I was growing up, I gleaned fragments of these stories but not the chronology of their lives, nor the historical context in which they unfolded. Now in retirement, I have time to remember, assess, analyse. To piece the fragments together, I have used the letters they wrote to each other, and to their friends, scraps of my mother's memoirs, letters that each of them wrote (separately) in attempts to obtain reparations, my father's witness statement at Amon Göth's trial in Kraków and numerous published and unpublished accounts of friends and extended family.

The first time my father publicly recounted his experiences since the trial of Amon Göth was in an article in *The Scotsman* in 1995[2] on the fiftieth anniversary of the liberation of Auschwitz. For my mother, this public 'coming out' was a source of acute embarrassment. She had been hiding her Jewishness, albeit rather unsuccessfully, from her Polish friends.

My mother tried on several occasions to put things down on paper. Once I gave her a primitive laptop. She got as far as her mother's death, when she slammed down the lid and lost it all. On another occasion, she wrote in longhand, but somehow her biro ran out of ink at just the same point. Over the past few years, I have read almost every book and online resource which touches on Kraków, Płaszów, Lwów, Warsaw and the death marches. I have made use of the comprehensive resources of the Wiener Library in London and the National Library of Scotland in Edinburgh. Throughout this process, I have so wished that my parents were here to answer my questions. I wished I had listened more intently on the rare occasions when they were willing to talk. I regret now that I never managed to record their oral testimonies. I did think about it, and my son Tim even bought my mother a machine for this very purpose, but somehow I never set it up, partly out of fear that it might bring on nightmares or angina attacks.

Since I started the research for this book, I discovered many second generation memoirs, the most memorable of which are: Philippe Sands' masterly *East West Street*,[3] inspired by his family's destruction at the hands Hans Frank and Otto Wächter (who between them were also responsible for the demise of several members of my own family), Rita Goldberg's *Motherland*,[4] about her mother's experiences in the Terezin and her father's colourful life in war-torn Europe and Israel, Göran Rosenberg's excellent prose poem to his father, *A Brief Stop on the Road from Auschwitz*,[5] written, like this book, in the author's retirement. All these memoirs have had the same effect on their writers that this is having on me: a setting down of a burden and as well as reconciliation with the past. Hadley Freeman, who is in effect third generation, spoke about her need to set it down in her book *A House of Glass*;[6] for her it was not an option, it simply had to be done.

Some parts of my family's story are unique; others corroborate well known Holocaust history. Corroboration is important, because events of history should be seen through many lenses, and besides not everybody is well informed. Holocaust denial, although thankfully a minority pursuit, is not unlawful in the UK – unlike in most European countries and the US. It can be seen here on Twitter every day. Denialist and antisemitic tropes are hurled at Jewish schoolchildren in London as though they should be held to account for the conflict in Israel. Speakers and pro-Palestinian militants on university and other public platforms loudly proclaim it in the name of free speech.

Although Holocaust education is part of the national curriculum compulsory in England, it is still not mandatory in Scotland. Even in England, the version they teach is minimised and sanitised, concentrating on life affirming topics like the *Kindertransport* or heroic resistance fighters. When I read Anne Frank's diary to my grandchildren, and they watched the film of the *Boy in the Striped Pyjamas*, they said, 'How sad', without realising the scale of the operation. I was recently outraged to find out that my granddaughter's GCSE history curriculum, while concentrating on the twentieth century, seems to have somehow missed out the Holocaust altogether.

In 2018, the Polish President Andrzej Duda signed into law a bill outlawing allegations of Polish complicity in the Holocaust. It is now unlawful for anyone, including teachers, journalists, and tour guides in Poland to bring to peoples' attention individual acts of antisemitism or collaboration. Under this law, Poland's innocence is protected and anyone who dares to question it risks jail. The premise is that it was the Germans, not the Poles, whose laws led to genocide; and Poles, none of whom ever participated in any collaborationist regime, must bear no responsibility. With the re-election of the Law and Justice party in 2020, Poland's 'historical policy offensive' continues. In April 2021 three members of the advisory council for the Auschwitz-Birkenau resigned, following the appointment of a right-wing politician to serve on the Council. Sanitising Poland's involvement in Nazi crimes deprives history of the unfortunate fact that neighbours can turn on neighbours, particularly when times are hard. To present it otherwise is to deny how easily this can happen – there and elsewhere.

'Being complacent about the past can have dark consequences', said Jo Ellison.[7] She also reminded us of the science of cliodynamics, the new trans-disciplinary area of research which aims to model long-term social processes mathematically. Peter Turchin,[8] its pioneer, detected that phases of mass destruction in human societies occur in predictable cycles. Tobias Stone[9] showed that these cycles occur in every other generation and suggested that this might be because our collective memory is limited to the experience communicated to us by the thread of direct memory from our parents and grandparents. If that is indeed so, there is a period of political instability and unrest due in the 2020s. It seems particularly expedient, therefore, to share the grit of my parents' and grandparents' stories with the next generation before the statute of limitations on the Holocaust runs out. Maybe we can extend the cycle a little, at least till after my grandchildren's generation have had their children.

In whole organism biological sciences, my professional discipline, we study the evolution of life on the planet. I am used to questions to which the evidence provides no clear answer. Historical research is like that too. Recollections are not always reliable; when the narratives from secondary and tertiary sources overlap with my parents' accounts, I have used them as confirmation. When they diverge, I cite the divergent accounts. I have explained my paternal grandfather's, Marek's, unenviable role in the early part of the German occupation based on my father's accounts and the testimonies of other survivors. When historical accounts have expressed criticism of him, I have exposed it, though I have tried – maybe subconsciously – to defend him by explaining the difficulty of his position.

One issue which has interested me as an observer from a distance of eighty years is what my parents knew or thought they knew at the time. Of course, we are now fully aware of the facts of history; the Holocaust happened, the war finally came to an end, and some of the perpetrators were tried for crimes against humanity and genocide. All my parents knew at the time was that the screws were tightening by degrees. Polish antisemitism started with snide remarks, turned to overt mockery, and then slid into unpunished murder. The occupier's edicts also came stepwise, starting with prohibitions in the uses of public amenities, then confiscation of radios, motor vehicles and property. They saw identification, enforced evacuation, then concentration in ghettos, the daily extermination of single individuals and the periodic deportations of masses, their friends among them. They got to know the terror of snarling dogs, barked commands, and shots. They did not think about the past or the future, just the horror of the present.

To start with, they would have thought optimistically that the deported, who had lost their jobs because of the wartime restrictions, were indeed being sent off to be resettled elsewhere where work was more plentiful. My father called the realisation that the deported did not come back his 'pivotal psychological moment'.

When I talk about the Holocaust, some of my friends remind me that 'my Holocaust' is one of many. There have been other genocides before and since then, they say, not least the one perpetrated by Stalin (my hero when I was growing up in communist Poland). Although the respective evils of Hitler, Stalin and Mao have been ranked and debated,[10] the fact that other mass murderers existed does not make my family's experiences any less significant. Besides, my mother was at one stage a prisoner of Stalin's cadres, and my aunt Jasia, who happened to be Catholic, was deported by them by cattle truck to Kazakhstan. Although I once believed in Stalin's ideology of 'all men are equal', which has left me with definite leanings to the political left, it has also left me with the knowledge of how easily people can be duped into following false beliefs. Of course, I do not now excuse Stalin, but nor do I pass judgement on the respective evilness of villains. As for other genocides, such as the ones in Bangladesh (1971), East Timor (1975-1999), Cambodia (1975-1979), Guatemala (1992-1995), Rwanda (1994), Srebrenica (1995), Darfur (2003-present), Nigeria (2002-present) and Syria (2018), I would urge anyone who has stories to tell about them to tell them now.

More recently, the perfidious ideology of ISIS has used vulnerable young men to kill innocents. In Iraq and Syria, these modern-day fascists daubed Christians' homes and businesses with the Arabic letter 'Nun', meaning Nazarene (a pejorative word for Christians). As I write this, Uyghurs are being annihilated in Xinjiang and Rohingya Muslims in Myanmar. But evils do not cancel each other out; the fact that these things still happen makes it more, not less, important to document all the atrocities of the past.

The book is divided into three sections: each with three or four chapters. Part I tells of my paternal side of the family; Part II deals with the maternal side of the family; Part III is entitled 'Living with the Past'.

Parts I and II are structured in the form of portraits. The chapter about my paternal grandfather, Marek, the first President of the Kraków Jewish Council, is based on my father's personal anecdotes backed up by the rich archival and internet sources which exist about him as a named individual. The short chapter on my great uncle Aleksander, whose testimonies helped Thomas Keneally visualise the scenes he portrayed in *Schindler's List*, is based on published accounts, but also precious conversations I had with him about his work as the ghetto doctor. The chapter on my father tells of his experiences in Jewish Self Help (JSS) in the Kraków Ghetto and Płaszów Labour Camp (later concentration camp), deportation to Flossenbürg, then Auschwitz and finally the gruelling 300 miles long death march. There is not much archival material relating to my mother and my maternal grandparents, but plenty about the dark places they inhabited and the evil that was perpetrated in them. The chapter on my mother describes her time in Lwów (now Lviv) under the Soviets (Lvov), then the Germans (Lemberg), her miraculous escape from the death train to Belzec, and her life in Warsaw and Berlin on false papers. These were the stuff of her nightmares. The chapter on my maternal grandfather, Alfred, tells how he survived by hiding in plain sight within the quasi-Nazi Organisation Todt.

Then there were those whose lives were unlived to their natural end. I never met my other three grandparents, nor my aunt Lula, whom I am supposed to resemble, nor the gifted pianist Kuba, my mother's cousin. Now, as a custodian of their extraordinary stories, I have finally got round to piecing together the fragments, filling in the gaps and adding a frame. I hope they would have approved.

Over the past few years my days and nights have been filled with ghosts of the victims and their perpetrators. But the process has brought a measure of resolution. It has at last allowed me to look upon my parents with awe. I feel so proud of the courage, nous and resilience that made their survival possible, albeit in different ways. Marcel Proust expresses what I feel almost exactly when he says: 'When we have passed a certain age, the soul of the child we were and the soul of the dead from whom we have sprung come to lavish on us their riches and their spells.'[11]

In Part III I enter the story. It follows our life in post-war Stalinist Poland until our emigration in 1958, and later our cultural transition to academic life in Edinburgh. I finish with a chapter on the effects of the trauma on my parents' post-war lives, even though they themselves would never have admitted to any such effects. My parents dealt with the traumas in very different, often diametrically opposite ways. I also address the effect of their experiences on me because these second-hand experiences have shaped me and my descendants and defined who we are.

Notes

1. Binet, L., *HHhH* (London: Vintage, 2013), chapter 150.
2. My father was interviewed by Thea Jourdan, a *Scotsman* journalist, published in *The Scotsman Magazine*, 26 January 1995.
3. Sands, P., *East West Street* (London: Weidenfeld and Nicholson,2016).
4. Goldberg, R., *Motherland* (London: Halban Publishers, 2014).
5. Rosenberg, G., *A Brief Stop on the Road from Auschwitz* (London: Granta Books, 2014).
6. Freeman, H., *House of Glass* (New York: Fourth Estate, 2021).
7. Jo Ellison, 'Why we forget the past at our peril', *Financial Times*, 9 February 2018.
8. Peter Turchin, 'Entering the Age of Instability after Trump', *Evonomics*, 17 November, 2016, retrieved from: http://evonomics.com/science-predicting-rise-fall-societies-turchin/ (accessed 23 May 2021).
9. Tobias Stone, 'History tells us what will happen with next Brexit and Trump', *Huffington Post*, 25 July 2016, retrieved from: https://www.huffingtonpost.com/tobias-stone/history-tells-us-what-will-brexit-trump_b_11179774.html (accessed 23 May 2021).
10. See for example Snyder, T.D., *Bloodlands; Europe Beween Hitler and Stalin* (New York: Basic Books, 2011).
11. Proust, M., *The Captive*, first published 1929, republished by CreateSpace Independent Publishing Platform, 2017.

PART I

The Biebersteins

1

Marek and Mila

'Without families you don't get stories.' Bart van Es[1]

Family Life

My paternal grandparents, Marek and Mila (Emilia) were born in 1880 and 1882 in Poland,[2] but then part of the Austro-Hungarian Empire. His name on the birth certificate is Mordhe Wolf Bieberstein, hers is Mirl Kaufler. Like many of the assimilated Jews of that generation they each had two or more different names, a Polish one, and a more official Jewish one. As far as I know neither was orthodox, but they followed the rites and rituals of Judaism, the main of which was to honour and sanctify family life. Did they meet each other and fall in love? Or were they introduced to one another by a matchmaker? I do not know, and I am not sure whether my father knew. In any case they grew up and met at the turn of the centuries, a golden time, politically, personally, and spiritually. Franz Joseph, the emperor of the Habsburg Empire, was tolerant of the Jews, and indeed all religions. Laws passed in 1849 prohibited antisemitism and conferred political and civil rights to all, so Marek and Mila felt free to practise their religion and traditions, while regarding Poland as their motherland and Polish as their language.

Unfortunately, Franz Joseph's benign reign ended when in 1914 he led the world into the First World War. As far as I know Marek never served in the war, which started in the first few months of my father's life, but his brother Aleksander did. The photo below shows the two brothers, Marek with his handle-bar moustache, smartly dressed for the photograph, and his younger brother Aleksander, who later became a doctor, resplendent in his Austro-Hungarian military uniform. It is sad to think that the joy, hope and the love of life which shone from my grandfather's young face, was so brutally extinguished three decades later. Sadly, I never knew my grandfather, but Aleksander (or Uncle Zyś, as I called him) was a constant presence in my early years in Poland. Later he made his home in Israel. I visited him there in 1967 and listened to his reminiscences. His collected memories were published posthumously in his definitive book on the destruction of Kraków's Jews.[3]

After their wedding in 1908, my grandparents made their home in Podgórze,[4] currently a district of Kraków, but then an ancient town in its own right. The name means literally 'under-the-hill' and the hill in question is the famous pre-historic man-made mound, thought to be the mythical resting place of Krakus, the legendary founder of Kraków. For present day visitors Kazimierz is promoted as the Jewish district, but in my grandparents' day accommodation there would have been expensive and occupied by long-established, mainly orthodox families. Podgórze, to the South of the river Wisła (Vistula), was a more affordable Jewish working-class suburb.

Kraków was then about a quarter Jewish, but Jews represented more than half of the city's doctors, lawyers, architects, musicians, and artists. In the inter-war years waves of antisemitic hatred swept through the city and the country, the swell of the wave depending on who was in power. Between 1918 and 1926 the antisemitic National Democrats (*Endecja*) ruled. Although officially the Treaty of Versailles demanded that Poland must offer citizenship rights to ethnic minorities, state-endorsed hooligans responded with pogroms, fists, and taunts. Then in 1926 the *Endeks'* toxic rule ended abruptly with a *coup d'état*, which saw the 'pro-Jewish' Josef Piłsudski installed as leader. Under him the pogroms ceased, and the waves subsided to mere ripples. Piłsudski was hugely welcomed by the Jewish population and deeply mourned when he died in 1935.

Marek and Mila had three children: Ludwik born 30.01.1910; Artur born 30.03.1914 and Lula born 16.11.1921. (Artur became my father.) The precious photo on page 13 shows the complete Bieberstein family assembled in their Shabbat best in Kraków, *c.* 1922. Of course, neither of my parents managed to save any family photos through the war, so you can imagine my father's delight when a few precious pre-war photos (pages 13, 15 and 17) surfaced several years later, sent by an Israeli cousin. My father's eyes scanned the family scene shown on page 13 eagerly, and then smiled. 'I remember, like it was yesterday,' he said. 'Ludwik got into a row for having stuffed something bulky into his breast pocket.' Then his eyes filled with tears.

The family spoke Polish, not Yiddish, at home. Marek also spoke fluent German, but it was Hebrew that my grandfather loved best. He would have impressed upon his children the beauty and the poetry of the Torah, while the weekly and annual rites of Judaism would have imposed on the family a sense of rhythm, security, and identity. Although my grandmother kept a kosher kitchen with different dishes for milk and meat, my father told me

Alexander and Marek Bieberstein (about 1908)

From left to right: Marek, my grandfather (aged 42), Ludwik (my uncle, aged 12), Lula (who would have been my aunt, aged 2), my grandmother (aged 40), and my father, Artur (aged 8)

that from time to time she brought home ham for the children. She would serve up the delicious juicy slices on the paper they were wrapped in, assuaging her guilt by keeping the plates kosher.

Marek had a deeply academic mind and loved teaching, a gift passed on to his son, my father, and I like to think also to me, his granddaughter. Hebrew was, moreover, a noble ancient language worthy of academic pursuit. He taught it going round Kraków schools, the Jewish Orphanage,[5] and at the Saturday school or *Cheder*, where boys would have been coached for their *Bar Mizvahs* (a sort of Jewish Communion). Various sources call him 'Dr' or 'Professor', although to my knowledge he never obtained a doctorate. 'Professor' is probably just a generic title given to senior teachers, but the 'Dr' reflects the esteem with which he was held.

In the mid-late 1930s Marek was a member of the Jewish Self-Help (JSS) committee (the *Presidium*) and the President of the Jewish Orphanage. Using his excellent contacts with the Jewish Community to good effect, he performed the role of care worker for the destitute and needy, providing soup kitchens, free medical care, accommodation, and interest-free loans. He performed these philanthropic deeds in addition to his day job of teaching Hebrew.

With Piłsudski's death in 1935, and under the pervading influence of the new Nuremberg laws, many Poles enthusiastically took up the Germans' antisemitic rhetoric. The anti-Jewish feeling amongst the Poles was made worse by the influx of thousands of Polish Jews from Austria following its annexation to Germany (*Anschluss*) in March 1938 and from Germany in October 1938. The numbers of Jews in Kraków swelled from 56,515 in 1931 to nearly 70,000 in the November of 1939.[6]

I am not actually surprised that the Poles felt threatened, when their independence, so hard won in the First World War, was fragile again. They were expecting an alliance between Russia, France, and Britain against Germany, and were disappointed when that never materialised. They were not at that time aware that on 23/24 August Stalin suddenly went into cahoots with Hitler, the two secretly overseeing the signing of the Molotov-Ribbentrop[7] pact of non-aggression, and that within weeks Poland would be erased from the map of Europe, its rivers serving as borders between the Germans and the Soviets. Nevertheless, in Kraków preparations went ahead for war. Trenches were dug in the *Planty* (a circular park round the centre of the city where the medieval walls had once stood), glass-fronted shops and windows criss-crossed with gummed paper, hide-outs were located.

My uncle Ludwik was the only one of the Bieberstein family who had the foresight to leave, just in the nick of time, a few days before the

Lula and Marek on their pre-war holidays. (1) Lula on a sledge c. 1927. (2) Lula with Marek at the seaside c. 1930. (3) Lula with Marek in winter c. 1933. These photographs, as also the ones on pages 13 and 17, were sent by my grandfather to their relatives in Israel.

German occupation. As a qualified doctor, he decided to try his luck in Hungary, which then seemed a less risky place to be. Indeed, Hungary was only occupied in 1944, by which time Ludwik had travelled half the world with the Anders' Army.[8] He survived the war, as I will tell in a separate chapter.

On 1 September 1939, the residents of Kraków were awakened in the morning by echoes of detonations, rattle of machine guns, smoke in the sky, and the distant drone of aeroplanes. Despite the ominous sounds, the news of the invasion had not yet percolated through, and there were lots of confused rumours going around. A few optimists thought it was just an army exercise, some thought that the Poles were fighting off the Germans and winning, others fearing imminent German bombardment, hid in basements. People listened to the radio, but there were no clear statements offered, only martial music and lists of Polish conquests.

On 3 September came the joyous news that Britain and France had declared war on Germany, so peoples' mood lifted, and everybody thought that the mighty West would surely rally quickly and save them. Their hopes were dashed on 4 September with the news that German troops were closing in. My great-uncle Aleksander heard the following words on the radio: 'The occupying forces do not consider the citizens of the country (Poland) as enemies. International laws will be adhered to and...Jews should feel secure about their fate.'[9] Possibly the messages of hope were just a ploy, to lull the Jews into passivity. Then two days later, on 6 September the Poles erected white flags of capitulation on Kraków's two hills, and the German occupation of the city began.

As the German soldiers marched in, they presented themselves as the good guys, offering sweets to the Polish children while being filmed for the World News. Many Poles welcomed them as fellow Jew-haters. Malvina Graf[10] in her excellent account of the life in Kraków, describes a street scene of a bearded Jew having his beard publicly shaved off to the raucous laughter of bystanders.

Marek Bieberstein, President of the Jewish Community

Within two days of the invasion (8 September), my grandfather, Marek Bieberstein, was ordered to lead the Jewish Community in Kraków, and instructed to establish a group which would act as the primary (and sole) source of communication with the German authorities. Local self-governing bodies known in Hebrew as *kehillot*, or in Polish as *gminy* had traditionally taken responsibilities for all community matters such as

Marek aged 56. The inscription of the other side reads: 'from Uncle Marek, August 1936'.

religion, marriage, burial, ritual slaughter, as well as social welfare and education. To head a group with such noble social aims might have seemed like an honour, but ten weeks later the same group became known as the *Judenrat* and its role came to be the execution of German orders.

It was his erstwhile friend and neighbour, Dr Stanisław Klimecki, the then acting Mayor of the City, who had recommended my grandfather for the unenviable position of leader. Marek, the social activist, well-connected, a fine organiser, fluent in German, was the obvious choice. Of course, Marek did not want to take the post, but he was threatened with arrest if he refused.[11] The fact that he initially refused indicates that he already feared that the Germans' intention was to enforce the compliance of the Jewish community towards its own destruction.

In May 2016, the Polish newspaper *Dziennik Polski* wrote an article entitled 'The Judenrats, on the Edge of Collaboration'.[12] That was indeed the problem, Marek, an honourable man, did not want to collaborate or represent the Germans. The article quotes reminiscences of Henryk Zwi Zimmermann, a contemporary of my father's, and later a prominent Israeli activist, jurist and politician.

I set about to look for Zimmermann's book[13] on various booksellers' websites here and in Poland, and everywhere found it was 'not available'. I sent a request to my cousin, Lucjan Wroński, to search for it in Poland. And he finally found it in his town library. He sent it to me, and I read it avidly

before posting it back. In the book Zimmermann describes a Shabbat scene
in my grandparents' house (my translation from the Polish):

> [It was] a Friday night and the Bieberstein family was in their flat in
> Podgórze at their Shabbat supper; table was laid with a white cloth,
> candles lit in the menorah. At the table was his wife Emilia, his
> younger son Artur [the elder son, Ludwik, left Kraków the day that
> war broke out], and 20-year-old Lula. [She was in fact only 18]...
> The father stood up, lifted the wine glass to his lips to recite the
> *kaddish*, when they were interrupted by a loud knocking at the door.
> At the door stood two SS men...In a loud, aggressive tone the older
> officer [He was *SS-Oberscharführer* Paul Siebert, the head of Sipo's
> Jewish affairs office] informed him that they had been sent on the
> instruction of the chief of the District, and that he is hereby bid to
> lead and organise the Jewish Council. Bieberstein refused and tried
> to make Siebert change his mind. He failed...Siebert gave him 48
> hours to choose his team.

Later he describes Lula as 'a charming dark-haired girl', with whom
Zimmermann became good friends. Apparently, it was she who related this
scene to him. The same Shabbat scene in my grandparents' home is also
described by Lov and Roth[14], and Grądzka-Rejak[15] in her recent book,
possibly based on the same evidence.

These accounts based on Zimmermann's reminiscences, which are
themselves based on my young aunt Lula's memories, may have a degree of
Chinese whispers about them, for the depicted scene is meant to have
occurred on the 8 September, while according to my father's CV, my father
was conscripted into the army on the 7 September. If the dates are correct,
he is unlikely to have been present at the Shabbat table. According to the
Holocaust historian, Agnieszka Zajączkowska-Drożdż,[16] an alternative
explanation for the formation of the Kraków *Judenrat* is to be found in the
testimony of Leib Salpeter, [17] who himself later became a *Judenrat* member.
He claims Marek was appointed by Klimecki a few days earlier, since the
previous leader had left the city, and the Jewish Community had been left
without representation.

Whether it was in fact Siebert at gun point, or Klimecki by persuasion,
who appointed my grandfather to lead the Jewish Community, Marek knew
very well that the position was not a favourable one. Resigned to his fate,
he then proceeded to choose the members of the Council wisely with 12
men who would be most likely to 'help the people under their charge'.[18] He

named Wilhelm Goldblatt as his deputy. Later when the Council became the *Judenrat*, the number of members was increased to 24. Marek's job turned out to be as horrible as he had feared – to act as a conduit for Nazi edicts, which as time went on was to force people to labour, leave their homes and strip them of their businesses and personal property.

The day after the Council members were named, Siebert and his entourage arrived at the Council offices. They were met at the door by Marek's deputy (Goldblatt) with cap in hand. Siebert was livid. Expecting to be greeted by the whole committee, he vented his anger by repeatedly punching Goldblatt on the head, shouting that he was affronted by the Council's disrespect. When the stunned and chastened Goldblatt showed the SS-men to the meeting room, all the assembled members rose to greet them. The SS-men promptly lined the council members up against the wall, while Siebert barked: 'You think that you were elected in order to have power? Your role here is to answer our demands and to execute our regulations.' He, Siebert, and his minions were all to be addressed as '*Herr Chef*' (Chief). They instructed Bieberstein to present himself promptly on the following day to receive further written instructions concerning their duties and competence. Then just to show who was boss, and to make sure that the Council did not consider themselves above themselves, he 'bid them to perform' humiliating gymnastic exercises – 'Rise, fall, rise, fall.' Afterwards the Council members were made to stand with their hands raised and faces to the wall.[19]

The early days of the war saw the streets of Kraków teeming with refugees from the neighbouring towns and villages.[20] In the meantime, others, usually the better-off like my mother's family, fled to the East. There was much confusion as mass movements clogged the roads, while Kraków's demographic changed, becoming more impoverished and needy. My grandfather's first job was to provide food and shelter for the refugees. Schools and synagogues were turned into shelters, task forces organised to ladle out soup and give out linen. The Jewish community, as always, was generous in its response.[21]

At about the same time (9 September) an edict was issued to mark all Jewish stores, cafés, restaurants and enterprises with a Star of David. The most likely benefit of such signage would be to facilitate legitimised robbery. By the end of September, the wealthier Jews who lived in better appointed, nicely located apartments had to vacate their homes. Their premises would be occupied by the Gestapo and their treasured possessions appropriated. Owners were given only two or three hours to leave their homes.[22] Faithful Catholic servants would often be entrusted with the family's jewels and small valuables and these treasures would then be used in the forthcoming years to buy false papers or serve as ransom to blackmailers. My grandfather's family home was luckily too modest for the Gestapo, so they were not evicted at this stage.

The Jewish public of Kraków found out about the appointment of my grandfather as president and of Wilhelm Goldblatt as his deputy, from placards dated 17 September 1939, distributed all over the city. His first official decree as head of the Community was on 21 September, when more placards were posted, this time signed by my grandfather, instructing the city's Jews to fill in the various anti-aircraft ditches that had previously been dug throughout Kraków. The task was to be completed by the 23 September, which happened to be, or was maybe deliberately chosen to be, Yom Kippur, the most solemn Jewish fast of the year. To add insult to injury, on the very same day Marek was forced to order the confiscation of all liturgical objects from the synagogues.[23] I can imagine how that would have upset him, but he would have been powerless to object. They confiscated *menorahs*, gold cups, antique ornamental lamps and other ceremonial objects made of silver or gold, but not before Marek had arranged for a complete inventory of the confiscated loot to be made.

Until the 26 October 1939, the city along with the rest of the occupied territories had been in the hands of the Wehrmacht (Unified German Armed Forces), but on that day it was placed under civilian rule known as *Generalgouvernement* (GG), with Hans Frank as the Governor-General of the whole territories and Otto Wächter as the Governor of Kraków.

The GG had no trouble in deciding to appropriate the beautiful medieval city of Kraków as their capital. Frank, together with his substantial entourage of subordinate SS-men, their families, and servants, took up residence in the historic Wawel Castle. A red flag with a black swastika was hoisted up its tower while Nazi forces arranged themselves in strict formation in its courtyards. Hans enjoyed playing King in Wawel's opulent royal private apartments, while his vain wife Brigitte, who robbed rich Jews of their furs for a pittance (it was called 'trading'[24]), fancied herself as the Queen of Poland. In 1939 the Nazis looted the valuable art works of the castle and sent them to Hitler's art collection in Berlin. Among them was the famous Lady with the Ermine by Leonardo da Vinci. In 1940 Frank with an eye for good art, requested that it be returned to Kraków, the capital of the GG for him to enjoy in his office rooms during his 'reign'. Later, when the Soviets started to close in, Frank arranged for the painting to be smuggled back to Germany. After liberation American soldiers found it in a country house in Bavaria and returned it to the Wawel Castle in 1946. I

Map of GG 1939-1941 with its four regions annexed from Poland: Kraków, Lublin, Radom and Warsaw. Beyond the green line the district of Galicia was added after September 1941 (https://en.wikipedia.org/wiki/Krak%C3%B3w_District) Wikipedia Commons License: CC BY-SA 2.0

loved that painting as a child, awed by the lit faces of the lady and the ermine, both turned leftwards towards an invisible third party. It now hangs in the National Museum in Kraków, and I revisit it on each of my tourist trips to Kraków.

Hans and Brigitte Frank were not the only ones with an eye to good art. Charlotta, the wife of Otto Wächter, the Governor of Kraków, furnished her apartment with carefully chosen looted national treasures. Some ended up in Germany and were not returned until February 2017.[25]

From the 18 November an order came from Otto Wächter, that all Jewish people older than twelve had to be identified by wearing Star of

David armbands on their right arm. The size and colour were specified: 'a white band with a blue Star of David sewn on it…the white band had to be 10cm wide and the star had to be 8cm in diameter'.[26] The *Judenrat* was ordered to produce them and the citizens to purchase them by 1 December. Anyone who refused to wear the identifying armband was punished, the punishment escalating higher and higher with time from the law's initial introduction. To start with the fine was 10 zloty, later a jail sentence, and later still, from 15 October 1941, the penalty was death by hanging.[27]

In other countries, or even cities, the specifications for the badge of identification were different. For example, in Austria and in Germany it had to be a canary yellow star, initially home-made from spare fabric, but later more official ones were issued with the word 'Jude' in black across the star. These had to be worn on the left breast, not as an armband. In Bulgaria the yellow badge was plastic. In Denmark and Norway no badges were introduced, so the oft-quoted story about the King of Denmark sporting a yellow Star of David is most probably apocryphal, though he is on record as saying that if the Germans introduce it 'perhaps we should all wear it'.

In Poland compliance was absolute. When baptised Jews made representations to the Polish Central Council for Social Welfare to intervene for exemption on their behalf, the result was the very opposite of what was intended; it gave the Nazis a ready-made list of converts to subsume into the Jewish population and all were later forced to move to the ghetto. In Poland there were no demonstrations by the Aryan population in opposition to the Jewish badge. In contrast French, Dutch, Czech, Bulgarian and even German Aryans often rose in support and sympathy.[28] (This view has now been challenged by the right-wing Polish government which claims innocence and victimhood during the Nazi occupation.)

The jeers from the Germans and the Poles continued unabated, especially now that the victims were labelled. Julian Aleksandrowicz recounts in his book[29] stories that I heard him tell when he visited us during my childhood. I remember playing with some toys in a corner, while he recounted how a German with a skull and bone cap apprehended two innocent Jewish men who were passing by, bid them to slap each other forcibly around the face, and when he thought their blows were too half-hearted, horsewhipped them mercilessly himself. Such scenes were performed simply for the occupants' amusement, but the Polish bystanders, albeit powerless to stop them, stood by, watched and smirked.

The visual identification of all Jews was the first step in the Nazis' programme of persecution. The orthodox Jews had always been easily identifiable and were used to being jeered at, but the assimilated majority

Armband seller – winter 1939/1940
From the Chris Webb Private Archive

felt uncomfortable at having to suddenly wear their ethnicity on their sleeve. Both Jews and Poles had to doff their hats and step off the pavement if they saw a uniformed German approaching, but antisemitic Poles also expected the same subservience from their Jewish neighbours, meeting any signs of resistance with overt hooliganism and violence. A strict hierarchy was soon established: a German was better than a Pole, and a Pole was better than a Jew.

The feeling of subservience intensified as a salvo of restrictions followed in quick succession. The orders came from the Germans but were announced to the Jewish community by means of memoranda signed by my grandfather. Bank accounts were blocked (20 November 1939), cars and motorcycles had to be first registered (27 November 1939), and then surrendered (4 December 1939), Jews are forbidden to move from one place to another (11 December 1939), Jews forbidden to travel by train (26 January 1940), a ban on collection of water (13 March 1940), denial of Jews to walk in the *Planty* and main square areas of Kraków (29 April 1940), and another demand for forced labour (29 April 1940).[30]

On 28 November 1939, a decree was passed to form Jewish Councils or *Judenräte* all over GG. For my grandfather, the thought that his was one of many such puppet councils, would have brought no comfort. What is certain is that the Council's role had changed. Whereas before the war its function was to educate the children, administer orphanages, and to help the sick, its new role was to mitigate the implementation of Nazi decrees.

By December 1939, all Jewish schools were closed, and those Jews going to Catholic schools excluded. Professional contacts between Jews and Aryans were forbidden, for example Jewish doctors could no longer treat Aryans; Jewish lawyers were forbidden to appear in courts. The enforcement of these regulations begs the question – how did they know who was Jewish, and how does one define Jewishness? The 1931 Census was what they would have consulted initially, but the *Judenrat* was ordered to do another one in November 1939. Given the circumstances, why on earth did people admit to their Jewishness? Was it a nationality or a religion? Duda[31] claims that 'the governor of Kraków defined a Jew as someone who is or was a believer in the Jewish faith'. This criterion seems untenable to me. How did they know who was a believer (or how much of a believer)? Graf,[32] I think, gets it right. She states that the criteria of Jewishness were based on ancestry, so anyone born a Jew was considered Jewish, regardless of their beliefs. Kraków was a city of culture and many of its wealthier and influential Jews would have held no beliefs of any kind. Yet there was no reprieve for them.

In December 1939 the Germans surrounded the Jewish district of Kazimierz, and also parts of Podgórze with police cordons, and proceeded to ransack the Jewish homes, confiscating (i.e. robbing) all gold, silver, cash, valuable pictures, carpets, binoculars, typewriters and radios, searching even the cellars and attics.[33] Of course, they were not meant to appropriate anything personally because Jewish property belonged to the Reich, but most Germans benefited materially, if not by pocketfuls of seized possessions, then by clandestinely acquired bribes. I suspect that some rare naively philanthropic 'good Germans' might not have survived the system and have become victims themselves.

About this time all prayer houses were closed, and the ritual slaughter of meat banned. Enforced labour continued on Saturdays and Jewish holidays. There was however, one perfidious exception. One Saturday they instructed that the synagogues be opened again, and all Jews invited to worship in their Shabbat best. The shuls were then invaded by reporters from *Der Stürmer* (a Nazi newspaper) who proceeded to carefully choose to photograph the disabled, the sick and the badly dressed, enacting strange dances, their faces raised in religious ecstasy. The aim was to jeer, caricature and ridicule the community and present them as *Untermenschen*.[34]

The whole process of human degradation, starting with identification, forced labour on starvation rations, exclusion, loss of property and of all dignity, was thus gradually implemented within a few months. The emaciated, overworked specimens of mankind (those that survived) were therefore even more the subjects of hatred and ridicule. They were carriers of disease, 'rats' or 'vermin', worthy at best of tittering finger-pointing, at worst of random acts of gratuitous sadism. To quote Berenstein and Rutkowski,[35] 'the Nazi Polish language press…strove unremittingly to whip up Poles against the Jews'. New posters continually appeared on walls, in trams, railway stations and poster pillars – all vilifying the Jews.

Antisemitic poster, Poland 1940. The wording reads 'Beware of spotted typhus – avoid Jews'. Reproduced with permission from the United States Holocaust Memorial Museum Collection – gift of the Katz Family

Marek Bieberstein tried in vain to protect the Jewish community from the growing persecution. Hans Frank announced on the 12 April 1940 that 'Kraków is to become the most cleansed town in the *Generalgouvernement* (GG)'.[36] The German words for this were *judenfrei* and *judenrein*, which with the guttural German 'r' would have sounded more chilling. They certainly wanted to be rid of the Jews, but another reason was that they needed to make room for the high-ranking German officials and profiteers flocking to Kraków from the Reich. Frank's intention was for only between 5,000 and 10,000 Jews to remain in Kraków. Later this was expanded to 15,000 to only include those needed for their handicraft, trade, and business skills. Since the population of Jews in the city was at that time about 68,000, this meant that less than a quarter could remain. Marek Bieberstein realised that mass deportations would shortly follow, so he and his team initially asked people to leave voluntarily. If they left now, they could take their family belongings with them, whereas if they were forcibly evicted, as would happen later, they would lose everything. As an extra incentive he offered some money for food and relocation expenses. When that did not work, he issued a decree reprinted on pages 27 and 28 in its original, and also in translation. 'Leave, if you can voluntarily, by any means at your disposal, take your belongings with you.' The deadline was 15 August 1940.

By mid-August 1940, many Jews left and went to live in the surrounding villages, or with relatives elsewhere. Some managed to find work on farms, others bought false papers or were hidden by 'righteous gentiles'. To be able to stay in Kraków, each Jewish citizen had to apply for a residency permit, or *Ausweis*. 15,000 was the maximum allowed to stay in Kraków, and so 15,000 *Ausweise* should have been printed. The *Judenrat* printed too many permits, offering a bribe to a Nazi official in return for leniency on this issue, but the plan misfired badly. An official investigation was conducted and when the bribery was uncovered, Marek was held responsible. Bribery might seem like an abhorrent crime to us, but it was not like that there and then. Crowe[37] calls it 'an honest desire to help fellow Jews'. In any case, backhanders (*łapuwki*) were part of the culture during the war (and also after – I remember it well). Even before August 1941, the *Judenrat* offered 'presents' to individual SS-men to blunt the force of minor Nazi rules.[38] Historian Isiah Trunk[39] in his book *Judenrat* devotes a whole sub-chapter to the issue of intervention and bribery, quoting numerous examples of *Judenrat* chairmen of other councils who used corruption and bribes to mitigate German edicts. 'Paying bribes to the Germans was a method widely practised by Jewish Councils before and even in the midst of resettlement actions.' So, when seen in the context of the times, the offer of

An die
Jüdische Bevölkerung der Stadt Krakau!

Die Behörden haben ursprünglich die freiwillige Umsiedlung eines beträchtlichen Teiles der in Krakau wohnenden Juden und Jüdinnen in andere Ortschaften des Generalgouvernements angeordnet mit der Einräumung der Berechtigung, dass [die]jetzigen, die bis zum 15. August 1940 von Krakau freiwillig abwandern, ihren neuen Wohnort selbst bestimmen und ihr ganzes Hab und Gut mit sich führen dürfen.

Gleichzeitig wurde seitens der Behörden [an]gekündigt, dass Juden Krakaus, die bis zum 15. August 1940 freiwillig nicht weggezogen sind, mit zwangsweiser Umsiedlung zu rechnen haben.

[D]a dieser Anordnung nicht in diesem gewünschten Ausmasse Folge geleistet worden ist, haben sodann die Behörden sämtliche Juden Krakaus der Aussiedlung grundsätzlich unterworfen.

Am 23. Juli 1940 bestimmten die Behörden die zwangsweise Evakuierung aller Juden und Jüdinnen aus Krakau bei Aufrechterhaltung der freiwilligen Umsiedlung bis zum 15. August 1940.

Mit dem 16. August 1940 beginnend, werden somit die Behörden an den Vollzug dieser angekündigten zwangsweisen Abwanderung der Juden bei Anwendung polizeilicher Massnahmen herantreten.

Wir fordern somit alle Juden und Jüdinnen Krakaus auf, mit der freiwilligen Umsiedlung aus Krakau in andere Städte und Ortschaften im Bereiche des Generalgouvernements und zwar in die möglichst weit von Krakau entfernten Ortschaften unverzüglich zu beginnen, um auf diese Weise den neuen Wohnort frei wählen und ihr Gut, insbesondere Einrichtungs- und Gebrauchsgegenstände mitnehmen zu dürfen, unabhängig davon, ob ein Umsiedlungsauftrag zugestellt worden ist, oder nicht.

Wer diese Aussiedlungsfrist überschreitet, setzt sich der Gefahr aus, der obenerwähnten Zubilligungen verlustig zu werden.

Es liegt somit im höchstpersönlichen Interesse eines jeden Juden und jeder Jüdin Krakaus, nicht die zwangsweise Evakuierung abzuwarten, sondern vor dem 15. August 1940 freiwillig und ganz möglichst bald Krakau zu verlassen.

Reisebewilligungen, Personalausweise, wie auch sonstige Auskünfte über etwaige Begünstigungen, werden den Umsiedlern im Umsiedlungsbüro der Jüdischen Gemeinde, Krakau, Brzozowagasse Nr. 5, gewährt.

Krakau, den 25. Juli 1940.

JÜDISCHE GEMEINDE IN KRAKAU
Obmann: Marek Bieberstein.

Do
Ludności żydowskiej m. Krakowa!

Władze zarządziły poprzednio dobrowolne przesiedlenie się przeważającej części Żydów miasta Krakowa do innych miejscowości Generalnego Gubernatorstwa, zezwalając wszystkim, którzy dobrowolnie opuszczą Kraków do dnia 15 sierpnia 1940 na wybór nowego miejsca osiedlenia i na zabranie ze sobą całego mienia.

Równocześnie zagroziły Władze przymusowym wysiedleniem wszystkich Żydów, którzy do 15. sierpnia 1940 dobrowolnie Krakowa nie opuszczą.

Ponieważ powyższemu zarządzeniu nie stało się zadość w dostatecznych rozmiarach, postanowiły Władze poddać przymusowemu wysiedleniu wszystkich Żydów Krakowa.

Ostatnio dnia 23. lipca 1940 postanowiły Władze rozpocząć przymusową ewakuację wszystkich Żydów Krakowa z dniem 16. sierpnia 1940, przy utrzymaniu prawa dobrowolnego przesiedlenia się do dnia 15. sierpnia 1940.

Z dniem 16. sierpnia 1940, przystąpią zatym Władze do przymusowego wydalania Żydów z Krakowa przy użyciu środków policyjnych.

Wzywamy zatym wszystkich Żydów Krakowa do natychmiastowego rozpoczęcia dobrowolnego przesiedlenia się z Krakowa do innych miast i miejscowości w granicach Generalnego Gubernatorstwa i to znadniczo do miejscowości odległych od Krakowa celem zapewnienia sobie w ten sposób prawa do dobrowolnego wyboru przyszłego miejsca zamieszkania oraz prawa zabrania całego swego mienia, a w szczególności urządzenia i przedmiotów użytku, bez względu na to, czy nakaz przesiedlenia został doręczony, czy też nie.

Kto się nie dotrzyma powyższego terminu dobrowolnego przesiedlenia się, narażonym będzie na stratę powyższych uprawnień.

Leży zatym w najistotniejszym interesie każdego Żyda i każdej Żydówki nie wyczekiwać na przymusową ewakuację, lecz jeszcze przed 15. sierpnia 1940 opuścić dobrowolnie Kraków i to możliwie zaraz.

Zezwolenia na użycie kolei, dowody osobiste i wszelkie inne informacje co do możliwych ulg, udziela Biuro Przesiedleńcze Gminy Żydowskiej w Krakowie, Brzozowa 5.

GMINA ŻYDOWSKA w KRAKOWIE
Przewodniczący: Marek Bieberstein.

Kraków, dnia 25. lipca 1940.

To the Jewish population of the City of Krakow !

The authorities at first announced the voluntary removal of a substantial number of the Jewish men and women who are living in Krakow to other places in the Generalgouvernement; those who have left Krakow voluntarily by 15 August at the latest may, as concessions, have the right to choose a new place to live and to take with them all of their belongings.
At the same time the authorities have announced that Jews who have not left by 15 August, will have to anticipate enforced removal.
If this announcement does not have the desired result, all Krakow Jews will be subject to official removal.
On 23 July 1940 the authorities decided on the enforced evacuation of all Jewish men and women from Krakow, leaving in place the provision for voluntary removal until 15 August 1940.
From 16 August 1940 onward, the authorities will thus commence the execution of the announced forced evacuation of Jews, by using police measures.
We therefore call on all Jewish men and women in Krakow to begin the voluntary removal from Krakow to other towns and villages within the Generalgouvernement without delay, preferably to places as far away as possible from Krakow, thus enabling you to choose your own place to live and to take with you all your belongings, especially furniture and utilities, no matter if there has been an order for your departure or not.
Whoever remains after the date of removal will face the risk of the treatment mentioned above. Therefore it is very much in the self interest of every Jewish man and every Jewish woman not to await the enforced evacuation, but to leave Krakow voluntarily as soon as possible, and before 15 August 1940.
Travel permits, identity cards and information on all facilities can be obtained from the Removal Bureau of the Jewish community, 5 Brzozowa Street, Krakow.

Krakow, 25 July 1940　　　　　　　　　　　　JEWISH COMMUNITY IN KRAKOW
　　　　　　　　　　　　　　　　　　　　　　　　Chairman: Marek Bieberstein

Placard instructing Jews to leave Kraków, 25 July 1940 – a Nazi decree authorised by my grandfather
Source: The Holocaust Education & Archive Research Team (Images from the Holocaust)
www.HolocaustResearchProject.org

a bribe to a Nazi official to exert his influence so that another 10,000 Jews could remain in their homes, seemed nothing unusual, and definitely worth trying.

When Thomas Keneally's *Schindler's Ark*[40] first came out, my father was upset that Marek was not presented sympathetically enough, especially as in the current world the word 'bribery' has seriously crookish connotations. He got in touch with Keneally about this and was promised that the matter would be resolved in a second edition. I don't think it ever was, but then I don't feel that Keneally's description of the situation was particularly unfair. One thing, however, is of interest. Finkel[41] reminds us of the fate of the chairmen of the 'Russian' and 'German' Minsk ghetto Judenrats, who were also arrested for allegedly trying to bribe a German official. Both lost their lives.

The full details of my grandfather's 'crime' are documented in the history books of the Holocaust.[42] The bribe was to be paid to the German *volksdeutsch* official, Mr Reichert, in return for his 'promise' of help to exert his influence. Probably the better-off Jews contributed to the ransom which amounted to 100,000 zlotys. As Trunk[43] puts it, he was arrested 'for the impudence of trying to rescind the expulsion of the Jews from Cracow'. He was tried and found guilty on 13 September 1940.

The Yad Vashem entry for Marek Bieberstein honours his integrity. It says (translated from Hebrew): 'While liaising between the German Nazi regime and the Jewish community, Bieberstein did his utmost to ease the dire state of the Jewish community by organizing assistance to those members in need. He also often aided the release of Jews from Nazi imprisonment.'[44] In the course of this research, I read many historical texts in which my grandfather is mentioned, and I have to say that in none is he treated unkindly. His full statement in defence of his 'crime' is cited in Polish by Low and Roth[45], but the significant part of his testimony are the heart-felt words: 'I decided to act in this way, in the belief that it was the best course of action I had in order to help the Jewish people under my leadership.' Furthermore, as the court in their judgement confirmed, Marek had in no way personally benefited, nor had he intended to do so, from this illegal transaction.

I put my grandfather's name repeatedly into the Google search engine and searched through both the websites and the images. I hoped to find a photograph of him as a member of the *Judenrat*, but I searched in vain. I was briefly excited to find a photograph entitled 'The Judenrat' in Kraków in Low and Roth,[46] and the same one on a website.[47] It shows a group of seven unsmiling men, each with the white and blue armband. Unfortunately, none looks like my grandfather of the pre-war photos.

However, in the course of these internet searches, I came across few surprises. The first was a shady connection between my grandfather and a thoroughly despicable character called Simche Spira, the head of the Jewish Police (OD)[48]. In a novelisation of the reminiscences of *Haftling Scheunemann*, John McKenna[49] talks of Bieberstein and Spira going together to see Hans Frank. I don't know if that ever happened. Since it was the *Judenrat* presidents who appointed the OD chiefs,[50] I worried that Marek might have been responsible for the appointment of this unscrupulous informer, who was (after the war) tried, sentenced and executed for his crimes. To research this further, I sent an email to the historian Evgeny Finkel, who had just produced a new definitive book, *Ordinary Jews: Choice and Survival during the Holocaust.*[51] I was delighted to get an immediate and reassuring reply. 'No', he said, 'Spira would have been appointed after your grandfather's imprisonment'.

The other surprises were pleasant ones. There was a videotape testimony of someone called David R.,[52] born in Kraków in 1925, so only about 14 when he came across my grandfather. He recalls 'assistance from Marek Bieberstein, the *Judenrat* chairman'. Another testimony from Samuel Offen[53] recalls Hebrew lessons from Dr Bieberstein, who was 'a very well known, very liked gentleman... very prominent in the Jewish Community'. Samuel Offen later wrote a book about his experiences.[54]

It was good to find these confirmations of my grandfather's acts of kindness and integrity, because I believe he tried to do some good in his horrible position which Low and Roth[55] describe as 'balancing above an abyss' – on the one side protecting the needs of the Jewish people, and on the other implementing Nazi orders. It's what Primo Levi in his book *The Drowned and the Saved* described as a 'grey zone'.

There are two opposing views from Holocaust historians. Hannah Arendt[56] was of the opinion, expressed in her book *Eichmann in Jerusalem*, that without the Judenrats' cooperation fewer Jews would have perished. In fact, she has nothing good to say about the *Judenräte* at all. While listing the different sins of each chairman in turn (though she does not mention my grandfather by name), she lumps them all together as a group of self-seeking, self-aggrandising oligarchs who enjoyed their new power while betraying their people. Likewise, Wroński and Zwolakowa[57] deride the *Judenräte*, claiming that they were 'opportunistic bourgeois members of the Jewish Community...with cannibalistic tendencies'. However, these views have been challenged by historian Isaiah Trunk who wrote: 'In the final analysis, the *Judenräte* had no influence on the frightful outcome of the Holocaust; the Nazi extermination machine was alone responsible for the tragedy, and the Jews in the occupied territories, most especially Poland, were far too powerless to prevent it.'[58] Historians Rubenstein and Roth,[59] who have studied other scholars' response to the *Judenräte*, claim that 'few scholars are prepared to agree with Hannah Arendt'. They believe that the tactic that the *Judenrat* leaders adopted of alleviation and compliance eased suffering and saved lives. They say that 'to think that they collaborated with the Germans would be a perverse distortion and to say that they cooperated with them blurs the fact that these men were compelled by terror to comply'. Pankiewicz,[60] of the famous pharmacy, who was a true 'righteous gentile', and who knew my family well, had nothing but good things to say about Kraków's *Judenrat*, and believed that the fate of the Jews would have been worse without them.

Imprisonment

Following his transgression Marek was removed from his post and imprisoned initially for 18 months and then three months more, first in Montelupich Street in Kraków, later in St Michal Street in Kraków and later still in Tarnów. It seems a shame, in retrospect, that the sentence was so short. He may have survived the war had he stayed in prison longer. My great-uncle Aleksander, who was by this time the doctor in charge of the hospital for infectious diseases, described how he used to visit him in jail delivering news and parcels of food, and how the move from Montelupich was deliberate, paid for by bribes because the St Michal prisoners were less at risk of deportation.[61] In any case his incarceration can't have been easy, as the jails must have been full of seriously nasty criminals. With the hindsight of history, we can feel grateful that he was removed from duties, because as the screws tightened, he was spared from aiding further acts of evil and for ever being classified as a villain in the history books of the Holocaust.

While my grandfather was in jail, my grandmother Mila received a demand from the JUS for his registration documents, which they thought he must have left at home. She wrote to them twice to say that she has looked for them everywhere and thinks he must have taken them with him (to prison). Although these are trivial documents maybe salvaged from the deserted offices of the Community Council after the war, I include them as they confirm the bureaucracy that existed; they are also the only sample of my grandmother's beautiful copperplate handwriting that I have.

According to the reminiscences of Pola Gerner (later Scheck),[62] Mila struggled financially while Marek was in jail. The American Jewish Joint Distribution Committee (known as 'the Joint')[63] elected to help Mila and her family using money received from overseas donations. Pola, who worked as a young administrative assistant in 'the Joint' offices, remembers that Mila was too proud to receive these shameful handouts directly, sending her nephew, Jerzy Scheck, to act as an intermediary. Incidentally, it was through Jerzy's visits to 'the Joint' to collect Mila's money that Pola first met and fell in love with Jerzy. They both survived the War,[64] emigrated to the United States and married. I visited them in New York in 1966.

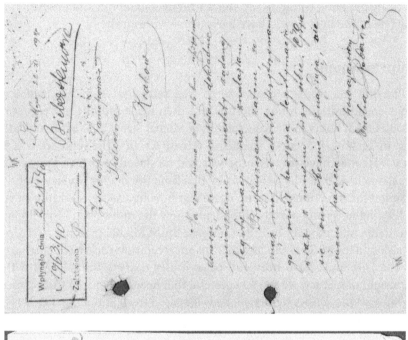

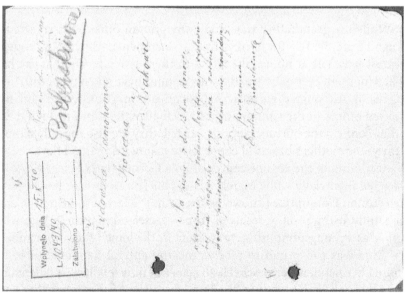

My grandmother's letters to the JUS written in her beautiful copper-plate handwriting

A photograph of my grandmother, Emilia (Mila), probably taken between 1938 and 1942

My great-uncle Aleksander describes visiting Marek in jail,[65] but he does not say whether his immediate family were also able to visit, or, whether this was not possible because any dealings with the prison guards would have required backhanders which the family members were simply not in a position to deliver. In June 1941, which was after the formation of the ghetto, Marek, along with other prisoners, was moved to another jail, in Tarnów which was 84km away. Aleksander describes how Marek was led out wearing no outdoor clothes, wrapped in a blanket. He visited him 2 or 3 times a month in the Tarnów jail, despite the distance and delivered food parcels and the all-important news.

The brothers were very close, so on his many visits my great uncle Aleksander kept my grandfather informed of the escalating horror of life in Podgórze – telling him of the new yellow *Kennkarte* (ID card) issued by the police with a stylised Hebrew 'J' in red on the left-hand inner page, and of the forced snow clearances in the freezing early winter of 1941. Later in March 1941 he brought news that a ghetto was being formed in the poorest part of Podgórze, that Mila, Artur and Lula had been evicted from their family home and were now living in a corner of an apartment on Limanowski Street 13, in the centre of the ghetto. Perhaps he brought him a map like the one on page 34.

The forced move to the ghetto must have been heart-breaking for Mila without her husband to lean on. Which possessions should she take, which bits of furniture to fit into a hand cart? Did she have the time or energy to unscrew the *mezuzah*[67] from the doorpost of her home at Zaułek Rejtana

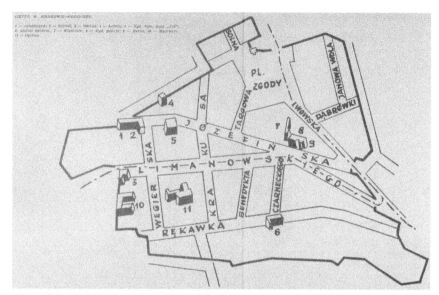

Scan of the Kraków ghetto map from Aleksander Bieberstein's book.[66] Note: 3 – Judenrat Offices, 5 – JSS/JUS, 8 – Optima Factory

10, and transfer it to the entrance to the room they shared in the ghetto? I don't know whether she ever accompanied her brother-in-law to the jail, but if she did not, Marek and Mila would certainly have yearned for news of each other, and longed for Marek's jail sentence to end.

In December of 1941 Aleksander would have told Marek about Pearl Harbour and America's entry into the Second World War. They would have rejoiced about that and maybe laughed a bit about the German soldiers dressed in ghetto ladies' furs shivering on the Eastern Front. Later still in 1942, Aleksander brought him news of concentration camps from which nobody returned but would have added that his family were not at risk because they all had jobs. Mila had found work in the Optima factory, Artur was the chief pharmacist with the JSS, and Lula was a nurse. He would have tried to cheer him up that his family was safe and that he still had a home to return to.

The Ghetto and the Orphanage

When my grandfather was released from jail in July 1942, he joined his family in their ghetto room. Their space was small and shared, but he was at last reunited with his family and it felt like home. July 1942 would have been after the first wave of deportations, which removed more than 7,000 of the ghetto's inhabitants. The shrunk population was clearly not in need of such a large area, so the ghetto boundaries were redrawn. Limanowski 13, which had initially been in the centre of the ghetto, was now at its edge. Fischler-Martinho[68] remembers that the even numbers, to the south of the street would be out-with its confines, but not the odd numbers to the north.

After two years of maltreatment and near-starvation, Marek was suffering from heart disease and poor blood circulation. The first thing to do was to look for a job, and he felt lucky to also secure one in the Optima factory where his wife worked. Both my grandparents were by now been numbed to the horrors they witnessed from its windows. Unable to perform physical work, Marek's helpful colleagues allowed him sedentary work in the office.[69] At this stage in the chronology of his life and the war, my grandfather must surely have felt relieved to be free of his *Judenrat* duties, for it was the role of his successor to compile the lists of deportees. It would have been a task in which he would have been constantly bombarded with hard-to-resist bribes or with heart-rending pleas of those who could not afford bribes. I am sure he felt well out of any involvement in the ugly work of the deportation machinery.

He was also no doubt relieved from participating in a particularly heinous crime described by Pankiewicz.[70] One day the Germans assembled all the high-ranking *Judenrat* and OD members, grouped them in rows of 4 and marched them out to Płaszów. The men were taken to the gallows, but instead of being hanged themselves, they were made to participate in the hanging of a batch of Polish prisoners. All this was done while the Germans filmed the spectacle to provide propaganda evidence of how Jews were systematically murdering Poles.

As well as his 'day' office job, Marek sat on the Board of the JSS under Michal Weichert (who was my father's boss). Other members of the *Prezydium* were Dr Chaim Hilfstein and Dr Eliasz Tisch, the former of whom played a major role in the 'Schindler Jews' story. In addition to his two jobs and despite his failing health, my grandfather maintained an interest in the orphanage, of which he had once been President, and after his release from jail he was once again elected to serve on its board. By this time, the orphanage has had to move twice.[71] Shortly after his return there was yet another move down the street to Józefinska 41 at the whim of the chief of the Jewish Ghetto Police (OD), Simche Spira, who requisitioned the building for his staff. It was not easy to move children, beds and equipment, and inevitably the children suffered. According to my great-uncle the first move was a catastrophe, the second move was a blow, the last move was a fatal blow.

Both my grandfather and my great-uncle would have witnessed the events of the next *Aktion*, which happened 28 October 1942. On the morning of that day a truck covered with flaps of black denim pulled up at the orphanage, loaded the screaming infants into wicker baskets and drove them to a location outside town where they were slaughtered. The older children were taken to *Plac Zgody* (Harmony Square), from which they were marched in rows of 4, led by the directors, Regina Feuerstein and David Kurzmann, to the railway station in Płaszów and from there by freight train to the Belzec death camp. Both the directors perished with the children, though the Germans had offered them safe houses to stay in the ghetto. Both had declined.

After the October *Aktion*, the Germans dissolved the orphanage. Any surviving children roaming disconsolately around the ghetto, or new orphans, as well as children whose parents were alive but working, were ultimately rounded up and placed in two different childrens' homes, the *Tagesheim* and the *Kinderheim*.[72] That is my great-uncle's version of events, but it is not corroborated by other testimonies, who remember only one home, interchangeably called *Tagesheim* or *Kinderheim* (discussed by Grądzka[73]). There are also some inconsistencies in the accounts regarding the management of the two homes. Benisch,[74] claims that the children were under Nazi management, but under the directorship of Aleksander Bieberstein, whereas Grądzka[75] and Sliwa[76] say that my grandfather, Marek Bieberstein and Dr Jakub Kranz assumed joint directorship as soon as the ghetto *Kinderheim*[77] was formed, soon after he was released from jail. During my grandfather's sojourn in jail Aleksander would certainly have been its President, and he may have been later. Or if there were indeed two homes, they may have managed one each between them, or Aleksander might have been President until the October *Aktion* and Marek later. It is also possible that the two brothers were confused for each other (although they did not look at all alike).

In any case, whoever was in charge, the situation was grim. After the numerous moves the new home(s) had no statutes or regulations regarding age and the conditions were not as good as in the original orphanage. The children of the *Tagesheim* were 'employed' gluing envelopes in the vain hope that this 'work' would give them immunity from deportation. Roman Polanski, the film director, in his memoir *Roman*, [78] remembers making paper bags as a day boy, 'folding and gumming sheets of brown paper for hours on end'. Despite the common knowledge of what had happened in the October *Aktion* many children who had become separated from their parents came begging for admission. Pearl Benisch[79] in her book *To*

Vanquish the Dragon describes a touching scene where my great-uncle interviews two girls, Sarah and Ruchka, as care-workers.

> Girls…each of these children has undergone an experience of the most traumatic kind. Some saw their parents being shot and ran away and hid. Some got lost during the deportation, could not find their mothers, and wandered by chance off the *Sammelplatz*. Others watched their families being taken away, and turned and ran, frightened out of their minds. Miraculously they escaped the *Aussiedlung*. Each child has his own tragic story to tell. We want to make them feel comfortable. We want to give them the warmth of home. 'You know girls', he stressed with emotion, 'we try, we do everything possible to make them feel they are still children'.

The girls got the job, but later report, 'There is no-one to cuddle them. No matter how hard Dr Bieberstein tries to make them feel like children, they are just haunted little Jews, scared, frightened, always on the watch. Knowing little Jews.' I don't know to which Dr Bieberstein they are referring, but it hardly matters. In a further section of the book, she describes a play which the children put on, where surprisingly they all wanted to play the parts of the OD or SS-men. Using sticks for truncheons they acted out the atrocities they had seen being committed.

By early 1943, the construction of the forced labour camp at Płaszow was underway in preparation for the fulfilment of Himmler's order.[80] Ghetto A was formed for the workers and Ghetto B for the unemployed, the sick, children and the elderly. Even then the inhabitants of Ghetto B knew that their days were numbered. The demarcation line was traced with barbed wires pinned to poles. It was the first step towards the ghetto's liquidation. The final step happened over two consecutive days: 13 March 1943 for Ghetto A, and 14 March for Ghetto B. SS soldiers roamed around accompanied by vicious dogs winkling out anyone left in hiding.

Regina Helken, a children's care-worker at the *Tagesheim*, described the following scene featuring my grandfather, which reputedly took place on 13 or 14 March 1943,[81] but I think that it would have been the 13th, given the events that followed.

> The little ones sat together in the large room, frightened, quiet, sobbing. Big, frightened eyes, pale, grey tragic faces. Marek Bieberstein, the director of the *Tagesheim* looked grim. He loved these little people, he had fought for them to get better food and

comforts; he'd always been gentle and calm. On that day...he told the entire personnel to go home, while he stayed on and was one of the last ones to leave.

Marek must have returned home desolate that afternoon surmising the fate of the children he had left behind, but hoping against hope that they would be moved to the camp with all the other inhabitants of Ghetto A.

Later that afternoon, my grandfather, my grandmother, and Artur lined up in columns with all the others, and made their way to the camp, carrying no more than a small bundle or suitcase of belongings each. The route took them past the junction of Węgierska and Limanowska Streets where the brutal Amon Göth, the newly appointed commandant of the Płaszów camp, was conducting selections. 'Whomever he did not like, whoever was too young or too old, whoever walked crookedly, or weakly, would be withdrawn and instructed to go to Ghetto B.'[82] Luckily to their surprise they all 'passed'; maybe Göth did not notice them, or maybe he thought them healthy enough to be able to make a contribution to the camp effort. It was just as well, as all those from Ghetto B perished. Some were rounded up and mercilessly killed in the streets and on Plac Zgody on 13 and 14 March 1943.[83] Others were loaded onto lorries, taken to the railway station, and from there transported by cattle truck to Auschwitz and certain death.[84] In all about 4,500 Jews were eliminated in the course of those two days.

Płaszów was going to be a labour camp, and the Nazis only wanted able-bodied workers, so parents were ordered to leave all children younger than 14 at the *Kinderheim* in Ghetto B. Any children found in the marching lines were torn from their parents' arms and either shot on the spot or consigned to Ghetto B, to be shot the following day. It would have been on 14 March that the same fate befell the children of the *Tagesheim* in Ghetto A and those in the *Kinderheim* in Ghetto B as befell the children of the orphanage a few months earlier – all were murdered. Among them would have been the little girl in a red coat, who is said to have so profoundly affected Schindler that he transformed from an opportunistic Nazi into a saviour. Although the time and geography of the event as depicted in Spielberg's film do not exactly match the evidence, psychologically and cinematically the little girl in red remains in peoples' minds as one of the most memorable icons of the Holocaust.

My poor grandparents trudging past the predatory gaze of Amon Göth would have had a more personal reason to be heartbroken. A few days earlier their daughter, Lula, had decided to defect to the Aryan side to be with her Catholic boyfriend Ryszard (Rysiu). I can imagine the pain my

Lula, between 1938 and 1942

grandparents would have felt when they hugged their daughter goodbye for the last time as she set off for her Aryan escape. They must both have hidden their pain pretending to themselves and each other that she would be safer 'on the other side', that the war would be over soon, that their separation would be short and temporary.

Płaszów

The forced labour camp was built on the outskirts of the city on swampy, hilly ground, which included two Jewish cemeteries. The hills had to be planed down, the swamps drained, and the cemeteries levelled, but after all there was no shortage of manpower. The remains were thrown into mass graves, while the tombstones were used to pave the road to the camp. The work was done quickly while the SS screamed orders and fired shots forcing the prisoners to desecrate the relics of their own ancestors.[85] The same trick of paving the road to the camp with tombstones was used in Majdanek, the Lublin camp, so it seems that the choice of tombstones as building materials was not just the happenstance of their availability but a deliberate act of humiliation and desecration.

At peak capacity Płaszów camp interned 25,000 inmates. Although it was never an extermination camp and no gas chambers or crematoria were built there, it became sheer hell on earth. Some people said that the conditions in Auschwitz were better.

Graf[86] remembers what it felt like to move from the ghetto to Płaszów: 'Upon leaving the ghetto we lost all hope and desire to survive...That one

Evacuation of the Kraków ghetto, 13 March 1943 (United States Holocaust Memorial Museum)

room in the ghetto that five of us had shared now seemed to have been a palace. In the camp we lost our privacy and the warmth of the atmosphere of home.' She describes the terrible conditions, including sharing one bowl between five women, a bowl which also doubled up as a container for their bodily functions. Wooden crates served as beds; there were no mattresses. To start with some people in the camp still kept their jobs in the ghetto; later all the workshops were moved to the camp. She reports what the deserted ghetto looked like after the liquidation: dead people lying in the street and 'the buildings empty, the windows and doors flung wide open… a ghost town'.

In the meantime, the Płaszów camp grew, built by the inmates themselves, to provide a basic existence for over 20,000 people. The walls were made of barbed wire five metres deep with high tension electrified wires running alongside. And there were watchtowers, 13 of them. The completed camp included separate barracks for men and women, a labour 'education' camp for Polish workers who had violated certain disciplines (Poles and Jews were always kept separate), the administrative buildings, an *Appellplatz* where prisoners had to check-in for their twice-daily roll call and a mass grave, into which more bodies were added every day. Of course, none of the inmates had watches, so a trumpet call would be sounded to announce roll call. Often this would be interminable, with the inmates standing frozen in columns 4 to a row. Why were they counted and recounted so assiduously? Benisch[87] remembers thinking 'were we so precious?'

The camp started off as a labour camp (*Arbeitslager*), supplying the workforce for the armament factories and a stone quarry, then it became a forced labour camp (*Zwangsarbeitslager*), and became a full-blown concentration camp (*Konzentrationslager*) on 10 January 1944. Scores of people were murdered daily, mostly by shooting on the killing hill, Chujowa Górka (a hill named by the inmates rather rudely after an SS-man called Hujar – it's meant to be a pun because the word also means 'prick').

Between March and September 1943 my grandmother and grandfather both still worked in Optima. In addition to this job, Marek was also still a member of the JUS (Jewish Aid Centre) which had its headquarters on Józefinska Street. At the same address was a special pharmacy where my father Artur directed the distribution of medications and drugs for all labour and concentration camps in Poland (now the GG)[88]. Having jobs in the old ghetto, while being interned in the camp, meant a trudge in guarded columns of four at daybreak and sunset, about 3km each way.

In the meantime, my grandparents' health was failing; Mila was suffering from abdominal pains, Marek from heart disease. My father did not think that his mother's medical problem was serious, just the result of an inevitable infection, but the severe pains she experienced led to a botched operation in insanitary conditions. She did not recover and died, aged 60, in September 1943. What I don't know, because I never asked, was whether my ailing grandmother knew of her daughter's fate before she died. I can't help hoping that she did not know that Lula, the beautiful, vivacious 21-year-old brunette, had been denounced in the autumn of 1943 and shot on Bochnia station.

So, by the end of that year, Marek had lost his wife, and he may or may not have known of the death of his daughter. What I do know is that Marek was very unwell. At the end of the working day he frequently visited his brother, Aleksander, who as the doctor in charge of the infectious disease hospital, [89] had a service room there (such luxury). Lonely and ill, Marek clung to his younger brother for support, both emotional and medical. Aleksander, a man of some influence, tried in vain to secure some sick leave for his ill brother, first appealing to the chief medical officer of the district, Dr Leon Gross. Unfortunately, Gross, was not sympathetic, invoking regulations signed off by yet somebody else called Kalfuss. At the end of April 1944 my grandfather collapsed and was transferred to the camp hospital.[90] Bau, in his testimony, calls it a 'death house'.[91]

My grandfather's death is described graphically in *Schindler's Ark* by Keneally.[92] It would appear that Płaszów was up to capacity and there was no further room for buildings inside its electrified fences. So, an order came out to further reduce its population, starting with the sick, called euphemistically *Die Gesundheitsaktion* or Health Action. Amon Göth explained that it would allow him to allocate work for all according to their physical abilities, and for these unable to work, light employment would be provided.[93] I quote from Keneally:[94]

> He managed it as any one would manage a county fair. When it began on the Morning of May 7th, the Appelplatz was hung with banners: *For every prisoner, Appropriate Work!* Loudspeakers played ballads and Strauss and love songs. Beneath them was set a table where Dr Blancke, the SS physician, sat with Dr Leon Gross and a number of clerks. Blancke's concept of health was as eccentric as that of any doctor in the SS. He tried to rid the prison clinic of the chronically ill by injecting benzene into the bloodstream. These injections could not by anyone's definition be called mercy killings. The patient was seized by convulsions which ended in a choking death after a quarter of an hour. Marek Bi[e]berstein, once president of the Judenrat, and now, after his two years' imprisonment, a citizen of Płaszow, had suffered heart failure and been brought to the Krankenstube (hospital). Before Blancke could get to him with a syringe of benzene, Dr Idek Schindel had come to Bi[e]berstein's bedside with a number of colleagues. One had injected a more merciful dose of cyanide.

Irka Scheck-Hirschfeld's testimony[95] suggests that it was Aleksander himself who administered the poison, having learned that his brother was on the list for deportation to Auschwitz. That might be true, or it might have been gossip, as other accounts disagree. Witness to his death was a prisoner called Petzenbaum, who lay on a neighbouring bed. He somehow survived and told the story as it is recounted by Keneally[96] to my great uncle many years later in Tel Aviv. Marek died on 14 May 1944. His body was burned on a communal pyre three days after his death together with all the others murdered that day.[97]

In Kraków after the war Dr Leon Gross, the doctor who 'selected' my grandfather for annihilation, and who was himself a Schindler's Jew, was held responsible for assisting the Nazis in their efforts. It was he who made up lists of people who were sick to satisfy the Nazis' quotas for extermination. He was put on trial, found guilty and hanged in 1946. It is possible that my grandfather would have died shortly anyway in the ghastly conditions of the camp, and I suppose I should be grateful for the mitigations of the kindly hospital doctors, for sparing him the agonies of benzene or the much worse indignities which befell other *Judenrat* chairmen. Nevertheless, I cry when I see that scene in Spielberg's film.

Notes

1. Van Es, B., *The Cut Out Girl* (London: Penguin, 2018).
2. Marek was born in Tarnopol, now in Ukraine, Mila was born in Kraków.
3. Bieberstein, A., *Zagłada Żydów w Krakowie* (Kraków: Wydawnictwo Literackie 1985). It was published after Aleksander Bieberstein's death in 1979.
4. Their home address was Zaułek Rejtana 10.
5. The address of the orphanage was Dietla 64.
6. Grądzka, M., *Jewish Women in the Kraków Ghetto. The Person and the Challenges* Volume 3 (2013) Number 2, p. 123-141; *The Kraków (Cracow) Ghetto During the Holocaust*, Holocaust Encyclopaedia, USHMM, https://www.ushmm.org/wlc/en/article. php?ModuleId=10005169 (accessed 4 July 2021).
7. Molotov was Stalin's protégé and Ribbentrop was the Foreign Minister of Germany.
8. Anders' Army was the informal yet common name of the Polish Armed Forces in the East, named in recognition of its commander General Anders. The army travelled 12,500 km from the Soviet Union, through mountains and deserts, through Italy, Iran, Iraq, Palestine and Egypt between August 1941 and May 1945.
9. These words were spoken by Walter von Brauchitsch, the Commander-in-Chief of the German Army, cited in Bieberstein, A., *Zagłada Żydów w Krakowie* (Kraków: Wydawnictwo Literackie 1985), p 18.
10. Graf, M., *The Kraków Ghetto and the Płaszow Camp Remembered* (Tallahassee: Florida State University Press, 1989).
11. Bieberstein, *Zagłada Żydów w Krakowie*; Löw, A. and Roth, M., *Krakwoscy Żydzi Pod Okupacją Niemiecką 1939-1945* (Kraków: Towarzystwo Autorów Wydawców Prac Naukowych Universitas, 2014).
12. Martyna Grądzka-Rejak, 'Judenraty: Na granicy kolaboracji', *Dziennik Polski,*9 May 2016, retrieved from http://www.dziennikpolski24.pl/aktualnosci/a/judenraty-na-granicy-kolaboracji,9968289/ (accessed 4 July 2021).
13. Zimmermann, H. Z., *I Have Survived, I Remember, I am a Witness* (Tel Aviv: Katarot, 2004). I read it in Polish: *Przeżyłem, Pamiętam, Swiadczę* (Kraków: Baran i Suszczyński, 1997).
14. Löw, A. and Roth, M., *Krakowoscy Żydzi Pod Okupacją Niemiecką 1939-1945.*
15. Grądzka-Rejak, M., *Kobieta Żydowska w Okupowanym Krakowie (1939–1945)* (Kraków: Instytut Pamięci Narodowej, Wydawnictwo Wysoki Zamek, 2016).
16. Zajączkowa-Drożdż, A., Lecture entitled 'Marek Bieberstein' in *Znani, Nieznani Krakowscy Żydzi na Przestrzeni Wieków*, Kraków, 2016 (transcript of lecture sent to me by the author).
17. Document 53, Testimony by Leon (Leib) Salpeter, Kraków, on the formation of the Jewish Council, undated (ca 1945). USHMMA RG 15.084M (ŻIH 301/832) (translated from Polish).

18. Bajohr, F. and Löw A., *The Holocaust and European Societies: Social Processes and Social Dynamics* (London: Palgrave Macmillan, 2016).
19. These three sources all describe the same scene: Zimmermann, *I Have Survived, I Remember, I am a Witness*; Bieberstein, *Zagłada Żydów w Krakowie*; Löw, A., and Roth, M., *Krakowscy Żydzi Pod Okupacją Niemiecką 1939-1945*.
20. Benisch, P., *To Vanquish the Dragon* (New York: Feldheim Publishers, 1991).
21. Ibid.
22. Bieberstein, *Zagłada Żydów w Krakowie*.
23. Kielkowski, R., *Zlikwidować na Miejscu*(Kraków: Wydawnictwo Literackie, 1981).
24. Sands, P., *My Nazi Legacy* (BBC Storyville, December 2016).
25. Uki Goni, 'Son of Nazi governor returns art stolen from Poland during second world war', *The Guardian*, 26 February 2017. https://www.theguardian.com/artanddesign/2017/feb/26/nazi-art-stolen-poland-returned-horst-waechter (accessed 1 May 2021).
26. Crowe, D., *Oscar Schindler: The Untold Story of His Life, Wartime Activities and the True Story Behind the List* (Boulder, Colorado: Westview Press, 2004).
27. Graf, M., *The Kraków Ghetto and the Płaszów Camp Remembered* (Tallahassee: Florida State University Press, 1989).
28. Friedman, P., *Roads to Extinction: Essays on the Holocaust* (New York: Conference on Jewish Social Studies, 1980).
29. Aleksandrowicz, J., *Kartki z Dziennika Doktora Twardego*(Kraków: Wydawnictwo Lietrackie, 2017), p 34.
30. The website of the Central Jewish Library (*Centralna Biblioteka Judaistyczna*) has digital images of several documents signed by Marek Bieberstein (http://cbj.jhi.pl)/ - accessed 7 July 2021).
31. Duda, E., *The Jews of Cracow* (Kraków: Wydawnictwo Hagadah, 1999).
32. Graf, *The Kraków Ghetto and the Płaszów Camp Remembered*.
33. Bieberstein, *Zagłada Żydów w Krakowie*.
34. Ibid
35. Berenstein, T. and Rutkowski, A., *Assistance to the Jews in Poland 1939-1945*, translated Edward Rothert (Warsaw: Polonia Publishing House, 1963).
36. Fischel, J.R., *Historical Dictionary of the Holocaust* (Washington DC: Rowman and Littlefield, 2020).
37. Crowe, *Oscar Schindler*.
38. Bieberstein, *Zagłada Żydów w Krakowie*.
39. Trunk, I., *Judenrat: The Jewish Councils in Easter Europe under Nazi Occupation* (University of Nebraska Press; New Ed edition, 1996).
40. Keneally, T., *Schindler's Ark* (London: Hodder and Stoughton, 1982).The United States edition of the book was titled *Schindler's List*. After Spielberg's film was released, the book was later reissued in Commonwealth countries under that name.
41. Finkel, E., *Ordinary Jews: Choice and Survival During the Holocaust* (Princeton University Press, 2017).
42. At least three sources document my grandfather's 'crime': Finkel, *Ordinary Jews: Choice and Survival During the Holocaust*; Löw, A. and Roth, M., *Krakowscy Żydzi Pod Okupacją Niemiecką 1939-1945*; Trunk, *Judenrat*.
43. Trunk, *Judenrat*.
44. Yad Vashem is Israel's official memorial to the victims of the Holocaust. The entry in its data base was sourced by my cousin, Talia Mor, and translated from the Hebrew.

45. Löw, A. and Roth, M., *Krakowoscy Żydzi Pod Okupacją Niemiecką 1939-1945.*
46. Ibid.
47. Kraków Judenrat. Retrieved from: https://www.google.com/culturalinstitute/beta/asset/krakow-poland-the-judenrat-members-in-krakow/0gFKclmhk0vGVA?hl=en (Accessed 5 March 2018).
48. OD is *Jüdischer Ordnungsdienst* or Jewish Ghetto Police.
49. McKenna, J., *Haftling Scheunemann* (California: CreateSpace Independent Publishing Platform, 2014).
50. Crowe, *Oscar Schindler.*
51. Finkel, *Ordinary Jews.*
52. David R. Holocaust testimony (HVT-2946) / 5 May, 1994: https://www.worldcat.org/title/david-r-holocaust-testimony-hvt-2946-may-5-1994/oclc/702155196 (accessed 7 July 2021).
53. Offen, S., *Oral testimony of Samuel Offen.* Voice/Vision Holocaust Survivor Oral History Archive. 27 December, 1981: http://holocaust.umd.umich.edu/interview.php?D=offens&section=13 (accessed 2 July 2017)
54. Offen, S.,*When Hope Prevails* (Livonia MI: First Page Publications, 2005).
55. Löw, A. and Roth, M., *Krakowoscy Żydzi Pod Okupacją Niemiecką 1939-1945.*
56. Arendt, H., *Eichmann in Jerusalem: A Report on the Banality of Evil* (New York: Viking, 1963).
57. Wroński, S., and Zwolakowa, M., *Polacy Żydzi 1939-1945* (Warszawa: Ksiażka i Wiedza, 1971).
58. Trunk, *Judenrat.*
59. Rubenstein, R., and Roth, J., *Approaches to Auschwitz: The Holocaust and Its Legacy* (Purdue University Press, 1987).
60. Pankiewicz, T., *The Kraków Ghetto Pharmacy* (Kraków: Wydawnictwo Literackie, 2013).
61. Bieberstein, *Zagłada Żydów w Krakowie.*
62. Brecher, E.J., *Schindler's Legacy: True Stories of the List Survivors* (UK: BCA, 1994), p.282.
63. The American Jewish Joint Distribution Committee (known as 'the Joint') was established in the United States by local Jewish charities to bring aid to Jewish communities in Central and Eastern Europe. It has been active since 1914, through the First World War, in the inter-war years, and in the Second World War. In 1940, the Germans transferred the headquarters of 'the Joint' out of Warsaw to Kraków, 85 Dietla Street.
64. They survived as *Schindlerjuden.*
65. Bieberstein, *Zagłada Żydów w Krakowie.*
66. Ibid.
67. A *mezuzah* is a small decorative case containing a piece of parchment inscribed with Hebrew verses from the Torah.
68. Fischler- Martinho, J., *Have you Seen My Little Sister?* (London: Vallentine Mitchell & Co. Ltd., 1998).
69. Bieberstein, *Zagłada Żydów w Krakowie.*
70. Pankiewicz, *The Kraków Ghetto Pharmacy.*
71. The moves were from its original address on Dietla 64, to Krakusa 8 to be within the ghetto, and then again to Józefinska 31 when the ghetto borders shrank even further.
72. Bieberstein, *Zagłada Żydów w Krakowie.*

73. Grądzka, M., *Przerwane Dzieciństwo - Broken Childhood* (Kraków:Wysoki Zamek, 2012).
74. Benisch, *To Vanquish the Dragon.*
75. Grądzka, *Przerwane Dzieciństwo - Broken Childhood.*
76. Sliwa, J., Clark University. Email communication 24/03/2017.
77. On Limanowski Street.
78. Polanski, R., *Roman* (Bern: Scherz Verlag, 1984).
79. Benisch, *To Vanquish the Dragon.*
80. Himmler's order was to make Kraków *Judenrein* (free of Jews).
81. Grądzka, *Przerwane Dzieciństwo - Broken Childhood*, p 443.
82. My father's witness statement at the trial of Amon Göth (included in the Appendix).
83. Graf, M., *The Kraków Ghetto and the Płaszów Camp Remembered* (Tallahassee: Florida State University Press, 1989).
84. The Kraków ghetto: http://www.holocaustresearchproject.org/ghettos/krakow/krakow. html (accessed 8 July 2021).
85. Plaszów-Kraków Forced Labour Camp: http://www.holocaustresearchproject.org/ othercamps/plaszow/plaszow.html (accessed8 July 2021).
86. Graf, *The Kraków Ghetto and the Płaszow Camp Remembered.*
87. Benisch, *To Vanquish the Dragon.*
88. Graf, *The Kraków Ghetto and the Płaszow Camp Remembered.*
89. The hospital in the ghetto still functioned after the ghetto's liquidation.
90. Bieberstein, *Zagłada Żydów w Krakowie.*
91. Plaszów Concentration Camp, Joseph Bau's – Journey Through the Past: http://www.holocaustresearchproject.org/othercamps/plaszow/bauplaszow.html (Accessed 8 July 2021).
92. Keneally, *Schindler's Ark.*
93. Transcript of Amon Göth's trial (Wiener Library).
94. Keneally, *Schindler's Ark.*
95. Brecher, *Schindler's Legacy*, p.291.
96. Keneally, *Schindler's Ark.*
97. Bieberstein, *Zagłada Żydów w Krakowie.*

2

Artur

'I wish I could protect the memory of us all.'

Kraków Before the War

I have described my father's family in the previous chapter, but will now explore how the events that took place shaped him to become the person he was. He himself described his family as 'modest'. Nowadays we would call them typical middle class – his father a teacher, his mother a bookkeeper. My mother thought that he may have had to compete for his parents' attention with his clever elder brother and cute baby sister and attributed his craving for affection to the 'middle child syndrome'. She found him difficult to love, while I loved him unconditionally, despite his terrible tempers, his ruthless despotism and his blatant dislike of almost all my friends. But then I used to hear his (and my mother's) ear splitting nightmares and knew that the terror had never really left them.

But first, I shall describe him as a young man growing up in pre-war Poland. They did not speak Yiddish at home; my father disliked its hard, guttural German-sounding tone, but that did not stop him from using some choice Yiddish words colourfully, as I do still. He enjoyed the warmth of the family Shabbat nights where his mother would light the candles and his father would lead the family in prayer. He would have joined in and known the meaning of the rituals of the Pesach, Yom Kippur, Purim and Chanukah. Unfortunately, he never passed this knowledge down to me, so now I have to Google them to find out what it is that my Jewish friends are celebrating. As a small child he accompanied his father to the synagogue, though not with any religious conviction. He always claimed that the synagogue was an important place – for conducting business.

As a youngster he was well-liked, sporty and academically able. He was also obedient, given to respecting the authority of his superiors (or so he said, and I believed him). He went to a Polish school, the Kościuszko School (first Primary school on Sokalska Street, then High School on Zamojski

Street). The latter remains a well-known Kraków High School, still at the same address. The school was, and is, Polish, not Jewish, though he told me he mingled mostly with other Jewish children in his peer group. On his application form to the Royal Society of Edinburgh in 1968[1] he wrote: 'since very early childhood [I was] fascinated with chemistry, particularly organic chemistry'. His other favourite subject was Latin. On our travels to foreign cities in post-war Europe he would gleefully spy Latin inscriptions etched in stone and consider their relevance to their place and time. It is a pity that I never revisited Kraków with him as an adult, because I would have liked to hear his comments on this one: *'Frustra vivit, qui nemini prodest'* ('He lives in vain who does no good to others'). It is etched on an old Lutheran church on Grodzka – right in the heart of the old town.

My father was incredibly self-disciplined, exacting from himself a regular physical exercise routine every morning until the day he died. In fact, physical exercise played a large part in his life. As a young man he enjoyed hill-walking in the Polish Tatras in the summer, and skiing and skating in the winter. I know that he was an accomplished and graceful skier and was later disappointed with my lack of enthusiasm and aptitude for this (or any other) sport. I don't know if he accompanied his father and my aunt Lula on their seaside and skiing holidays, snaps from which I show in the last chapter. He may, by then, have wanted to spend holidays with his peers. He could do a passable crawl and breast-stroke, so he must have learned to swim somewhere.

I think my father's adeptness in sport is very relevant here, because at the time when war broke out, he would have been in excellent physical shape. The other attribute which would have helped him to survive, was his scrupulous cleanliness. Until the end of his life my father would boil water in a kettle in the morning and then use it to wash and shave adopting a strict order of progressively less hygiene-demanding tasks. At the end, the same water would serve to wash his socks. My mother's and my frequent use of the immersion heater provoked endless arguments.

My father and his friends travelled widely before the war, including hill-walking and skiing trips to Austria, and summer sightseeing trips to Hungary and former Yugoslavia. My mother was one of the party on their Yugoslavian holiday in the summer of 1939, but they were not boyfriend and girlfriend at that time.

He passed his *Matura* (School Leaving Certificate, required for admission to college or university) in 1932 and wanted to study medicine at the Jagiellonian University of Kraków. He had the required qualifications, but it was very difficult for Jews to gain entry. Although the *numerus clausus* (literally a 'closed number'; in reality a racial quota), did not officially come in until 1937, an unofficial bar already existed. Only 10 per cent of the places were allocated to Jewish students, whereas something like 40 per cent of people who qualified for University were Jewish – and most wanted to study either medicine or law. The only way to get in was to seek 'protection' from someone well connected, such as a doctor, lawyer or politician. Artur's uncle Aleksander could certainly exert some pull (he had managed to get his brother Ludwik in a few years earlier), but Aleksander had his own son Edwin to consider and did not want to be seen exercising his influence too often. So, my father elected to study philosophy in his first year, and then transferred to pharmacy, thinking it would give him a more useful career. Edwin, by the way, did indeed gain entry to study medicine in 1936; he finished his studies after the war and became a well-respected doctor.

During my father's studies there were already unofficial 'ghetto' benches designated for the Jews at the back of the auditorium. Some more socially-minded Poles would disregard the racial segregation rules and come and sit with their Jewish friends at the back of the class. Another form of protest by both Jews and their Catholic friends was not to occupy any seats at all, but stand throughout the hour-long lecture, causing a serious disorder. Uncle Edwin told me about this when I had a long chat with him in the 1990s. He also mentions it in his audio testimony.[2] According to my father's reminiscences, during his student years (1932-1937) ghetto benches had not yet come in legally but were practised unofficially by many of the professors. The practice was institutionally legalised in Polish universities in 1937. Throughout my father's studies the greatest threat came from the strongly antisemitic Polish nationalists, 'Endeks',[3] whose objective was to eliminate Jewish presence wherever possible. At that time, the *Endeks* were gaining strength within the student community and pogroms were a frequent occurrence. Between 1935 and 1938, 500 Jews were murdered in Poland, including 30 university students, and more often than not the police took the side of the attackers.[4] I give these facts and figures so as to paint a picture of the scene prevalent throughout my father's student years.

The subject of pharmacy suited my father's kind of skills well. He had an exceptional, deep-seated grasp of chemistry, able to envisage the shapes of molecules in 3-D and understand how they fitted together. Also, unlike me, he never forgot anything. When I was studying chemistry, I managed to do well enough in the exams but forgot it all the following day. His effortless understanding of my undergraduate level chemistry 30 years later never ceased to impress me. Latin also proved very useful in his study of medicinal plants. He knew them all, their properties, their Polish and Latin names and later their English names as well. While he was a student his favourite place to revise was the Botanic Garden on Mikołaj Kopernik Street in Kraków. I remember being taken there as a child, and shown the bench he used to sit on, near a ginkgo tree. According to his CV (submitted to the Royal Society of Edinburgh) he studied chemistry and pharmacology between 1932 and 1937. He graduated *summa cum laude* as *Magister Farmcji* (Master of Pharmacy) from the Jagiellonian University in Kraków in 1937. He was right, of course. Medicine would have given him the best chance of survival, but pharmacy was a good second best. It offered him a skill which he could later put to use in a chemists' commando, and allow him to avoid back-breaking labour, and several, but not all 'selections'.

After graduation, he was conscripted to the Polish Army and served with them for one year in Warsaw and Wilno until 1938. Military service was a requirement from which no man could be excused. He never talked about that year, probably because it was uneventful, compared with the horrors of the Occupation. What the army would have done, though, was offer him plenty of physical exercise and to hone his already rigorous self-discipline. John McKenna[5] makes an interesting observation in his novel about *Haftling* (Prisoner) *Scheunemann* saying, 'it was easy to tell which prisoners had been in the army…as they reverted to a military bearing'. Certainly, a military bearing was more likely to aid survival than the cowed look of a typical victim.

After his return from the army in November 1938, he started work as a pharmacist in *Farmacja Pod Słońcem* (Pharmacy under the Sun) – this was the pharmacy where he received his practical instruction as a student – but his real ambition was to do a doctorate, so after his graduation he enrolled in the Department of Pharmacology, using his earned money to fund his fees. He had barely started when his studies were interrupted by the war.

Kraków under German Occupation

What amazes me now is why the Bieberstein family, and indeed the entire Jewish population of Kraków did not simply pack their bags and emigrate in early 1939. They knew about the Nuremberg laws of 1935, they had heard about *Kristallnacht*, which took place all over the Reich in November 1938. Austria was annexed, Sudetenland seized. According to Gribetz[6] even after the commencement of the Second World War the Nazis maintained a policy of permitting emigration, issuing exit visas right until October 1940. So, what were they waiting for?

It could be of course, that those people who did apply for emigration papers found themselves behind 43,000 others on the waiting list,[7] though I am sure that greasing the palm of some minor official would have speeded up the process. In addition to all these problems, exit visas were expensive, or as Kaplan[8] put it, 'the way of the Polish emigrant is paved with Polish zloty amounting to as much as 20,000 apiece'. And of course, the Germans made the possession of that amount of money impossible because by the end of 1939 Jews' bank accounts were frozen. In addition, anyone who decided to emigrate had to forfeit his property.[9] It is easy to see now, with the benefit of hindsight, that the whole of my family (both sides of it) would have been saved if only they had pooled their resources, sold up while they still could, and emigrated lock, stock and barrel. However, you have to put yourself in their place and time. The Holocaust had not yet happened, and they simply did not know how bad things were going to get.

For Jews emigration to Palestine should have been the obvious option, and some of my extended family did do this in the 1930s. However, by the time the Jews of Kraków took the threat of Nazis seriously, the British mandate made immigration to Palestine difficult. In March 1939 Great Britain put out a 'white paper' restricting Jewish immigration to 75,000 for five years and limiting the purchase of land by Jews. At the same time the US, espousing the work of the eugenicist Madison Grant,[10] shut its borders to Jews and other 'inferior' races. Anyway, by September 1939 Marek was responsible for his community and escape for the whole family was not an option.

Some of the Polish Jews did predict the apocalyptic disaster which subsequently unfolded, notably Chaim Kaplan, a resident of Warsaw, who kept a meticulous and politically prescient diary between the first days of the occupation and his deportation to Treblinka in December 1942.[11] The original notebooks, which were written in a beautiful Hebrew script at the height of the Nazi terror, were translated into English in 1966, so that is the reference I give. The diarist was aware from the very beginning of the occupation that the Nazis aimed to eliminate the Jews. With an uncanny premonition of what was about to happen, he predicted that Hitler would eventually lose the war, and that most Jews would not live to see his downfall.

My uncle Ludwik was the only one to have had the sense to leave while he still could. In the summer of 1939, he had just qualified as a young doctor. He bought a train ticket to Budapest and spent the first year of the war in Hungary and France. Why did my father not decide to leave with him? I never asked him this question. Maybe he did not have the money or maybe he did not want to leave his family. It is also quite possible knowing him, that he was so engrossed in his studies, that he simply hoped the disruption would be short-lived.

With the start of the war, in September and October 1939, my father was briefly drafted into the Polish army, and took part in offence initiatives in the areas of Przemyśl and Lwów in Eastern Poland. The main aim of the army was initially to delay the advance of German troops, and when that did not work out, to see to their other enemy, the Soviets. While the Germans were advancing from the West, the Soviets were advancing from the East. As Pivnik[12] put it, 'Poland was a nut in the powerful steel jaws of a nutcracker'. The conflict lasted 20 days, ending on 6 October with the annexation of the entire Polish territories by Germany and Russia. In the skirmish at Przemyśl, which fell to the Germans after a fierce defence by the Polish troops, my father was captured and imprisoned as a Prisoner of War (POW) between 7 and 29 September 1939 (my father's CV, which I found among his papers).

This is where the dates don't quite add up. In the previous chapter I describe how in September 1939 my grandfather was forced to become the President of the Jewish Council. Henryk Zwi Zimmermann[13] describes the Shabbat scene in my grandparents' house when *SS-Oberscharführer* Paul Siebert, the head of Sipo's Jewish affairs office, hammered on the door and forced him to form a group, which would later become the *Judenrat*. According to Zimmermann's account my father was there with his parents that night alongside his younger sister Lula, 'a charming dark-haired girl'. If that is indeed so, and according to Crowe[14] the date was 8 September, then my father could not have been present. It could also be that either of the sources might not have remembered the date exactly.

His CV goes on to state 'I escaped from prison and returned to Kraków'. I do not know how he escaped or even why. I filled in the details through the memories of his colleague Poldek Pfefferberg, whose escape is described by Keneally in *Schindler's List*.[15] I know that my father and Poldek were in the Army together, and it could be that they escaped at the same time.

Maybe he should have stayed a POW, because in Kraków things were deteriorating fast. From the very start of the German occupation, the Jewish population was removed from the protection of the law, so any acts of discrimination, violence and later murder, whether by Germans or Poles went unpunished. And it all happened by degrees, starting with discrimination. The first thing to affect my father would have been his expulsion from the university. I can imagine how that would have upset him when he could no longer go the lab where he had interesting experiments on the go.

Being well acquainted with the uses of medicinal plants, my father would have foraged whenever he could, harvesting such common weeds as nettle, camomile, coltsfoot and St John's wort. He would have dried these and dispensed them along with conventional medicines. Of course, after the formation of the ghetto, there would have been no opportunity for 'urban botany' as there was no green space within its congested confines. And the next stop, Płaszów, which is within the green belt now, would then have been a mud and blood bath.

The famous interrupted trumpet call of Kraków (*Hejnał*) from St Mary's Basilica (*Kościół Mariacki*) sounded for the last time on 3 September 1939, but strangely enough the playing resumed from 24 December 1940, albeit only twice a day.[16] Of course, whether it sounded or not would have been irrelevant to the Jewish residents, because they were in any case by then excluded from the Main Market Square. When the playing resumed even the proudest of Poles must have been bemused by the celebration of an act of thirteenth century heroism in the face of current atrocities being perpetrated on a daily basis.

Through the winter of 1939 until February 1940, the *Farmacja Pod Słońcem* continued to employ my father, but when the pharmacy was taken over by a German director, he was dismissed with no severance pay. Around that time other restrictions to individual freedom followed, each becoming ever tighter by degrees. Bank accounts were blocked (November 1939); radios confiscated (1 December); cars and motorbikes had to be submitted (4 December 1939); Jews were forbidden to change address (11 December 1939); travel by train was banned (26 January 1940); Jews were not allowed to walk along the paths and squares of the famous Planty Park, and were banned from Cloth Hall and the Main Market area (April 1940).[17] Until 21 February 1941, Jews were still allowed to travel by tram, though in segregated compartments. After that date all means of transport were banned.[18]

A lot of the restrictions were regrettable blows to self-esteem, but my father was used to that; otherwise, they did not affect him too much. After all he had no car, and he had nowhere to travel to, but the main issue at hand was how to find a source of income. Any capital he might have had in a savings account would have been blocked, restricting his available wealth to no more than 2,000 zloty. Unfortunately, the Biebersteins, unlike my mother's family, did not have jewels to trade or hide.

My father found work at the JSS (or *Jüdische Soziale Selbsthilfe*) with which my grandfather had close links. Crowe[19] said it was the only Jewish aid society allowed to work in the *Generalgouvernement* (GG) and was, unlike the *Judenräte*, founded due to Jewish initiatives. My father applied there and got a job, first as a lowly pharmacist, and then in 1940 as director of its pharmaceutical and medical supplies dispensary centre.[20] Early in 1940 one of his first jobs was to dispense – free – to all Jewish children, a consignment of cod-liver oil and condensed milk. A dispensary was attached to one of the hospitals and the children lined up to be offered a spoonful of cod-liver oil, a spoonful of sweet, condensed milk and a white baked roll.[21] I can imagine the children's twisted faces from the fishy medicine radiating into grateful smiles as soon as they tasted the sweet, thick milk. I can remember the contrast well, for as a sickly child I was given the same combination.

Throughout its existence the JSS (which later became the JUS) did good work to alleviate the suffering of impoverished Jewish communities all over Poland.[22] They received donations from abroad, particularly the US, through the American Joint Distribution Committee (also known as the Joint) and the International Red Cross.[23] Pharmaceutical products were often included in these donations. It became my father's job to dispense these to hospitals and chemist shops all over Poland (now the GG). The pharmacy not only distributed donated goods to other outlets, but also sourced pharmaceutical and medical supplies from all over the GG from factories such as Wander[24] and Vita, which still exist. In fact, his official summary notes, signed by him, as director, are now available in digitised form on the internet.[25] Among lists of dates of issued medicines, dressings and cod-liver oil to individual institutions, German permits signed and stamped by the Heath Board of GG, are also lists of his employees. Later, in 1940 and 1941, proof of employment was essential and the inclusion of names offered the workers exemption from deportation. The lists of employees that my father compiled would undoubtedly have saved lives.

The Ghetto

On 3 March 1941, Otto Wächter, the Governor of Kraków, announced in the *Krakauer Zeitung* (a Kraków newspaper), that all Jews must move to a special district specially designated for them. People tend to think that the ghetto was in Kazimierz, the Jewish District – and now a major tourist attraction – but the area designated for the purpose was in fact in the poorest part of Podgórze. Initially the authorities called it the *Jüdischer Wohnbezirk* ('Jewish Residential District'); it was only later that it became known as the 'ghetto'. The German directive claimed that it was created for the health and security of its citizens, but the real reason was that Kraków had to be decontaminated and the Jews, like lepers, contained.

The ghetto was encased by a three-metre wall shaped like Jewish tombstones, which according to Otto Wächter's wife were 'elegant in the Hebrew taste'.[26] Each person was allocated approximately four cubic metres of space, with each apartment housing four families. Janina Fischler described the ghetto as sixteen square blocks of slum[27] (see the map in the previous chapter), 3,000 rooms in all. All windows and doors overlooking or leading to the 'Aryan' side were closed off with bricks and four guarded entrances were created. Altogether the ghetto was to hold 18,000-19,000 people, though over time the numbers ebbed and flowed, as following each attrition more inmates from other parts of Poland were brought in.

My grandfather was at that time in jail (details of his 'crime' are given in full in a previous chapter), so my father as the head of the household, had to oversee the eviction of the family from Zaułek Rejtana, to Limanowska Street 13, right in the middle of the ghetto. It must have been

The Kraków ghetto walls, September 2010. Note the irony of the shape – resembling *matzevahs* (Jewish tombstones)

heart-breaking for them to leave their home and their cherished family possessions to move in with some unrelated others. According to the database[28] the Bieberstein household consisted of Artur, as head of the household, his mother Mila (Mirl), and his sister Lula (Felicja). My father recounted how my poor grandmother tried to make a home in these strange and cramped surrounding. She cooked with what meagre scraps came her way, and kept their new ghetto home nice – with a table-cloth on the table and candles for Shabbat. Forlornly she counted her chicks, saying, 'I think your father will come back, but will I ever see my little Luduś again?' Word had just reached them that Ludwik had joined the Anders' Army, and she feared for his life. Little did she know that he was the safest of them all, but at that time none of them knew the horrors that the future would bring.

Although those terrible words *Arbeit macht frei* had not yet appeared in their daily vocabulary, they all knew that they needed stable work to stay alive. Lula already had a job as a nurse, but my grandmother having lost her job as a book-keeper for a Polish firm, was a *hausfrau*. She felt lucky to find work in the Optima factory (see map on page 34) to make boots and sew uniforms for the German soldiers. In the 1920s the Optima building had housed a chocolate factory producing confectionery for the citizens of Kraków and beyond. My father remembered the delicious smells that used to emanate from its pores and reminisced that as a child he would deliberately lurk in its doorways in case, as sometimes happened, a kind worker would offer him a bag of chocolate rejects. That particular memory was triggered four decades later by a chocolatey smell while we were walking past a biscuit factory in Edinburgh's Causewayside. After the occupation, the Germans expanded the Optima premises and converted them to produce military uniforms and boots. I saw the factory with its original Optima sign on the wall of the building on my trips to Kraków, but its true place in my family's history only became real to me when I started to research material for this book. No sooner did I key in 'Optima' into the Google search engine, then I was taken on a virtual globe-trotting tour of the factory and instructed in its gruesome history.

My father occasionally talked about the anguish and terror, the all-pervasive cold and hunger and the forced snow clearance which he had to carry out, despite his 'important' work at the JSS, much of which benefitted the GG. The ghetto was a place where honourable people perished. To work was not enough; only those that knew how to trade stayed alive. Trading (and also theft and bribery) would have taken place all the time. People swapped jewels for a loaf of bread, or a warm coat. A heart-breaking

testimony of survivor Gerda Weissman Klein[29] tells how her mother
swapped her diamond ring for an orange. I don't think my father's modest
family would have had any jewels, so my father traded hard work. He was
strong, healthy, and tenacious and so would have performed jobs for which
he might have been rewarded with food.

The Kraków tram (No. 3) ran through Podgórze as it had always done,
except now it shot through the heart of the ghetto without stopping.[30] I
wonder what its Aryan passengers must have thought as they sat in its
walnut-panelled carriages inscribed with the words *Juden Verboten*. Out of
its windows they could have been able to see straight into my father's ghetto
home. According to a website for present-day tourists,[31] the Polish citizens
generously donated food and other valuable commodities through the
tram's windows. I hope that is true, though my father certainly never
mentioned any such shows of Polish beneficence.

A notable exception to Polish indifference was the famous Catholic
pharmacist, Pankiewicz, now celebrated as Kraków's most famous
'righteous gentile'. The *Pod Orłem* pharmacy, where he worked, is now a
five star-rated tourist attraction, and a branch of the Kraków Historical
Museum. Over the two and a half years of the ghetto's existence the
pharmacy became a strategic social centre in which people congregated to
obtain contact with the outside world, to collect smuggled food and
medicines and false documents, and to drink alcohol (medicinal ethanol)
long into the night. Pankiewicz and his staff were the only Poles allowed to
remain and trade within the ghetto. From its windows Pankiewicz bore
witness to one of the greatest atrocities ever perpetrated. His book, which
was initially published in 1947 in Polish, has since been translated into all
the European languages and is available in many editions, most published
after his death.

The first edition of *The Cracow Ghetto Pharmacy* by Pankiewicz[32],
which I read in Polish as a teenager, and re-read when I started on this
project, was written within months of the end of the war. It is probably the
most accurate account, unbiased and un-faded by the passage of time. I
was, however, disappointed to find it has only one brief reference to my
father. After keying in 'Pankiewicz' and 'Artur Bieberstein' into Google, I
discovered that my father was mentioned in a much longer stretch of text
in the second edition of the book. I bought an English edition of the book
and was very pleased to see Pankiewicz refer to my father as 'my junior
colleague…a truly good man'. He also recounts how my father 'performed
miracles' to save the life of one stunningly beautiful woman, Mrs Dora
Schmerzler. He obtained a stamped blue ID card for her (*Blauschein*), thus

allowing her to live in the ghetto and to work outside it. Previously Dora had been hiding with some other Jews on the outskirts of the city. The day after my father's intervention Dora's companions had been found and shot. Sadly, my father never mentioned the exquisite Dora, or what subsequently happened to her, in any of his reminiscences. Nor did he mention that this incident very nearly cost him his life. Apparently one of the infamous SS-men, one Rottenführer Ritschek, found a letter Artur had begun writing to Dora. Ritschek beat him up and arrested him. He was saved by Dr Weichert, his boss.

Pankiewicz[33] also describes another daily visitor to his pharmacy, a physician called Dr Roman Glassner, who was the great-grandfather of our relatives Lukasz and Patrycja. He describes Glassner as 'an extremely cultured man'. He also describes the denunciation and incarceration of Roman Glassner's daughter Stanisława Skimina (my aunt, and Lukasz and Patrycja's grandmother) in an isolation cell in a prison for imbeciles, and her subsequent escape under cover of darkness. She was quite likely to have been pregnant with my cousin Hanka at the time. Hanka was born in 1943 but suffered from ill health most of her life, possibly resulting from her *in utero* privations; she died too young, aged seventy, in 2014. She was a wonderful person, and my favourite playmate when we were growing up in post-war Kraków. Her grandfather, Dr Roman Glassner, died in one of the sub-camps of Płaszów at Bieżanów, but until then Pankiewicz kept in touch with him sending him medications and news of his daughter.

There are other memorably good accounts of life in Kraków ghetto. The memoirs of Graf,[34] Fischler-Martinho[35] and Muller-Madej[36] provide colourful accounts of the diet, clothes, and emotions of the inhabitants. In the early days of its existence people got on with life despite the overcrowding, the curfews and restrictions. People just 'adapted'.[37] There was even a Jewish newspaper, called *Gazeta Żydowska*, published under the control of the GG two or three times a week, which included 'Hints for Housewives' and recipes.[38] It could be that the whole thing was a massive smokescreen, serving to dupe the West, to show them how well the GG was serving its Jews. Very close to my father's ghetto home there was an excellent coffee house, where one could buy real coffee and home-made cakes, and next to the ghetto gate a restaurant served tripe, gefilte fish and chulend. People said, 'we will survive, if only it does not get any worse'.[39] Not far from my father's ghetto home was a post office and it even issued its own ghetto stamps inscribed with Hebrew lettering. Of course, the Nazis liked to foster an appearance of normality to facilitate the implementation of further phases.[40]

I don't know how much my father would have made use of cafés and restaurants; he never liked to eat out even after the war, but he would have made frequent use of the bath house in which Janina Fischler-Martinho's grandmother worked. Despite the impoverished conditions, the ghetto was 'home' and he did not feel a prisoner. One day, in the summer of 1942, while working at the JSS, he received a list, delivered from Lublin: '*Liste der Häftlingsernährung*' (List of food for Detention Prisoners). This included details of the daily rations and it was my father's job to assess the calorie intake. However, it was not the content of the document but its title that brought on what my father called 'a pivotal psychological moment'. 'Why *Häftlingsernährung*, why should we be prisoners; of what were we guilty?'[41] The document talked of Majdanek, a camp on the outskirts of Lublin, where mass exterminations were being carried out in gas chambers.

Further corroborations of the destruction of whole Jewish communities came in the form of letters marked 'returned to sender'. The letters were initially sent out by Michal Weichert, my father's boss, to various branches of the Jewish Social Self-Help Organization (JSS) from their central office in Kraków. The Polish postal service returned them to their office, a while after they were sent, with various handwritten additions on the envelope: 'Left the address'; 'The Jews were deported' or 'The Jewish council no longer exists'.[42]

Brought up as he was in a culture of antisemitism my father had until now dismissed the Germans' rhetoric of annihilation as a vacuous metaphor. It now seemed that Hitler's wish had become an order.

People claim that the Poles, and indeed the West, did not really know what was happening, that they were ignorant of the Germans' intended total annihilation. Without a doubt, the Polish postmen were fully aware of what had befallen the addressees whose letters were returned to the sender. Furthermore, the speeches of Hans Frank, which were printed in German and Polish newspapers, made the situation crystal clear. Even much earlier, in October 1940 he said – 'My dear comrades, I would not eliminate all lice and Jews in one year [public amused, he notes in his diary], but in the course of time, and if you help me, this end will be attained'. Then in December 1941 he repeated:[43]

> As far as the Jews are concerned, I want to tell you quite frankly that they must be done away with in one way or another...Gentlemen, I must ask you to rid yourself of all feelings of pity. We must annihilate the Jews. Difficult to shoot or poison the three and half million Jews

in the *Generalgouvernement*, but we shall be able to take measure which will lead, somehow, to their annihilation.

My great-uncle Aleksander Bieberstein writes in his book [44] that in the first few days of the occupation he personally witnessed the Germans' instructions:

> …which were to have the firm consequence of total annihilation of Jews through: segregation from the Polish population, economic ruin, removal of personal freedoms, incarceration in ghettos, physiological extermination through enforced labour, deportation to work and concentration camps, and in the end to extermination camps and gas chambers.

It seems unlikely that Aleksander did not share this information with his family, so they should all have been aware of what was coming. It could be that they simply did not believe him and they, along with the whole world, kidded themselves that the Germans were good at spouting metaphorical rhetoric and just put their heads in the sand. According to Cesarani[45] they still considered antisemitism to be 'no more than an advertising slogan'. Pola Gerner (later Scheck) remarks in her testimony: 'The Nazis were very smart. They must have had terrific psychologists. It went step by step down. They took the silver: what's the big deal? Tomorrow they take the fur coats: what's the big deal? And that's how it went.'[46] Like that frog in the water which gets steadily hotter, people simply tolerated the decrees, hardly noticing that each incremental step was more punitive than the last.

The deportations, once they started, came in waves. The first, which was just a 'taster', took place when my grandfather was still in jail. In early March 1942 they removed 50 intellectuals and deported them to Auschwitz. Had Marek been around, he may well have been sent with them. Then came the 'Operation Reinhard'[47] deportations (1 June, 5 June, 28 October 1942),[48] which between them systematically removed the old, the young and the infirm.

Each one of these waves of deportations was preceded by a wave of intense bureaucracy. My father described the events of early June 1942. The JSS offices, where he worked, were transformed into rows of tables with typewriters and clerks from the Gestapo labour office with stamping equipment at the ready. Permission to remain in the ghetto would only be granted to those who managed to get their *kennkarte* stamped there and then, and this only happened upon the presentation of the appropriate work documents. Often permission to remain was granted purely on the whim of a minor clerk. Often sizeable bribes changed hands. It all took a long time, while long queues of people waited to be served. All those over 55 were automatically denied a stamp, said my great-uncle, though he did not say how my grandmother Mila managed to get one. The fact that she was not taken, though she was 59, suggests that my father might have offered a 'present' to an appropriate official. Then registration ceased and all those without stamps scurried about looking for hiding places. The following day the SS and the OD (Jewish Police) rampaged through the ghetto in a game of cat and mouse. Without too much difficulty they managed to round up 2,000 from cellars and attics, from inside wardrobes and behind false partitions. Those they caught were all taken at gun-point to *Plaz Zgody* (Harmony Square) to sit on their bundles in the full glare of the hot sun.

On 1 June, the assembled victims were formed into marching lines and led to the train station at Płaszów, and thence by cattle trucks to the extermination camp of Belzec. The bundles they were made to abandon were collected for sorting. Then *Plac Zgody* was again filled and the scene

Jews applying for identification and work permits c. 1941 (United States Holocaust Memorial Museum)

repeated, again and again. However, by 4 June, the Germans still did not have enough victims; they wanted more, still more. They filled the Square again, this time shooting at random. 'The sight of blood and the corpses excited their bestiality, and the killing mania empowered their sadism', wrote Pankiewicz.[49] But the Germans were still not satisfied. First, they sacked Marek's successor, the Judenrat Chairman, Artur Rosenzweig, for failing to supply the required numbers, and thrust him and his family within the thronging crowds destined for deportation.

Then on 5 June, the Germans thought of yet another bureaucratic ploy, to call in all those in the possession of stamped *kennkarte* to supplement it with a new work card, the *blauschein* (blue card). Again, crowds gathered at the JSS offices, again there were queues and stress of an uncertain outcome, again bribes changed hands, some successfully, others not so. All those who failed to qualify for a blue card were immediately taken, this time to the courtyard at Optima where my grandmother worked, watching the nightmare scene through its windows. The assembled victims in Optima were kept for two days without food or water, until 8 June, when they were marched like the others without a *blauschein* out of the ghetto to the railway station for 'resettlement' in the East.

News of what was going on in Optima soon filtered through to the rest of the ghetto inhabitants. My great uncle, Aleksander, the chief doctor in charge of the Hospital for Infectious Diseases, knew that until now hospital patients had not been deported, so he proceeded to cram the wards intended for 40 with some 300 pretend 'patients'. It was a high-risk strategy and he nearly came unstuck. One Gestapo man did enter the hospital, noticed the civilian clad crowds and thrashed Aleksander. Bruised, but not defeated, Aleksander cunningly persuaded the German not to get too close to the patients as they were convalescing from seriously infectious diseases.

Most sources quote the total figure of deaths from the June actions to be 7,000, leaving about 12,000 still in the ghetto.[50]

At that stage in the extermination programme the Germans tried to keep the fate of the Jews sent for resettlement secret,[51] and most of the remaining ghetto inhabitants were ignorant of what was really happening. Some were duped into a false sense of security by letters they received from their deported loved ones. What they did not know was that the victims were forced to write these letters shortly before they were gassed.[52]

As I researched the history of the Holocaust in Kraków, I became increasingly more curious about how and when people began to find out about the mass murders, suffocation by gas and the burning of corpses in crematoria. My father's 'psychological moment' came in the middle of 1942, which is probably after the June deportations. Pankiewicz[53], who watched the deportations from his vantage point within the ghetto, also tellingly describes the ghetto people's inability to take in the reality of the situation. He recounts various tales that were circulating: they talked of deportees left in wagons on sidings without food or water, they talked of armament factories staffed by forced labour but, he says, nobody suspected that the deported victims were just simply and swiftly annihilated. It was about this time that Aleksander brought home the story of railwaymen who had just returned from delivering their last convoy to Belzec with descriptions of 'trains arriving full and leaving empty and the smell of death in the air'.[54]

While pondering on what the victims knew, a mirror question was forming in my mind, as it would have been forming in my father's mind at the time. At what stage did the transition from mere antisemitic vandalism to full-blown genocide take place in the minds of the perpetrators? Was it incremental by degrees, a simple tightening of the screws, or were there some sharp radicalisation transitions affecting the process? It is easy now to click the internet button and find out how it happened and when, but for the Jews on the ground, it was all guesswork and the stuff of gossip. Most historians now agree that a change of intention took place in the middle of the war just after the German victory in the East. Historians Dwork and van Pelt[55] believe that this did not happen as a slippery slope. According to historian Browning[56] the transition time happened during a five-week period from 18 September to 25 October 1941. The old fairy-tale idea of shipping all of Europe's Jewry to Madagascar had been initially revived in 1940, but finally shelved early in 1942 when they realised that Germany simply did not have the means to transport 4 million people. The fact that Madagascar did not actually belong to the Germans was merely a minor impediment, which could be solved by paying off the Malagasy Frenchmen using money gained from confiscated Jewish property, but it was the matter of transport that finally scuppered the plan. They had hoped to defeat Britain and requisition its Navy, but when that failed there was no way to implement the evacuation. So, at that stage they had two possible courses of action: one was to work the Jews to exhaustion, like for example in draining the newly-conquered Pripet marshes, and the other was simply to kill them outright on a mass scale.

The decision to do the latter was officially rubber-stamped at the Wannsee conference on 20 January 1942. It was led by Heydrich and attended by 15 senior Nazi bureaucrats, including Eichmann. The conference itself was short and to the point; it barely lasted two hours. Europe's remaining 11 million Jews (numbered country by country) were to be disposed of. It was the details that took time – like what to do with half Jews and quarter Jews and those decorated in the First World War fighting for the Fatherland. Of course, the conference was held in secret, so the decisions made would have taken a few months to percolate through to the perpetrators who were charged to enact them.

Although annihilation was the general aim, the Germans were also keen to enslave and harness the able-bodied Jewish workforce for the good of the Reich. To that end the Germans created some places of work, special workshops where they used Jewish skills to make sellable products for both civil and German war-effort needs. The most famous such factory was the Emalia factory, which produced enamelware and ammunitions. Its director was Oskar Schindler, made famous by Thomas Keneally's *Schindler's Ark*.[57]

At first, Schindler ran the factory as a business, a lucrative one, because he could pay the Jews less that the Poles, but later he became sympathetic to their plight and employed them deliberately to save them from deportation. To be one of his workers meant survival, and so people queued (and no doubt bribed) to be hired. The factory was situated outside the ghetto perimeter, but its workers all got a special pass to enable them to leave and enter through the manned ghetto gates. Later Schindler even arranged living quarters for his workers. My immediate family never made it onto the list, but my great-uncle, Aleksander Bieberstein, did. His testimony informed some of the material covered in Keneally's book and Spielberg's film. Also on the list were Marek and Aleksander's nephew and niece, Jurek/Jerzy (George) and Irka Scheck, and Pola Gerner (who later became Jerzy Scheck's wife), together with her parents, Adele and Ignacy Gerner. All of them survived the war, emigrated to the US and settled in Long Beach, Long Island near New York. When I visited them there in 1966, I was amazed to find Pola's elderly parents still alive. In my family's circle of survivor friends, old people were a rarity, and few of the survivors' children had grandparents. That is when I first heard of Schindler.

In July 1942 my father was delighted to welcome his father back from his 22-month jail sentence. I can imagine the conversations that Marek, Mila, Artur and Lula would have shared that first Shabbat meal after his homecoming. They would have discussed Artur's 'psychological moment' and Aleksander's tales from the railwaymen of Belzec. There was much to pray for, but was there a God? Did they have food to eat? Did Mila still light candles? Or did she maybe feel the need to do it, now more than ever, to pray for peace and light in a world which had become so very dark.

By then the June deportation had already happened and with the population reduced by more than a third, the ghetto boundaries were redrawn and the redundant bits of wall partly demolished; the perimeter was demarcated with barbed wire. The Bieberstein family ghetto home in a corner of a room at Limanowskiego 13 now lay at the ghetto's southern periphery. Nevertheless, life in the reduced ghetto went on; it was tough, and permanently lined with grief. I know that my father was parsimonious, but maybe it was a habit learned, rather than inherited. I remember how he would stick the thinnest sliver of an old cake of soap to the next one, so as not to waste it. And he boiled and re-boiled tea leaves with fresh water until the day he died. However, his miserliness, which my mother complained of so bitterly, did not extend to other people. He was capable of acts of selfless kindness to people in need.

By this time nightly arrests, shootings and deportations were a regular occurrence. Two of the victims were the parents of a six-year-old girl called Basia. When my father found the tearful orphan in the street, he took her home rather than to the orphanage, and cared for her lovingly. Basia would not have had her own ration card, but the family offered to share their meagre living space and supplies. She lived with them for several months, but luckily Basia was old enough to be lucid, to converse and remember. She told them of some Aryan relatives in the country, so my father traced them, phoned them, and looked for a way to deliver her there. A foray into Aryan territory without any valid papers, and with a child who might not be entirely discreet, was fraught with danger. Ultimately, he risked both their lives by illegally boarding a train (Jews were of course forbidden to travel). He feared being apprehended without his armband (this was punishable by death), but he also feared the indignity of being told to drop his trousers. When many years later I gave birth to my first son, I asked my father's advice about whether I should have him circumcised. 'No', he said, 'Why would you want to disadvantage him so?'

Basia survived the war in hiding with her country relatives. After the war she used to visit us in Kraków in the 1950s, and on several occasions accompanied us on our holidays. I looked upon her as a sort-of half-sister and looked forward to her visits and her reminiscences about my father's kindness. I particularly liked the one about how he cut her fingernails on that memorable train journey. He was always good at that. She corresponded with my father regularly and, I remember that in one of her letters she expressed her intention to study agricultural botany in Odessa. My father phoned her and said typically and rather curtly, 'why not medicine?' just like he did to me ten years later. I know she qualified and married and then we lost contact with her. I don't remember her surname.

'How did the Poles view this turn of events?' I asked my father. 'They would have been free to earn money, travel, shop, and feed themselves. Did any of them offer help?' He said that Pankiewicz (the author of *The Cracow Pharmacy*) was an exceptionally good man. He helped a lot of people. 'But, no', he said, 'no one helped me personally'. Occasionally a Pole would sell him a loaf for a fair price, but most were too scared to fraternise with Jews, and hiding Jews was of course punishable by death. Many were antisemites and denounced Jews, a few saved them, but most just stood by and watched. After the June '*Aktions*' there was very little contact with the Aryan population. Initially the blue card enabled him to get in and out, but that ceased to work by the summer of 1942. Lula fraternised with an Aryan; she had a Polish boyfriend who used to come to the ghetto on some sort of business. Most Poles talked openly that the Jews were getting the punishment of history, implying that they got their comeuppance. The best one could hope for would be a meeting of the eye, a friendly smile, a kindly look, instead of a jeer and a vicious kick. While not offering to help (except for the 'righteous' few), the Poles criticised Jews for going to their deaths like sheep.

I wondered about that too of course. 'Why was there not an uprising, like they had in Warsaw', I asked. 'After all, what did they have to lose?' He said that the geography of the ghetto in Kraków made resistance very much more difficult. The ghetto was easily sealable and visible from its boundaries, laid out like on the palm of the Germans' hand. There was in fact a resistance movement called ŻOB (*Żydowska Organizacja Bojowa*), which used the ghetto as a base from which to attack targets throughout the city of Kraków. The most important attack took place in December 1942 at the *Cyganeria* café in the centre of Kraków, killing 12 German officers. This act of defiance lifted Jewish morale, [58] but many more Jews died in the subsequent reprisals. Now a plaque commemorates the heroism of the Polish *Gwardia Ludowa* (Polish Underground Organisation). As so often happens, monuments erected in Poland after the war whether to heroes or victims, mention the heroism of the Polish population hardly distinguishing Jews from the Poles. Unfortunately, that is not how it was on the ground at the time.

It is of course true that there were many Polish underground activists and sympathisers who provided counterfeit documents, brought in food, hid people for no personal gain, while risking their own lives. There were also some decent Germans, SS-men who pretended to arrest Jews only to lead them out to safety. Pankiewicz[59] also names and shames some despicable Jewish informers.

Happy post-war summer holidays with Basia

The JSS was dissolved in July 1942 but reopened under a new name *Jüdische Unterstützungsstelle* (JUS), after Weichert's[60] successful negotiations with the Nazis. My father transferred there and continued as the director of the pharmaceutical section. Between December 1942 and March 1943 my father also worked in the radiology unit of the Kraków hospital, under someone called Dr Otto Schwartz. It is possible that this placement required pharmaceutical knowledge. The JUS, like the JSS before it, was responsible for providing Jews in German slave labour camps with aid from abroad. It continued to operate even after the ghetto was liquidated, with Weichert and a few of his key workers (including my father) acting as useful go-betweens taking medicines to and from Pankiewicz.[61] They also had a soup kitchen which provided extra nourishment for the inmates; they called it *Zupa Jusowa* (JUS soup). In the summer of 1944, the JUS was disbanded and Weichert went into hiding.

However, I need to backtrack a bit to the summer and autumn of 1942. After the June deportations and the reduction of the ghetto's boundaries there was a short lull, during which the residents of the ghetto fell into apathy and depression.[62] 'And somehow people began to get used to it (the *status quo*) and to regard every savage event as perfectly normal and understandable.'[63] Most had lost their loved ones, but the hardships of everyday life made grieving difficult. The reduced size of the ghetto also meant that new strangers were thrust into close proximity, and inevitable quarrels about space and furniture ensued. Another reason for disputes was adherence (or lack of) to religious dietary laws (*kashrut*). In the cramped conditions of a shared kitchen the preparation of food and the separation of milk and meat dishes, was almost impossible. I can imagine the ghastly rows that would have ensued if a non-religious Jew was lucky enough to find some pork. Those that flouted the rules were seen as infidels, while those that stuck to them were mocked for their narrow-mindedness.

When in October 1942 the new Judenrat Chairman, Dawid Gutter, was called into the SS offices at Oleandry (later my primary school), people realised that a new deportation was imminent, and panic was in the air. On 27 October, the SS and the Gestapo again surrounded the ghetto, just as they had done prior to the June deportations, and announced that all those leaving for work in the morning of the following day are to assemble in front of the Judenrat offices the following morning. There on 28 October, despite the protestations of some of the German factory managers, a selection took place. Those chosen to stay were destined for deportation, and those chosen to go went with their German bosses back to their places of employment. The selection scenes topped everything they had hitherto experienced in brutality and sadism amid loud laments of families torn apart for ever. The selection process depended on a whim of the individual SS-man. Often essential workers with a valid blue card were deported to their deaths.

On this day of the October *Aktion* my father was saved by the foresight of his uncle Aleksander.[64] Aleksander, who always had his wits about him, had heard that medical staff would be exempt from deportation but that they planned to eliminate the patients. In fact, the ploy he had in mind was the very opposite of that which had worked so well in June, when he crammed the hospital full of pretend patients. This time he evacuated the patients into a nearby dwelling, while filling the hospital with pretend doctors, dressed in spare white uniforms with stethoscopes round their necks. An SS inspector, surprised by the empty wards, was simply informed calmly that there were no infectious diseases at the time, a story which was immediately corroborated by a friendly Polish policeman. Aleksander was so right to have done this, as all the inmates of another hospital were exterminated that day. Invalids deprived of their crutches were brutally kicked down the stairs onto a courtyard where they were made to jump and dance for the Germans' amusement; then they were shot. The sad fate of the orphanage children has already been described in the previous chapter. Almost all perished that day. The total losses from the *Aktion* were 4,500 by deportation and 600 in random shootings.[65] I am not sure of total numbers of residents left in the ghetto, because sources differ, and the figures don't always match up. In any case after each deportation more Jews were crammed in from Silesia and beyond. It was probably at least 10,000.

After the October *Aktion*, the ghetto area was again reduced, and the residents living outside the new confines forced to relocate yet again, given 24 hours to complete their move. No further walls were built, just rolls of barbed wire separated the restricted area from the rest. Although there were no organised deportations for a few months, random shootings continued. The SS-men would arrive in the ghetto by car and hunt down their prey indiscriminately irrespective of age or profession. The very sight of such a vehicle was enough to clear a street instantly as the inhabitants scattered and hid. At that time there was confusing gossip going around about the Nazis' future intentions. Some said that the Gestapo would not want to liquidate the ghetto, because without this 'civil' job (it was obviously considered a bit of a cushy number), they would be sent to the Russian front. It was probably to this end that a new project was being prepared – the building of the camp in Płaszów.

In December 1942, the SS inflicted on the residents yet another wave of bureaucracy. Both the cards (*Kennkarte* and *Blauschein*) were replaced with a new *Judenkarte*, and each Jewish worker who left the ghetto had to prominently display a 'W', 'R' or 'Z' patch on their outer clothing. The 'W' stood for *Wehrmacht*, for the military workers, the 'R' stood for *Rüstung*, for armament, and 'Z' for *Zivil* or civil workers.[66] If my family were lucky enough to be thus identified, my grandfather and grandmother would have had the 'W', since they worked in a military uniform factory, and my father and Lula would have had the 'Z'. However, all this is conjecture, and in the end no classification was good enough to save people.

On 6 December 1942, the ghetto was divided into ghetto A for the workers and ghetto B for the unemployed. My father yet again witnessed scenes of overt misery as families were torn apart. This time people only took their personal belongings with them, smashing any furniture they possessed for firewood, or throwing it out of the window onto the courtyard. Luckily both my father's ghetto home and the JUS where he worked fell within the precinct of ghetto A, so he did not have to move. Pankiewicz's pharmacy, which was in Plac Zgody, was in ghetto B, so medicines and prescriptions changed hands at the barbed wire fence. To start with people could move from one half to the other on the presentation of a special pass, which was obtainable from the OD. Later the pass became null-and-void and movement into Ghetto A was prohibited. In the meantime, the camp at Płaszów was taking shape as ever more barracks (*Barackenbau*) were being built for the rest of the ghetto's inhabitants.

Płaszów

On 13 March 1943, the German police surrounded the ghetto, milling thickly at the entrance between ghetto A and B. Instructions were passed by loudspeaker, then word of mouth – the ghetto was to be liquidated, and only those in ghetto A would be eligible for entry into Płaszów. The lucky ones in ghetto A were informed that they could take with them personal belongings, such as clothes, footwear and bedlinen. The items were to be packed in carefully labelled suitcases and to be delivered to Józefinska Street, from which they would be transported to Płaszów. Adele Gerner (she was later a relative by marriage) had delivered her beautifully monogrammed suitcase bearing 'AG'. Later someone spotted it in the possession of Amon Göth, the Commandant of Płaszów.[67]

The inhabitants of ghetto A had to pass a further selection process before being admitted to Płaszów – only the fittest would be allowed entry.

Amon Göth stood at the junction of Jósefinska and Krakusa Streets, conducting with a whip, like a maestro in an orchestra – to the left or to the right. Miraculously Marek, Mila and Artur all 'passed' and were herded into the newly-built barracks in the Płaszów forced labour camp, not together of course, for families were split apart. They were the lucky survivors of the ghetto's liquidation.

Pankiewicz[68] documents the barbarities taking place for those left behind, sparing us none of the detail. The next day, on Sunday 14 March, the inmates of ghetto B were taken to *Plac Zgody* and most were shot. Children were lined up next to one another in order of size, so that one bullet would kill all and the same went for babies in prams. The wind of death blew through every tenement, every flat. Left were only the abandoned possessions of the departed strewn in the streets, and the corpses. After a few German hyenas had picked them over, a group of miserable prisoners were given the job of undressing the dead and stacking them up as if they were railway sleepers. In the course of that day, 2,000 people died on the streets and 3,000 more were sent to Auschwitz.[69]

The reason why Lula was not with the family at this stage was that she had fled from the ghetto with her Polish boyfriend, Rysiu, and assumed an Aryan identity. It is not clear how Lula met Rysiu, or for how long they had known each other but love, perhaps made more poignant in such challenging times, made her feel free and reckless. Rysiu managed to obtain some Aryan papers for her (what did they have to sell to get these?), and to smuggle her out of the ghetto. He took her home to his family in Bochnia, a small town about 50 km to the East of Kraków. She lived with him there over that terrible summer of 1943, but her luck ran out in the autumn. It was inevitable, I suppose, because times were hard, and there was money to be made from denouncing Jews. Lula did not look particularly semitic, but maybe someone recognised her. She was handed over to the Gestapo and summarily shot somewhere near Bochnia railway station in the autumn of 1943.

Nobody knows what became of Rysiu. After the war people felt too numb to reignite painful memories. Maybe my father knew Rysiu's surname, but if he did, he did not tell me and I did not ask. It has been said that I look like my aunt Lula. How sad that I have not had the privilege of meeting her and knowing her. However, here is the good news. In 2016 my younger son, Tim, had a beautiful daughter, named Louise. I often call her Lula after her great-great aunt.

The camp 'for the workers' held about 6,000 people at the beginning, just after the liquidation of the ghetto, but at its peak it held 25,000 inmates.[70] Sources disagree on how many people were incarcerated there over the two years of its existence. The Polish Supreme National Tribunal estimates that it was 35,000, Eldar[71] says 50,000, but the website of the Kraków-info.com gives the figure of 150,000.[72]

More interesting than numbers are the details of what the inmates found on arrival. An accurate description is available from a diary of an eighteen-year-old boy, Juliusz Feldman, who died at Płaszów, leaving the diary mid-sentence. After the war Polish builders on the site of the camp discovered it tucked in behind a brick. Juliusz, like my father, passed through the scrutiny of Amon Göth on the day of the ghetto's liquidation. After an hour's walk up-hill to the camp this is what he saw: 'For the first time I saw the panorama of our future residence, the barbed wire, and the guard towers all around and in the middle the tiny barracks, huddled up against one another that are supposed to hold the entire ghetto.'[73]

The ghetto was left deserted, but various German factories and places of work were still functioning. Among them was the Optima factory where my grandparents worked making military uniforms and the JUS (previously the Jewish Self-Help or JSS) where my father worked. To get to these they were formed into work detail columns and marched out of Płaszów in the morning and back in the evening. Many such columns were formed to serve the different factory outlets still operating within the old

Joseph Bau's map of Plaszów camp (Source: Chris Webb Private Archive)

ghetto boundaries. Although the columns were closely guarded, many people managed to escape, either hiding in the deserted ghetto, or in the sewers, or helped by Poles. The trouble about escapees was that the rest of the prisoners had to pay for it. For every Jew that escaped ten were shot the following morning.[74]

The camp was built on two cemeteries divided by Jerozolimska Street – the Old Cemetery (Podgórzny Cmentarz, approximately two hectares in area) and the New Cemetery (Krakowski Cmentarz, about eight hectares in area).There were several sections: German living quarters, Jewish male barracks, Jewish female barracks, all separated by barbed wire (in places electrified wire), with gates in-between. There were 13 outlook towers 5-15 metres high with machine guns, reflectors, telephones, and loudspeakers, staffed mainly by Ukrainian guards. Electrification was supplied by a 5,000-volt transformer. There was another area housing the bakehouse, kitchen, cold-room, the butchery, coal store and other storerooms which were out of bounds to the inmates. Also out of bounds to the inmates (not surprisingly), was a store-room for items which had been confiscated.

Amon Göth, the camp commandant, was a sadist. His two ferocious dogs called Rolf and Ralf, were frequently unleashed to tear prisoners apart, literally from limb to limb. The dogs, which were to be addressed as *Herr* (Sir), were trained to attack when Göth cried *Jude.*[75] Natalia Weissman remembered the dogs being called *Mensch* (man), while the prisoners were called 'dog'.[76] 'Run like a dog', said Göth to my father on one occasion. There are accounts that the dogs got fond of a Jewish prisoner (Adam Sztab), who was given the job of dog minding, and Göth got so angry and jealous that he shot him.[77]

Thea Jourdan[78] quoted my father as saying: 'I saw the commandant shoot people for fun, he was a beast, a cruel creature'. The same memories were revealed by Helen Jonas-Rosenweig. In a Podcast series of the US Holocaust Memorial Museum she quotes, 'When you saw Göth, you saw death'.[79] My father's testimony of Göth shooting Jews at random was used at Göth's trial after the war. It also helped to inform the portrayal of Göth in Spielberg's film by Ralph Fiennes. Nevertheless, Spielberg's immensely powerful scene with Fiennes aiming his gun from the balcony of his villa, could not have taken place, because Göth's real villa sat at the foot of a steep hill. When I took both my parents to see the film when it came out in 1994, my father started to whisper loudly at this point, to the consternation of those around them. I apologised on his behalf, adding – 'please excuse my father, but he was there'.

Amon Göth on his balcony. The photograph was taken by Raimund Titsch, the gentile factory manager of the Madritsch factory. He reputedly hid the film and had it developed after the war.[80] (United States Holocaust Memorial Museum, courtesy of Leopold Page Photographic Collection)

At Göth's trial in 1946 my father described the events he witnessed in more fulsome detail. (The oral statement is translated in full in the Appendix.) One day before 6am when the prisoners were gathering on the *Appellplatz* in their work squads before being marched off to their places of work, Göth arrived to survey the columns. He was in a bad mood because some prisoners had escaped, and to vent his anger he mercilessly beat and then shot one prisoner at random, and then another. He then proceeded to slowly make his way down the column to where my father was standing in his row of four, saying 'If anyone does not like what he sees, maybe they should step forward. I am a fair person. I can talk with him. Please.' Luckily, he and the man nearest to him avoided looking him in the eye and so the rest of them were spared that day. In his statement my father wondered whether Göth was inebriated at the time. This is interesting as historians have often said that the perpetrators were fuelled by alcohol.

In January 1944, the camp changed status from a forced labour camp to a concentration camp. Contrary to what the words evoke, the change in status brought certain improvements for the inmates, as new orders from Berlin demanded that prisoners could no longer be shot without a hearing.

It was this alleviation of Göth's powers that saved my father's life in his second face-to-face encounter with the commandant. One day in the early months of 1944, my father went to a tailor's workshop, intending to hand in his jacket for mending. Suddenly word passed round that Göth was on his way and panic was in the air. My father, who should not have been in the tailor's shop during work hours, was told to go. He was just leaving when Göth appeared on his white horse, boots level with my father's eyes. '*Was machst du denn hier?....Comm näher*' ('what are you doing here, come closer'), he yelled. He whipped him raw with his horse whip, but because of the new regulations he refrained from shooting him. My father said, he must have been one of only a handful of prisoners who were beaten but not shot. Later, people said that Göth blatantly disobeyed the Berlin rules and the shootings continued.

The wanton violence against himself and others must have left a deep and indelible impact. The weals from the beatings healed to become silvery scars that criss-crossed his back, but Göth on his white horse repeatedly terrorised his dreams.

Amon Göth riding his white horse round Plaszów, photographed by Raimund Titsch in 1943 or 1944 (United States Holocaust Memorial Museum, courtesy of Leopold Page Photographic Collection)

At the time, his daily priority was to appear as clean, healthy, neat, and as inconspicuous as possible. It was with this aim in mind that he would have visited the tailor's shop. The phrase 'unseen but seeing' used by Kehane[81] describes it well. Another inmate recalls making himself 'not too erect, not yet slouching; not too smart, yet not sloppy; not too proud, yet not too servile, for I knew that those who were different died...while the anonymous, the faceless ones survived'.[82]

My father claimed that what really saved him was his fanatical yearning for cleanliness because to be clean meant you looked healthy, and if you were healthy, then you were of some use to them as a worker. His most prized possession in Płaszów camp, and all the subsequent camps, was a razor, which he cherished and hid from others. This was never intended to be used as a weapon against others or himself; it was to enable him to shave each day. To be clean-shaven meant that you looked younger and healthier, and to look healthy meant that you were more likely to be deemed fit for work and thus escape selections. The same advice to shave is recounted in the excellent little book *Man's Search for Meaning* by Victor Frankl, first published in German in 1946: 'Shave daily, even if you have to use a piece of glass to do it...even if you have to give your last bit of bread for it. You will look younger, and the scraping will make your cheeks ruddier.'[83]

I wonder how often starvation would have tempted my father to part with his razor. But he never did, not even on the death march that followed. You can imagine his utter dismay when, in the liberal, hairy sixties, I brought home a boyfriend who sported an untidy, long beard. My bearded boyfriend, David, later became my husband, and though eventually my father became reconciled to my choice of mate, he never really forgave me. Until the end he believed that both David and I would have clearly belonged in the 'victim' category within the camp hierarchy.

In his accounts of the camp, he inevitably talked of the latrines and the washing facilities (lack of), and of his endeavours to overcome these problems. The latrines were communal, about 30 holes in a bench above a cesspit, where prisoners sat side by side at obligatory times. The smells were terrible, from both ends. Bad teeth and a constant state of ketosis gave people appalling bad breath. Washing of clothes was impossible. As Feldman wrote in his 1943 diary: 'washing is forbidden, but you have to be clean; heating or boiling or washing anything is forbidden, yet you have to walk around in clean clothes; you are not allowed to have a chamber pot in the barracks at night, and it is also forbidden to go to the toilet'[84]. My father probably used the facilities of the JUS to wash himself and his clothes, as he later did at the Institute of Animal Genetics in Edinburgh (because hot water was free). The JUS may also have provided soap and toothpaste, but that would all have stopped when the JUS was disbanded in the summer of 1944. To start with he had underwear, which he would wash and dry meticulously. Later, underwear was not provided nor even allowed. One could not avoid fleas, bedbugs and lice (three species of them), since they slept several men to a bunk, three tiers deep, 200-300 people per barrack, but they could be held in check. At night, the jackets would be taken off, folded, and used as pillows, but before that my father would carefully debug his.

Before the camp became a concentration camp, the prisoners wore their own clothes with a yellow star.[85] From January 1944 they were issued with thin striped concentration camp clothes, presumably to better identify escapees. Scanning the map of Płaszów as it was then (see page 72), I see that there was a laundry. However, according to the accounts of prisoner Bau, the laundry was only used by a special squad to wash the clothes of the SS men, and those stripped off cadavers. I should think that the tailor's shop was similarly out of bounds for ordinary inmates, so my father's irregular visit there on the fateful day when he came face-to-face with Göth, can be explained simply by his desire to appear untattered.

The Płaszów camp, part of which is known to have been built on wet, swampy ground[86] must have been swarming with mosquitoes in the summer months. The interminable evening roll calls in the summer when each prisoner was called out by his six-digit number must have been unbearable, yet interestingly, mosquitoes are never mentioned in the holocaust history books, nor were they by my father. Obviously in the face of the brutality of daily life, the minor annoyance of mosquitoes would have been a complete irrelevance. My friend, Joyce Caplan, noticed this omission in the accounts of the camps, and brought it to my attention in a poem she wrote. On her tourist's evening walk round Auschwitz the mozzies came out, while 'she stumbled to her own freedom'.

The food rations dealt out to Płaszów prisoners were meagre. Each prisoner was allotted 1.4 kg of bread per week and 2 teaspoons of jam, but the jam contained nothing of value, such as vitamins. The label on the container bore the words '*Nur für Häftlinge*' ('only for prisoners').[87] In the morning they got a cup of ersatz coffee and a slice of bread. I always thought that the 'Camp' coffee, which the Scots are fond of, was named after the concentration camps, but apparently it really is a Scottish product, invented in 1876. In the evening he would get a bowl of thin soup with a cabbage leaf or two (the Germans called it *Judensuppe*). Each prisoner got between 700- 800 calories (sometimes 900) per day, whereas the normal ration for labourers should amount to 2,200-2,500. Hence each prisoner received a third of the recommended calorie intake.[88] In another scene reported by my father at Amon Göth's trial, the accused pretended to a camp inspector that each prisoner got two loaves of bread per week. The reality was that only one loaf was given. Some reports claim that Göth sold the 'saved' rations on the black market in Kraków.[89] He would have had plenty to sell, and not just food. This did not in fact go unnoticed, for in September 1944 Göth was arrested by the SS and charged with black market activities.

Between March and August 1943, my father continued to work in the JUS.[90] The day started with reveille at 5am; then a horn blast would announce roll call at 6am; then he would stand on the *Appellplatz* as one of 8,000 prisoners of his cohort, arranged in columns of work units, four to a row. They would often wait interminably for the laborious issue of the passes and when that was done, set off on the 3km march into town. While he worked in the JUS he would march together with a column of cleaners, whose job it was to sort the remaining furniture and household goods in the now deserted ghetto. Later in August 1943 when the JUS was shut down, he had to labour physically, lagging cement bags or stones. I remember that he described the back-breaking work and the cruel guards shouting, 'Work – you are not a statue of a worker'.

In the early days of the camp my father met up with his ailing parents after the evening roll call. Mila was suffering from abdominal pains, Marek from heart disease. My father did not think that his mother's medical problem was serious, but she was operated on in the camp hospital and did not recover. She died aged 60, in September 1943. My grieving father did not want her body to be hurled into the communal pit, so he carried her corpse on his shoulder to the old Podgórze cemetery and buried her in the furthest corner in soft earth under a tree. Here he dug a shallow grave with a small wooden knife. He knew where the spot was, and visited it whenever he was in the area, even on his last visit to Poland in the 1990s. He said there were trees there still, and that he would take me there sometime. Sadly, he never did.

My grandfather's death is documented in history books and in detail in a previous chapter.[91] It was 14 May 1944, the day of the 'health roll call'. The slogan for the day was 'work according to ability', and in order to pass the selection procedure all male prisoners had to strip naked and run past Dr Blancke, who stood on a small raised platform. Clad in a big fur coat, he pointed left or right to decide an individual's fate. The people shunted to the left were exterminated. There were 20,000 male prisoners in Płaszów at the time,[92] so my father would almost certainly been subjected to this humiliating selection process. Probably by May 1944 'saving' his father's dead body from the heaped pyre would not have been possible, nor would it have seemed like a priority. I don't know when he would have been informed of his sister's death – I can't help hoping it would have been after his parents' death. By then the struggle to exist would have left him with little energy for mourning.

At this stage in the camp's existence those selected for deportation, mostly young, old and infirm, knew what fate awaited them, yet Göth at his trial said he had not been aware that the prisoners were being sent to Auschwitz to be killed. His mendacity on that one was later exposed by a document produced by the prosecuting counsel. The document, signed by Göth, requested that 'Auschwitz return the camp uniforms from the May 14 transport of "special treatment prisoners".'[93]

Despite the bleakness of the situation, camaraderie of some kind existed between the fellow prisoners and bed mates. Artur would have been the first to help others within his circle of friends, but also knew how to look after himself, and sometimes survival had to depend on exploiting the weaknesses of others. For example, he would have had to fight for a place on the top bunk, because he did not want to be dribbled on by the ever-present diarrhoea. Social Historian Griselda Pollock (quoted in the Guardian[94]) made a useful distinction between the extermination camp and the concentration camp. The concentration camp exists not to extinguish life but to extinguish the human. 'You are removed from moral action, you become a number and, finally, you are reduced physiologically to a bundle of reactions, as the body struggles to survive extreme emaciation.'

I don't know to what extent my father abandoned his moral values, but an inevitable consequence of his experiences thereafter was to start with the premise of initial distrust when he first met somebody, and this stayed with him until the end. He could not understand, and repeatedly questioned my own philosophy, which was to trust people unless you are proved otherwise.

In retrospect historians find it hard to agree why all the camps were not liquidated anyway, and all their inmates sent to extermination camps to be gassed, but the prevalent view is that the Germans had to balance the aims of the 'Final Solution' with the opportunity to exploit cheap slave workers. Furthermore, the camp personnel knew that their job in the camp was a bit of a cushy one, compared with the bloody alternative of the Russian front. However, to keep the camp from liquidation they had to present good production figures, preferably of output essential to the war effort. Inmate Mietek Pemper, who was chosen by Göth to be his administrative assistant, explains in his memoir *Road to the Rescue* how he, more or less single-handedly, twisted the production facts so as to impress Berlin. He suggests, perhaps a bit immodestly, that his uniquely successful 'act of non-violent resistance', extended the survival of the camp and thousands of its inmates. Afterwards Pemper, who was through his work well acquainted with Oscar Schindler, survived as a *Schindler Jude*. Unfortunately, Pemper's excellent little book does not mention the background and aims of the chemists' commando, which ultimately saved my father.

The Chemists' Commando

The unit was initially organised by the SS General Wilhelm Koppe to invent new products to further the German war effort, and into this unit came selected chemists, mathematicians, engineers and other potentially clever scientists. I can imagine how relieved my father would have been to be excused from his back-breaking stone carrying and drafted into a desk job. 'The food was the same, but the conditions were better for us. We sat at a bench indoors, and wrote instead of using shovels', he said to Thea Jourdan during his *Scotsman* interview.[95]

I don't know what they did in the chemists' commando. I so wish I had asked my father and maybe I did, but the main answer was always, 'it saved me, because I did not have to work physically'. Very little is written about their work but the German boss of the commando, Wilhelm Koppe, claimed that some significant scientific discoveries were made by the internees.[96] Of course, Koppe would have wanted to present his outfit in a favourable light, but it is also entirely possible, as other reports suggest, that the whole chemists' commando concept was a phoney idea, a smokescreen that the Germans invented for their own benefit. Henry Orenstein, another chemist commando internee (who went on to be an exceptionally successful toy manufacturer in the US – he invented Transformers), remembers how his brother was asked a simple question by way of a test to qualify for admission, 'how many legs has a fly got'. The Eichmann witness, Dr Beilin (see later) remembers being asked 'what is the chemical formula for water?' The work they were given was inconsequential. The mathematicians were set to solve simple problems using calculators, the 'engineers' and 'inventors' were gathered around an automobile engine, turning it on and off. They had been told they would be inventing a gas that could immobilize cars, planes and tanks, but were told that their materials had not yet arrived. The chemists sat translating books on insects from Polish to German, while a prisoner who could not read or write German had been appointed librarian of the group.[97]

The above testimony is much more detailed than any of my father's accounts, but I doubt whether any work my father did there benefitted science or the German war effort. In contrast, Primo Levi's accounts of the chemists' commando in Auschwitz suggest that he was set some 'real' tasks. All the scientists would have been lucky to be part of a group which saved them from hard physical labour.

But by the middle of October moves were afoot for the chemists' commando. My father, along with 50 other members of the chemists' commando, was deported by freight truck to Flossenbürg concentration camp in Bavaria (a distance of 723km). Various sources state the deportation date as 10 October.[98] According to the Flossenbürg records he arrived there on 15 October and was given the prisoner number 28983 (see below). The departure date is left blank.

In Flossenbürg the prisoners took up their *Chemiker Kommando* jobs again, but my father never talked about what it was that they did there. Henry Orenstein[99], in a book which was published before my father died (but which he did not seem to have been aware of), provides further details. Felek Orenstein, the author's brother, was with my father in the same *Chemiker Kommando* in Flossenbürg and in his opinion the work they were engaged in there was 'phoney'. This is his description of what happened: reunited with their professor from Kraków, they set up a 'lab' in an empty

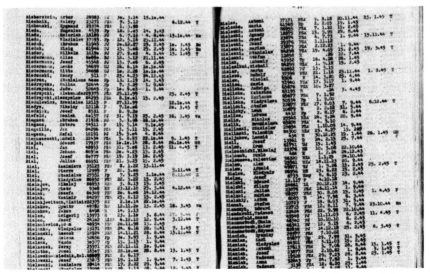

The extract from the original Flossenbürg records sent to me, when I requested them from the archival holdings of the United States Holocaust Memorial Museum. My father's name is at the top of the first page.

barrack and continued their work on the immobilising gas for cars, planes and tanks. There was talk of collaboration with the Wilhelm Institute for Applied Chemistry and Electrochemistry and the invention of a gas protection filter (*Gasshutzfilter*) called EO2, 11,[100] but what this was all about remains a mystery. Then on 15 November, a month after they arrived, for some unexplained reason the group was split. My father along with 22 others was sent back again to Płaszów, whereas the others, including Felek Orenstein, stayed on in Flossenbürg.[101] Why the group was split and why some were returned has never been explained.

Just for the sake of historical detail I have collected all the names I could find of other *Chemiker Kommando* internees who were with him at the time in Płaszów and compiled them in a table in the Appendix. From what I can gather, there would have been about 50 of them to start with. The table, which lists about a dozen, includes the fates and subsequent professions of those that survived.

By the end of 1944, the Russian Army was approaching from the East, and Płaszów's days were numbered. My father together with all the others who remained in Płaszów was marched to Auschwitz on foot (78km) to arrive there and enter through its sinister gates.

Auschwitz

According to one source [102] the final clearance of Płaszów took place on 14 January 1945, when the remaining inmates were sent on foot to Auschwitz. It must have taken them a few days to get there, which would mean he was there for only a couple of days. However, from my father's reminiscences, I thought he was there for maybe ten days; in the *Scotsman* interview he mentions three weeks.

Of course, my father's timeline can only have been a surmise. He had no watch and no calendar, only the positions of the sun and the phases of the moon would have indicated the passing of time. Was it really the same sun, the same moon? Goran Rosenberg, in his beautiful second-generation memoir *A Brief Stop on the Road from Auschwitz*, which reconstructs his parents' experiences from their fragments of memories, comes across the same sort of date inconsistency issues:

> Assuming it's necessary to make all the fragments fit together. But that isn't necessary at all. In this context it makes absolutely no difference on precisely which day you reach Auschwitz. Your journey has no timetable and no direction. You have no exact dates behind

you and no dates ahead of you. On your journey exact dates have no function. It's me they have a function for. I'm the one who needs them.

My father was placed in Auschwitz II-Birkenau, a short bus drive from the main camp, and nowadays part of the Auschwitz tourist experience. By then, in the final stages of the war, the prisoners were no longer branded with a tattooed number, nor were the gas chambers operational, but he would have been fully aware that Birkenau was where it all happened. He never met my hero, Primo Levi, though both were chemists and there at the same time.

There is no record of my father's time in Auschwitz, because the administrative block was blown up even as he was there. The SS also set about destroying the gas chambers and the crematoria. It is easy to understand why the Nazis wanted to destroy the evidence, but why would they want to march out the prisoners? The last roll call on the *Appellplatz* took place on 17 January, the day before they left. A total of 31,894 men were counted that day[103]; those capable of walking thirty miles were separated from those who could only walk to Auschwitz station, and those who could not walk at all.[104] When the Red Army entered on 27 January, they found about 7,500 alive and 600 corpses. The rest had been marched out. [105]

The Death March

At the start of the march on 18 January my father weighed 40 kg. He felt like there was almost nothing of him left to be hungry. He was winkled out of the latrines, where he was attempting to hide, to be deemed capable of walking and joined a cordon of prisoners to embark on the infamous death march. Daniel Goldhagen called death marches the 'ambulatory equivalent of a cattle car'. Primo Levi called them 'biblical marches'. From the sky, allied pilots called them 'human rivers'. The SS, however, euphemistically called them *Evakuierung* (evacuation). The term 'death march' was coined by the prisoners themselves, and later adopted by historians.

They took place on foot in the winter of 1944-45 from most of the concentration camps in the GG, 59 of them altogether.[106] The evacuations from Auschwitz went in two directions. Some cohorts headed northwest towards Gleiwitz, and others headed west towards Wodzisław. My father's column headed towards Gleiwitz, though of course at the time they did not know where they were going, nor did they know that the Red Army was closing in from the east and the Allies from the west. I suppose they would have surmised the westward direction of the march from the position of the sun. However, by then they would have been in no state to question the Germans' logic, which had proved to be so bizarrely idiosyncratic on so many occasions, as to where they were being led and why.

My father later reconstructed the death march route, painfully remembering each bit.

The route, carefully reconstructed on a present-day map, sets out the stops; the table below the map gives the German and Polish place names, and the distances. I was hoping to go on a car journey pilgrimage one day, but unfortunately Covid-19 got in the way of these plans.

On January 14, 1945:   Evacuation from K.L. Plaszow on foot
                              to Auschwitz-Birkenau

On January 18, 1945:   Evacuation from Auschwitz-Birkenau -on foot

From January 18 to April 4,1945: Evacuation march via the following
                              places (we usually stopped in smaller
                              K.Ls): Gleiwitz II (K.L.); Ratibor (a
                              prison); Loebschütz, Neustadt, Glatz,
                              Frankenstein, Langenbielau, K.L.
                              Rechenbach, Waldenburg, Landeshut (a mine),
                              Schmiedeberg, K.L. Hirschberg, Greiffen-
                              berg, Blumendorf and K.D. Reichenau near
                              Gablonz.

On May 8, 1945:   Liberation from camp Reichenau near Gablonz

May 10- June 22, 1945:   hospitalized in Tannvald near Gablonz.

Fragment of my father's letter to a friend- detailing the evacuation march.

The death march route from Auschwitz (the stops are marked with current names) – drawn by Andy Quinn of Emma Quinn Designs.

From		To		Distance (km)
German name	**Current name**	**German name**	**Current name**	
Auschwitz KL	Oswiecim	Gleiwitz (subcamp of Auschwitz)	Gliwice	65.5
Gleiwitz (subcamp of Auschwitz)	Gliwice	Ratibor	Racibórz	46.2
Ratibor	Racibórz	Leobschütz	Glubczyce	37.7
Leobschütz	Glubczyce	Neustadt KL (subcamp of Auschwitz)	Prudnik	31.5
Neustadt (sub-camp of Auschwitz)	Prudnik	Gladz	Kłodzko	81.8
Gladz	Kłodzko	Frankenstein	Ząbkowice	22.9
Frankenstein	Ząbkowice Sląskie	Langenbielau KL ((sub- camp of Gross Rosen)	Bielawa	22.0
Langenbielau KL ((sub- camp of Gross Rosen)	Bielawa	Reichenbach	Dzierżoniów	5.7
Reichenbach	Dzierżoniów	Waldenburg	Wałbrzych	36.4
Waldenburg	Wałbrzych	Landeshut	Kamienna Gora	23.8
Landeshut	Kamienna Góra	Schmiedeberg KL (sub-camp of Gross Rosen	Kowary	21.4
Schmiedeberg (sub-camp of Gross Rosen	Kowary	Hirschberg	Jelenia Góra	19.3
Hirschberg	Jelenia Góra	Greiffenberg	Gryfów Sląski	28.8
Greiffenberg	Gryfów Sląski	Blumendorf	Kwieciszowice	21.1
Blumendorf	Kwieciszowice	Reichenau	Bogatynia	43.3
Reichenau	Bogatynia	Reichenau b. Gablonz (sub-camp of Gross Rosen)	Rychnov u Jablonce	48.3
Liberated from Reichanau b. Gablonz on the 8th May 1945. Total = 555.7				

The place names of the death march stops and the distances between them. My father would have known these locations by their German names. They may of course have used short cuts, or footpaths or minor roads, so the distances are only approximate.

Historians have argued about the purpose of these enforced evacuations. Some say that the main aim was to remove the eye-witnesses and to conceal the crimes that had been committed. I would not be surprised, though I have no evidence, that the pockets of the SS officials who accompanied the bedraggled prisoners were filled with stolen gold. Might they also have wanted to use the prisoners as a human shield? Maybe they would have felt safer from attack from the planes of the allied forces overhead? Daniel Goldhagen[107] wrote that the marches' one and only purpose was to kill those Jews who had hitherto survived, but other historians do not agree. Neander[108] believes that the marches saved the SS men from military service (on the front line), and moreover, they could more easily escape and thus avoid eventually being called to account for their deeds. Whatever the motivation for the death marches, Himmler's rather retrospective edict given out on 18 April 1945, just two weeks before liberation, was '*Kein Häftling darf lebend in die Hände des Feindes fallen*' ('No detainee must fall into enemy hands alive').[109]

My father said that about 10,000 started off on that march, but the witness statement of Dr Aharon Beilin[110] cited 25,000. The latter figure fits in better with the camp statistics given above. My father was obviously on the same march as Beilin as he describes the same transit stations.[111] I think that when you are walking in a column in rows of 5, counting such large numbers stretching far in front and far behind is not something you would be in a position to do. Anyway, the number was diminishing daily, as stragglers were eliminated. The only thing they counted were the shots, which according to Beilin numbered up to 500 a day. As they walked, they frequently passed patches of red snow soaked with the victims' blood. Freddie Knoller (whom I heard when he came in 2015 to talk to an Edinburgh school), described how it was: 'We went westward, walking in our wooden shoes on icy, snow-covered roads. We were still in our striped, thin clothes. Many collapsed and were immediately shot on the spot. We had to take the corpses and throw them into the ditch next to the road.' An Aryan who followed the evacuation route a day or two later said 'the road ran between two hedges of bodies'.[112]

Yet one more account of the death march is that of Prisoner B3087[113] from Auschwitz to Gross-Rosen, so they would probably have shared the same experiences. He observed: 'As we walked past the frozen corpses, I wondered who else used this road. Somebody else had to, surely – someone besides the German Army. Who were these people, who passed the bodies of dead Jews in the ditches every day...How could they not see what was happening? How could they be all right with this?'

Elie Wiesel in his memoir *Night* describes the same march, also from Auschwitz when snow fell, and icy wind lashed like a whip.

> I was putting one foot in front of the other, like a machine. I was dragging this emaciated body that was still such a weight. If only I could shed it! Though I tried to put it out of my mind, I could not help thinking that there were two of us: my body and I. I hated that body. I kept repeating to myself: 'Don't think, don't stop, run.'

Elie was sixteen-years old at the time; he may or may not have been in the same cohort as my father. He started from Buna (Auschwitz III), while my father started from Birkenau (Auschwitz II). My father and I both read *Night* soon after it came out in English (it was first written in Yiddish), and I stupidly asked my father if he had ever met Elie. 'No', he said, 'there were too many of us, but what he describes is just how it was'. He too remembered how the SS-men changed when they got tired, but the prisoners just kept walking, sometimes running, on and on.

Another memoir that describes the same march from Birkenau to Gleiwitz was that of the child survivor Thomas Buergenthal. In his lovely book *A Lucky Child*,[114] written 50 years after the event, he describes the three-day march of that leg of the journey, where they slept on the road or in ditches overnight. He too tells of the attrition as people died or were shot along the way. At one point the SS decided that the children were slowing the column down and offered to take them off to a nearby convent. Thomas and his two friends wisely did not believe this too-good-to-be-true promise and mingled with the adults. Later he found out that his premonitions had been right, that all those taken had been shot. As he walked, he willed himself to live, for 'staying alive had become a game I played against Hitler, the SS and the Nazi killing machine'.

Survivor Sam Pivnik[115] describes thousands 'in every makeshift uniform you can think of, the stripes of the concentration camp most evident'. He describes the icy roads and sub-zero temperature, often left to sleep outside, and he also tells of a night he spent in Gleiwitz, which would have been at the same time as my father was there. 'We got no food that night and precious little sleep.' Elie Wiesel also says of this time, 'We stayed in Gleiwitz for three days. Days without food or water. We were forbidden to leave the barrack. The door was guarded by the SS.' Thomas Buergenthal's account of his time in Gleiwitz included a selection procedure; all those that could run across a field passed and all those who failed were eliminated. Elie Wiesel and Thomas Buergenthal were transported from

Gleiwitz by cattle truck to Buchenwald and Berlin, respectively, while my father continued to journey through Lower Silesia on foot.

Edwin Opoczyński, my father's cousin, in his testimony, albeit of a different death march cohort, describes how they passed through villages with streams and wells, but the guards would not let them stop. Nor did the villagers take pity on the marchers. 'Could they not have thrown us some bread?'[116] My father described how people were shot if they crouched down to defecate, or even bent down to pick a dandelion leaf to chew on. My father did not say what they ate, just that they were very, very hungry, except one day when they suddenly happened upon a store full of bread and a limitless supply of fresh water. The Germans let them eat and drink their fill, and many of the prisoners did, and subsequently died. Eating too much at once brings about what physiologists call the 're-feeding syndrome' caused by dangerously low phosphate levels. My father, being a chemist knew about this, so he restrained himself, and tried to restrain others. He stuffed his pockets full of bread and carefully rationed it over the next few days.

The Mine Shaft

However, his worst moments, the absolute nadir, of all his experiences were spent in a uranium land mine shaft in Landeshut (Kamienna Góra), described in Beilin's witness statement.[117] They did not know it was a uranium mine at the time – it looked like a bunker, at the entrance of which it said 'Entry Forbidden by Order of the Police'. The guards crammed them in and then shut the door. Beilin's testimony at Eichmann's trial fills in the details:

> It was a very long bunker like a labyrinth with lanes leading off to the sides…we began feeling that we had no air, that there was a lack of air there. The groups that were far from the door felt this much more and then the tragic shouts began – '*Luft*' (Air) – and naturally the SS men did not open the door until six a.m.

It was this night that my father lived and relived through countless nightmares, shouting out '*tlen, tlen*' ('oxygen, oxygen'). He told me how he would have suffocated if he had not made his way towards the entrance, where 'a little oxygen was coming in and climbed over bodies to get to the front'. He told that story to Thea Jourdan in the *Scotsman*, but not the other part which he told me, about how at one stage, feeling so frightened and thirsty, he cupped his hands to catch a stream of water, but it was only a man urinating.

I don't know how many people suffocated in that mine. My father thought 1,000 men entered and 250 died, but Beilin thought the numbers were much larger, that 5,000 entered and 1,000 died. Whatever the number, the fatalities were significant enough for that mine entrance now to bear

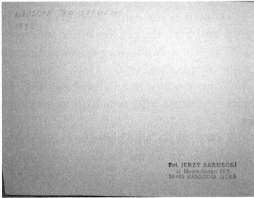

Photo of the mine entrance, and the inscribed back of the photo taken by Jerzy Sarnecki in 1990

an explanatory memorial to those who perished that dreadful night. With that in mind my father wrote to man called Jerzy Sarnecki , then the director of a local textile museum in Kamienna Góra. I don't have a copy of the letter he sent, but I do have the reply (dated 12 August 1992). It was a kindly letter enclosing some photos of the entrance to the mine.

It appears that the mine was once part of 'underground Poland', a labyrinth of passages, cellars, dungeons and caves, part of which at 'Arado' once housed Hitler's secret laboratory, and in another part a buried train full of Nazi gold, which apparently still remains hidden in a secret tunnel.[118] The labyrinth is now a favourite haunt of troglodytes and speleologists (with its own reviews on Trip Advisor), despite the slightly raised radioactivity levels. However, there is no sealed section any more in which 250 to 1,000 people died of suffocation and still no monument exists to mourn their passing. The Wikipedia entry for Kamienna Góra tells of the town's heroic medieval history, but there is no mention whatever of the death march and the mine shaft casualties.

'Shaft' is of course the wrong word as it implies a vertical entrance. The underside of Sarnecki's photograph uses the noun 'Sztolnia'. I had never come across this Polish word before; it struck me as useful for further internet searches. Google Translate offered the word 'adit' (which comes from the Latin 'aditus' meaning entrance). The word 'adit' twinned with 'Kamienna Góra' offered an interesting article in English on the geology of the area, but no mention of the death march. So, I continued my internet searches in Polish. Surely someone local from Kamienna Góra can corroborate my father's oral accounts of this terrible night. I keyed in 'sztolnia' and 'Kamienna Góra' into Google and hey-presto, I struck lucky with a couple of websites.[119]

The 'sztolnia' (known by the name 'Brodno') is now recognised as the site of the tragedy, and both the articles quote several testimonies from witnesses. As well as citing Beilin, they quote testimonies from Roman Granowski, Antoni Grządka and finally a letter from my father, published in 2000 (after my father's death) in a Polish magazine *Słowo Polskie*. That must have been the very same letter which my father sent to Jerzy Sarnecki a decade earlier.

A statement by Granowski, who happened to be in the same place and time as Aharon Beilin, confirms Beilin's testimony, though not the numbers:

> In January 1945, in Kamienna Gora we were herded onto a minor road running next to the stream. To the left of us was quite a high

hill; we were on the outskirts of Kamienna Góra. The SS-men who were escorting us decided that we should sleep in the tunnel, which was closed at the other end. I noticed a man, who I think was the foreman of the Organisation Todt, who seemed to oppose the SS-men and tried (unsuccessfully) to prevent us from being herded into the tunnel. Despite this the SS men forced us to go in. After a short while they brought us soup from a branch of the Gross-Rosen camp, which was located in Kamienna Góra. We came out of the tunnel onto a field at the entrance, and having finished the soup, I together with some colleagues, took back the cauldron. The Germans could not be bothered coming back with us, so they left us under supervision in the barracks of the enforced labour prisoners. At about 4 to 5 a.m. we were woken up and told that people were suffocating in the tunnel. We hurried to the entrance of the tunnel, and I together with a Dutchman, who knew about breathing apparatus, went into the tunnel with lamps, and we pulled out whoever we could, altogether several dozen people.

Antoni Grządka, who was a prisoner at KL Landeshut, relates the same event(s): 'We looked on in horror at the continuous cordons of prisoners evacuated from Auschwitz and other concentration camps to the East of us. We witnessed how they were herded into the dungeons excavated in the mountainside, from which after *each such night*, they removed piles of corpses of men who had suffocated because of lack of oxygen.'

What is truly frightening, especially from the last of these witness statements, is that the suffocation event might have been one of many. The articles go on to query, as I do, whether the witnesses describe one night, or whether, as Antoni Grządka implies, this was one in a series of such events. If the guards knew what the outcome would be, then we are talking about a different type of crime altogether. Knowingly suffocating prisoners to reduce their load (so to speak) is a crime against humanity. If, however, as is possible, fresh SS staff came with each cohort, it could be that they never expected people to suffocate and may indeed have attempted to resuscitate the dying, as remembered by Roman Granowski. He also remembered that a foreman warned the guards of the likely consequences. If that were so, then their crime is merely that of ignoring the foreman's warnings. This case should clearly have been examined in a Nazi crime tribunal. However, despite all these testimonies, the Central Commission for the Investigation of Nazi Crimes in Poland has entirely ignored it.

A similar suffocation event is described by survivor Ernest Levy in his book *Just One More Dance*.[120] Four hundred marching prisoners were herded into a warehouse, which could only hold about 80. That night 'the building became like a mincer: bodies became mattresses, layer upon layer, and those underneath were crushed to death'. Out of the 400 that entered, only 100 survived that night. It was only years later that the impact of this experience hit him. He wrote: 'Images of people drowning in an ocean of bodies, shouting for help, pushed under by the stronger – myself included – will always haunt me'.

My father's memories of his night in the mineshaft left similar feelings of guilt for having survived at the expense of others. Only a few of my father's friends survived that dreadful march. Among them was Bernard Aronczyk, in Canada and Julek Hochman (Wysocki) in France (both now deceased). Their shared history is evident from a correspondence bundle which Bernard Aronczyk's grand-daughter, Melissa Aronczyk, has collected carefully from her grandfather's effects. They make fascinating reading. In one my father writes to Bernard: 'I have no idea how much my fate depended on the close friendship which united us during the march, but I think that our mutual support meant a great deal', and in another, 'we both survived shoulder to shoulder...supporting each other psychologically and morally, helping one another as much as our frail strength would allow. From all our friends of our *Chemiker Kommando*, I only keep in touch (with you) and Julek Hochman, who lives in France'. Another snippet praises Bernard as the strongest of them all:

> I remember how you have been an example of resilience and both physical and psychological support to us all, with not a hint of a break-down, how you managed to be in solidarity with everyone and bring help as much as you could. Your friendship was most valuable to us during our dreadful trudge when we looked after one another in case anyone should get lost, because moral support was what we needed most.

The diminished group marched on and on. My father's perception of complete indifference from the resident population, while they were passing through what is now 'Polish' Silesia, is echoed in the words of the bystanders, 'these are just Jews...they are the enemy of our people'.[121] The testimony of Gerda Weissman[122] relates a difference in attitude between the Poles and the Czechs. While the Poles were hostile or at best indifferent, the Czech villagers were much kinder, throwing gifts of bread along the way. Only my father's last stop was in what is now the Czech Republic.

The war was now nearing its end, but then so was he. As someone said, 'only another half an hour till freedom, but only a quarter of an hour till death' (cited by Wiesenthal[123]). He was exhausted, his senses dulled with hunger. For him at the time, there was no future, no past, only a state of sub-existence.

The Liberation

He had endured so much that the liberation, when it came, on 8 May 1945, was almost a surprise. He was freed from Reichenau b. Gablonz (sub-camp of Gross-Rosen KL) by Czech partisans. The moment of liberation is described by several holocaust survivors as a moment of disbelief. Henry Orenstein[124] said, 'When it finally sank in, our reaction was very odd. No one shouted with joy. No one screamed with excitement. No one jumped up and down with happiness. There was no hugging, no kissing, no tears, no laughter.' Dan Stone[125], a holocaust historian, agrees: 'the moment of liberation was not one of complete joy, but rather a moment of mixed emotions and confusion'. My father was, however, always very sentimental about that moment. Thea Jourdan wrote how his face softened: 'we gathered and he [the commandant of Gross Rosen] told us "*Meine Herren, Sie sind frei*" [Gentlemen you are free]'. That must have been the first time for a long while that anyone called them 'gentlemen'. Then they sang all the national anthems one by one, as he drove away.

As soon as peace was declared, the International Red Cross scooped up the emaciated remnants of humanity and took them to hospital[126] to recover. He was there between May and the end of July 1945. My father told me often about how good they were to him, and how cleverly they brought him back to life, offering morsels of food at a time. Dr Beilin, in his witness statement, remembered a white bed and flowers on the cupboard. Sam Offen[127] remembered what it felt like to see himself in the mirror, for the first time in two years. My father reminisced of undreamt-of luxuries such as baths, toothbrushes, socks and scissors to cut his nails.

He considered what to do and where to go, except that there really were no options. Poland was his homeland, Palestine, of which some others talked, seemed too foreign and too far away. Anyway, any faith he might have had as a child with its romantic allusions to a Promised Land was killed stone dead by his experiences. He did not yet know that his brother was alive in London, and the small hand-out he got from the Red-Cross would not have covered travel to foreign lands. He went to the railway station, found that trains were running smoothly, checked the timetable and bought a ticket to Kraków. With two hours and some small change to spare, he wondered off into a nearby market. And it was there on a stall that he saw a small plaster dog. It was not a cute sort of dog, rather a severe looking terrier, not one of many such dogs, just one, alone, like he was. He put his hand in his pocket and took out some coins. It was the first thing that he paid for legally for over two years. What made him want to spend his money on a plaster dog, when he had no change of clothes and no food for the future? Why a dog, when after his camp experiences he became pathologically scared of dogs and remained so for the rest of his life? But he saw it and wanted it and cherished it, exhibited it behind glass on a bookcase shelf, then brought it here to Scotland. I have it still.

The plaster dog

Notes

1. A photocopy of his application was sent to me by the RSE administrator.
2. Oral history interview with Edwin Opoczyński. USHMM Accession Number: 1995.A.1280.23|RG Number: RG-50.225.0023, retrieved from: https://collections. ushmm.org/search/catalog/irn507785 (accessed 5 July 2021).
3. *Endek* stands for ND (National Democrats). The party had (like its modern-day successor, *Ruch Narodowy*), a strongly antisemitic stance.
4. Cooper, L., *In the Shadow of the Polish Eagle* (London: Palgrave Macmillan, 2000).
5. McKenna, J., *Haftling Scheunemann* (California US: CreateSpace Independent Publishing Platform, 2004).
6. Gribetz, J., Greenstein, E.L. and Stein, R.S., *Timetables of Jewish History* (London: Simon and Schuster, 1993).
7. Browning, C.R., Hollander, R.S. and Tec, N., *Every Day Lasts a Year: A Jewish Family's Correspondence from Poland* (Cambridge: Cambridge University Press, 2007).
8. Kaplan, C.A., *The Scroll of Agony: the Warsaw Diary of Chaim A. Kaplan* (London: Hamish Hamilton, 1966).
9. Hilberg, R., *The Destruction of the European Jews* (Boulder CO: Lynne Rienner Publishers, 1986), p 35.
10. Grant, M., *The Passing of the Great Race: or, the Racial Basis of European History* (New York: Charles Scribner's Sons, 1918). His theories espouse the idea that the 'Nordic race' is inherently superior to other human beings. His theory and this book were praised by Nazis and were admired by Adolf Hitler.
11. Kaplan, C. A., *The Scroll of Agony.*
12. Pivnik, S., *Survivor* (London: Hodder and Stoughton, 2012).
13. Zimmermann, H.Z., *Przeżyłem, pamiętam, świadczę* (Kraków : Wydawn. Baran i Suszczyński, 1997).
14. Crowe, D., *Oscar Schindler: The Untold Story of His Life, Wartime Activities and the True Story Behind the List* (Boulder, Colorado: Westview Press, 2004).
15. Keneally, T., *Schindler's Ark* (London: Hodder and Stoughton Ltd, 1982).
16. Chwalba, A., *Okupowany Kraków (rozmowa),* 2004 http://www.kedyw.info/wiki/ Andrzej_Chwalba,_Okupowany_Krak%C3%B3w_(rozmowa) (accessed 3 March 2021).
17. Agata Szostkowska, 'At the heart of pre-war Jewish world', *Central and Eastern Europe, International Journalism and PR, Tourism,* 2016, retrieved from: http://www. communications-unlimited.nl/at-the-heart-of-pre-war-jewish-world (accessed 3 March 2021).
18. Duda, E., *The Jews of Cracow* (Kraków: Wydawnictwo Hagadah, 1999).
19. Crowe, D., *Oscar Schindler.*
20. Bieberstein, A., *Zagłada Żydów w Krakowie* (Kraków: Wydawnictwo Literackie 1985); Graf, M., *The Kraków Ghetto and the Płaszow Camp Remembered* (Tallahassee: Florida State University Press, 1989).
21. Bieberstein, *Zagłada Żydów w Krakowie.*
22. Andrea Löw, 'Jewish Administrations', *European Holocaust Research Infrastructure Online Course in Holocaust Studies,* 2017, retrieved from: https://training.ehri-project.eu/jewish-administrations (accessed 3 March 2021).
23. Ibid.

24. Wander merged with Novartis.
25. Jagiellonian University Collection, 1939-1957, *United States Holocaust Memorial Museum Archives*: retrieved from: https://collections.ushmm.org/findingaids/RG-15.245_01_fnd_pl.pdf (accessed 3 March 2021).
26. Kraków Ghetto, *Action Reinhard Camps*, 2006, retrieved from: http://www.deathcamps.org/occupation/krakow%20ghetto.html (accessed 3 March 2021)
27. Reggie Nadelson, 'Two who survived without Schindler', *The Independent*, 17 February 1994, retrieved from: http://www.independent.co.uk/life-style/two-who-survived-without-schindler-not-all-the-jews-in-krakows-ghetto-were-on-oskar-schindlers-list-1394670.html (accessed 3 March 2021)
28. Ancestry.com. *Kraków, Poland, ID Card Applications for Jews During World War II, 1940-1941 (USHMM)* [database on-line]. Lehi, UT, USA: Ancestry.com Operations, Inc., 2013.
29. Oral history interview with Gerda Weissmann Klein, 1994, retrieved from https://collections.ushmm.org/search/catalog/irn507376 (accessed3 March 2021).
30. The No.3 tram went along Limanowski Street, Lwowska Street and then out at Plac Zgody.
31. 'Remembering the Jewish Ghetto in Kraków', *In your pocket: Kraków (no date)*, retrieved from: https://www.inyourpocket.com/krakow/The-Jewish-Ghetto-in-Krakow_73758f (accessed 4 April 2021)
32. Pankiewicz, T., *Apteka w Getcie Krakowskim* (Kraków: Nakladem Instytutu Wydawniczego, 1st edition, 1947).
33. Pankiewicz, T., *The Kraków Ghetto Pharmacy* (Kraków: Wydawnictwo Literackie, 2013).
34. Graf, M., *The Kraków Ghetto and the Płaszów Camp Remembered* (Tallahassee: Florida State University Press, 1989).
35. Fischler-Martinho, H., *Have You Seen My Little Sister?* (London:Vallentine Mitchell, 1997).
36. Muller-Madej, S. and Brand W.R, *A Girl from Schindler's List* (Kraków: DjaF, 2006).
37. Grądzka, M., Jewish *Women in the Kraków Ghetto: The Person and the Challenges*, Vol. 3, No. 2, 2013, pp. 123-141.
38. Weisgard, G., 'The role of women in the Jewish Community of Kraków', 2016, retrieved from: https://www.academia.edu/40337059/The_Role_of_Women_in_the_Jewish_Community_of_Krakow_from_the_16th_Century_to_1939_An_Unwritten_History (accessed 12 July 2021)
39. Pankiewicz, *The Kraków Ghetto Pharmacy*.
40. Grądzka, *Jewish Women in the Kraków Ghetto*, pp. 123-141.
41. My father's statement at AG's trial.
42. Weissblei, G., 'Letter returned to sender: the Council no longer exists', 2018, retrieved from: https://blog.nli.org.il/en/jewishlettersreturn/ (retrieved 3 March 2021).
43. The Nizkor Project, 'The "Final Solution": Hans Frank's Cracow statement, December 16 1941': retrieved from: https://www.jewishvirtuallibrary.org/hans-frank-cracow-statement (accessed 12 July 2021).
44. Bieberstein, *Zagłada Żydów w Krakowie*.
45. Cesarani, D., *Citizenship, Nationality and Migration in Europe* (Abingdon-on-Thames: Routledge, 1996).

46. Brecher, E., *Schindler's Legacy: True Stories of the List Survivors* (New York: Penguin Books, 1994).
47. These deportations were thought to be triggered as reprisals for the assassination of Reinhard Heydrich, 'the architect of the Holocaust'. He was critically wounded in Prague (in 'Operation Anthropoid') on 27 May; he died from his wounds on 4 June 1942. The 1 June deportation in Kraków took place even before he had died. The killing machinery was thereafter ratchetted up in centres of Belzec, Sobibor and Treblinka code-named 'Operation Reinhard', in his honour.
48. Kraków Ghetto: Key Dates, United States Holocaust Memorial Museum (no date): retrieved https://www.ushmm.org/wlc/en/article.php?ModuleId=10007458 (accessed 3 March 2021)
49. Pankiewicz, T., *Apteka w Getcie Krakowskim*.
50. Figures obtained from 3 texts: Bieberstein, *Zagłada Żydów w Krakowie*; Crowe, *Oscar Schindler*; 'The Kraków (Cracow) Ghetto During the Holocaust', The United States Holocaust Memorial Museum (no date), retrieved from: https://www.ushmm.org/wlc/en/article.php?ModuleId=10005169 (accessed 12 July 2021)
51. Breitman, R., *The Architect of Genocide* (London: Grafton, 1992).
52. Offen, S. ,*When Hope Prevails* (Livonia MI: First Page Publications, 2005).
53. Pankiewicz, *Apteka w Getcie Krakowskim*.
54. Bieberstein, *Zagłada Żydów w Krakowie*.
55. Dwork, D. and van Pelt, R.J., *Holocaust: a History* (New York: W.W. Norton & Company, 2004).
56. Browning, C.R., *The Origins of the Final Solution, September 1939-March 1942* (Lincoln: University of Nebraska Press and Jerusalem: Yad Vashem, 2004).
57. *Schindler's List,* the film (based on Keneally's book *Schindlers Ark*), dramatised by Steven Spielberg, 1993.
58. New Cracow Friendship Society, 2017. https://www.newcracowfriendshipsoc.org/krakows-history.html (accessed 8 July 2021)
59. Pankiewicz, *The Kraków Ghetto Pharmacy*.
60. Michal Weichert was my father's boss and my grandfather's Co-President at the JSS. After my grandfather's imprisonment he headed the Jewish Social Self-Help committee which organised social assistance for Jews in camps and ghettos. His son, Joseph, has recently (February 2018) published his father's collection of hand-written messages about the destruction of Polish Jews: https://www.jpost.com/diaspora/1940-41-letters-describe-destruction-of-polish-jewry-5403848 (accessed 12 July 2021)
61. Crowe, *Oscar Schindler*.
62. Bieberstein, *Zagłada Żydów w Krakowie*.
63. Pankiewicz, *Apteka w Getcie Krakowskim*.
64. Aleksander told me this story when I visited him in Israel in 1967.
65. Bieberstein, *Zagłada Żydów w Krakowie*, p. 75.
66. Crowe, *Oscar Schindler*.
67. Brecher, *Schindler's Legacy*, p. 282.
68. Pankiewicz, *Apteka w Getcie Krakowskim*.
69. Kraków Ghetto: Key Dates, United States Holocaust Memorial Museum (no date): retrieved https://www.ushmm.org/wlc/en/article.php?ModuleId=10007458 (accessed 3 March 2021)
70. Bieberstein, *Zagłada Żydów w Krakowie*, p. 104.

71. Eldar, M., Kraków - Płaszów Camp Remembered, 1999, retrieved from: https://www.yadvashem.org/download/education/conf/Eldar.pdf (accessed 12 July 2021)
72. Strzala, M., Płaszów Concentration Camp in Kraków, retrieved from: http://www.krakow-info.com/plaszow.html (accessed 12 July 2021)
73. Feldman, J., *The Kraków Diary of Julius Feldman;* trans. W. Brand, written by J. Feldman in 1943 (Lincoln, NE: Quill Press, 2002).
74. Bieberstein, *Zagłada Żydów w Krakowie*, p. 103.
75. Pemper, M., *The Road to Rescue* (New York: Other Press, 2008).
76. Karpf, A., *The War After* (Sydney: Minerva, 1996).
77. Crowe, *Oscar Schindler*.
78. Thea Jourdan, 'Arthur Jurand's List', *The Scotsman Magazine*, 26 January 1995.
79. Helen Jonas, Holocaust Survivor. *Voices on Antisemitism: A Podcast Series.* United States Holocaust Memorial Museum, presented by Aleisa Fishman 26 February 2009, retrieved from: https://www.ushmm.org/antisemitism/podcast/voices-on-antisemitism/helen-jonas (accessed 10 May 2021)
80. Ibid.
81. Kehane, D., *Lvov Ghetto Diary* (Amherst MA: University of Massachusetts Press, 1991).
82. Hilberg, *The Destruction of the European Jews*, pp.35, 247.
83. Frankl, V.E., *Man's Search for Meaning* (London: Rider, 2004). The book was first published in 1946.
84. Feldman, *The Kraków Diary of Julius Feldman*.
85. Natalia Weissman's testimony in Anne Karpf's book *The War After*.
86. Płaszów Forced Labour Camp, *Action Reinhard Camps*, 2006, retrieved from: http://www.deathcamps.org/occupation/plaszow.html (accessed 12 March 2021)
87. Copy of trial proceedings of Amon Göth (Kraków, September 1946), Wiener Library.
88. Aleksander Bieberstein's witness statement at Amon Göth's trial.
89. Lewis, R., *Encyclopaedia Britannica*(no date), retrieved from: https://www.britannica.com/biography/Amon-Goth (accessed 12 March 2021)
90. Its location changed to premises on Jósefinska Street after March 1943 (Pankiewicz, 1947).
91. We now know the details of my grandfather's death from various published accounts, including the one in Kinneally's *Schindler's List*. It's all described in a previous chapter.
92. Offen, *When Hope Prevails*.
93. Transcript of Amon Göth's trial.
94. Zoe Williams, 'Totalitarianism in the Age of Trump', *The Guardian,* 1 February 2017.
95. Thea Jourdan, 'Arthur Jurand's List'.
96. Dachau KZ, Płaszów KL/KZ Schindler's List Part 3, 2012, retrieved from: http://dachaukz.blogs pot.co.uk/2012/08/plaszow-klkz-schindlers-list-part-3.html (accessed 28 February 2021)
97. Orenstein, H., *I Shall Live: Surviving against all Odds* (New York: Touchstone Books, 1989); Abigail Jones, 'Meet Henry Orenstein, the Man who Changed How the World Plays', *Newsweek*, 21 December 2016, retrieved from: http://www.newsweek.com/2016/12/30/henry-orenstein-holocaust-survivor-transformers-toy-poker-king-533912.html(accessed 9 March 2021)
98. Dachau KZ, Płaszów KL/KZ Schindler's List Part 3, 2012, retrieved from: http://dachaukz.blogs pot.co.uk/2012/08/plaszow-klkz-schindlers-list-part-3.html (accessed 28 February 2021); Bieberstein, *Zagłada Żydów w Krakowie*.

99. Orenstein, *I Shall Live.*

100. Fritz, U., 'Flossenbürg Subcamp System', in G.P. Megargee (ed.), *United States Holocaust Memorial Museum Encyclopedia of Camps and Ghettos, 1933-1945, Vol. I: Early Camps, Youth Camps, and Concentration Camps and Subcamps under the SS-Business Administration Main Office (WVHA)* (Bloomington IN: Indiana University Press, 2009), retrieved from: https://www.jstor.org/stable/j.ctt16gzb17.22 (accessed 13 July 2021)

101. Dachau KZ, Płaszów KL/KZ Schindler's List, Part 3, 2012, retrieved from: http://dachaukz.blogs pot.co.uk/2012/08/plaszow-klkz-schindlers-list-part-3.html (accessed 28 February 2021); According to my great-uncle's account there were 19 Jews, one Pole and 2 Germans in the group that was sent back.

102. Ibid.

103. Hilberg, *The Destruction of the European Jews*; Pivnik, *Survivor.*

104. Hilberg, *The Destruction of the European Jews*, p. 254.

105. Strzelecki, A., 'The Liquidation of the Camp', in Długoborski, W. and Piper, F. (eds), *Auschwitz, 1940–1945. Central Issues in the History of the Camp. V: Epilogue. Oświęcim: Auschwitz-Birkenau State Museum*, 2000, pp. 9-85.

106. Death Marches, Jewish Virtual Library (no date), retrieved from: http://www.jewishvirtuallibrary.org/death-marches (accessed 13 March 2021)

107. Goldhagen, D., *Hitler's Willing Executioners: Ordinary Germans and the Holocaust* (New York: Alfred A. Knopf, 1996).

108. Neander, J. *Das Konzentrationslager 'Mittelbau' in der Endphase der NS-Diktatur*, Dissertation zur Erlangung des akademischen Grades eines Dr. phil, 1996 (University of Bremen).

109. Zamecnik, S., Kein haftling darf lebend in die Hande des Fendes fallen. *Dachauer Hefte* 1, 1985, pp. 219-31.

110. Nizkor Project, The Auschwitz Testimony of Dr Aharon Beilin, 2004, retrieved from: https://forum.axishistory.com/viewtopic.php?t=51877 (accessed 12 March 2021)

111. Until Hirscheberg where Beilin parted from the transport.

112. Levi, P., *The Drowned and the Saved* (London: Abacus, 1989).

113. Gratz, A., *Prisoner B 3087* (Jacksonville IL: Perma-bound, 2013).

114. Buergethal, T. A., *Lucky Child* (London: Profile Books, 2010).

115. Pivnik, *Survivor.*

116. Oral history interview with Edwin Opoczyński. USHMM Accession Number: 1995.A.1280.23 | RG Number: RG-50.225.0023, retrieved from: https://collections.ushmm.org/search/catalog/irn507785 (accessed 5 July 2021)

117. Beilin's witness statement. The relevant part is reproduced in the Appendix.

118. Jake Halpern, 'The Nazi Underground', *New Yorker*, 2 May 2016, retrieved from: http://www.newyorker.com/magazine/2016/05/09/searching-for-nazi-gold (accessed 14 July 2021)

119. Rafal Swiecki, 'Kamienna Góra: tajemnicze pogranicze', 11 September 2020, https://kamiennagora.pl/eksploratorzy-skanuja-sztolnie-brodno/ (accessed 11 July 2021);
Piotr Maszkowski, 'Tajemnice Kamiennej Góry', *Menway in INTERIA pl.*, 23 December 2010. https://menway.interia.pl/militaria/news-tajemnice-kamiennej-gory,nId,449703, nPack,2 (accessed 11 July 2021)

120. Levy, E., *Just One More Dance* (Edinburgh: Mainstream Publishing, 1998).

121. Lanzmann, C., *Shoah*. Film, 1985, The Masters of Cinema Series.
122. Oral history interview with Gerda Weissmann Klein, 1994, retrieved from: https://collections.ushmm.org/search/catalog/irn507376 (accessed 3 March 2021)
123. Wiesenthal, S., *The Sunflower* (New York, Schocken Books, 1999).
124. Orenstein, *I Shall Live*.
125. Stone, *The Liberation of the Camps: the End of the Holocaust and its Aftermath*.
126. The hospital was at Tannwald b. Gablonz (Tanvald, now in the Czech Republic). An internet search of the hospital revealed that it was once a TB sanatorium, but I could not find out whether the building still exists.
127. Offen, *When Hope Prevails*.

3

Aleksander

'...*remembrance is the highest form of posthumous justice...*' Maria Stepanova[1]

My great uncle, Aleksander, whom I mention several times in other chapters of this memoir, was my grandfather's younger brother. He was born in 1889, so was nine years his junior; yet in their later years my grandfather looked up to him and valued his support. He was the only relative from my father's side that I knew in Kraków when I was growing up. I called him *Wujciu* Zysiu (Uncle Zyś) and loved him. He was married to *Ciocia* Lola (Aunt Lola), who also survived the war, as did their two children Edwin and Inka. Inka's daughter Krysia (who was two years younger than me) was my childhood playmate, until she emigrated to Israel with her family just before we left. Edwin's first son Igor was only about four at the time, but I remember vying with Krysia for a turn of pushing him on a swing. His second son Oleś (diminutive of Aleksander) was born later, after we had left for the UK.

Like my grandfather, Aleksander was born in Tarnopol. He was educated in Kraków, so the family must have moved there at some time during his schooling. He always knew that he wanted to be a doctor. Under Franz Josef's benign rule, the *numerus clausus* which came in a few years later, had not yet been imposed, so all the medical school places in the Austro-Hungarian Empire would have been open to him. He chose Vienna and graduated from there before the outbreak of the First World War. In the inter-war years, he worked as an army doctor (see page 13). During the ghetto years he organised and directed the Hospital for Infectious Diseases, first in Rękawka Street, and later after the June deportations he masterminded its transfer to Plac Zgody. Throughout the whole of this period, he kept meticulous notes of all the events that were taking place.

The most significant infectious disease that threatened the ghetto and concentration camp inmates was typhus; indeed, the Germans, believing the Jews to be vermin, claimed that the forced confinement of Jews in designated districts was simply a protective containment measure. Aleksander, an expert in infectious diseases, determined to put his expertise to good use. Typhus, which must not be confused with typhoid fever, is caused by the bacterium *Rickettsia* and transmitted through faeces of the body louse (rather than the head louse or the pubic louse – all different species). Lice infected by feeding on the blood of typhus victims move from host to host, biting and wounding, while at the same time excreting infected faeces onto the skin. The bug bites itch and when rubbed become infected with the louse faecal material – enabling the bacteria to be delivered into the bloodstream.

Aleksander made sure that the baths were supplied with disinfectant, that the ghetto laundry functioned efficiently, and instituted a strict programme of health education and hygiene. The bio-modelling studies by the mathematician Lewi Stone, showed how similar measures in the Warsaw ghetto stopped the disease in its tracks in the winter of 1941.[2] The German occupiers were so surprised by the lack of epidemics within the ghetto that they came up with a cunning alternative explanation. The Jews, they said, were doubly dangerous; they were naturally immune to typhus but acted as asymptomatic carriers and spreaders of the disease.

Aleksander's other interventions in the ghetto are well documented. In June 1942, when a wave of *Aktions* was sweeping through, he used the Germans' fear of infections to good effect. He proceeded to cram the hospital intended for 40 patients with 300 civilians, hiding them under beds and in wardrobes. As expected, the SS duty officers were too frightened of infection to do a thorough inspection and left them alone. On another occasion in the October deportations, he used the opposite ploy. He dressed his friends and family (including my father) in white coats and evacuated the patients. Many of the patients died anyway, but some were saved, whereas all the inmates of the other hospitals in the ghetto were brutally murdered that day.Tadeusz Pankiewicz, the famous Polish pharmacist, philanthropist and 'righteous gentile', who rescued many Jews, described my great-uncle as 'a wonderful human being'.[3]

Aleksander was also involved in a rescue operation carried out by another 'righteous gentile', Dr Ludwik Żurowski, Kraków's medical officer.[4] Żurowski, who was responsible for the health of Jewish workers at a major ammunition factory in Kraków, fabricated a story that a fictitious disease was rampant amongst the factory's workforce and specified that the help of a Jewish doctor was essential. Aleksander Bieberstein, who had previously been his boss, was the doctor Żurowski specified.The German factory director, fearing he would be shot if production stopped, agreed.

The regular surgeries that the doctors subsequently held, treated, fed and saved the Jewish factory workforce.

In addition to being the ghetto's doctor, Aleksander was also President of the Orphanage. Pearl Benisch[5] describes him as 'renowned physician, a man of integrity, greatly devoted to children'. After the liquidation of the ghetto, he was interned in Płaszów, and then Gross-Rosen. His integrity and innate charm must have brought him to the attention of Oscar Schindler because he was added onto the famous List, albeit late, when he was already in Gross-Rosen. With them he went on to the relative safe-haven of Brünnlitz. This labour camp was created in the autumn of 1944, after Oskar Schindler had learned that his workforce of over one thousand Jews were to become victims of the Auschwitz-Birkenau gas chambers. Using the last of his considerable black market wealth, Schindler bribed SS and Nazi officials to transfer his entire workforce to Brünnlitz. While officially a sub-camp of Gross-Rosen, Brünnlitz was simply a factory complex, with barracks for the workers, and no real external security to speak of. Schindler bribed the SS-men with alcohol and good food to leave his workers alone.[6]

קבוצה של נצולי המחנה בריגליץ עם דר אלכסנדר ביברסטיין
ררגדי פאסיס ועם חיילים צ'כים.

Brünnlitz, Czechoslovakia. Group photograph of camp survivors with Dr Alexander Bi(e)berstein in camp stripes (Yad Vashem Photo Archive)

While at Brünnlitz, in January 1945, Aleksander personally witnessed Schindler's rescue operation of a batch of 120 starved prisoners locked in freezing cattle cars. The consignment, which came with transport documents, stamped with the words 'Merchandise: Jews', was left abandoned up a siding. When Schindler heard of this he immediately sent for the cars and brought them to Brünnlitz. Aleksander, who assisted in opening the wagons, said: 'The sight was appalling. Dozens of shadows covered with filthy rags, half-frozen bodies were lying in frozen urine and excrement. The stench was unbelievable. We found about 12 dead and 74 just about alive. All of them were French, Dutch, Hungarian, Czech and Polish Jews.'[7] The 'just alive' were brought back to life by Schindler's wife, Emilie, who fed them 'special porridge' while Aleksander and the other doctors administered medical help.

It was at about the same time in the early months of 1945 that Amon Göth, who considered himself to be a friend of Schindler, came to visit the camp. The brutal tyrant, the 'butcher of Płaszów', now looked faded and pathetic. He was suffering from digestive problems, and it was Aleksander, as one of five physicians in Brünnlitz,who had the dubious honour of examining him.[8] Eighteen months later when Göth was being tried in Kraków for his war crimes, Aleksander was surprised to be asked to be one of the witnesses for his defence. Aleksander replied that he could not possibly do this because he was already a witness for the prosecution.

The Göth trial took place in September 1946 about six weeks before I was born. I was the first baby to be born in Aleksander's surviving family and I was very dear to him, as he was to me. We visited them often in their beautiful flat on Karmelicka Street, about one kilometre from our flat. Olek's

Kraków 1947/1948. I am being adored by my uncle Aleksander and Aunt Lola. The second photo shows us a year or so later (left to right: My mother, Aunt Lola, myself and Uncle Aleksander)

mother, Aleksander's daughter-in-law, Hania, lived in it until her death in January 2022. When I visited it as an elderly adult on one of my recent tourist trips to Kraków, I felt the years peel away amongst the familiar furniture.

Aleksander's detailed diary notes, which meticulously described this most tragic period of Kraków's history, survived the evacuation of the ghetto and his time in Płaszów, but were sadly lost on the transport to Gross-Rosen. When the war ended, he recreated them while they were still fresh in his mind, later adding the memories of his friends, patients and family members.

After the war Aleksander's professional career flourished; he was the Director of the Department of Health of the Provincial National Council in Kraków from 1945 until his emigration to Israel in 1959. When he and his wife Lola arrived in Tel Aviv airport they were eagerly welcomed by Mordechai and Dawid, his twin nephews, whose father Moses (Aleksander's eldest brother) had the good sense to emigrate in the 1930s. When I visited Israel in 1967 (two weeks after the Six-Day War), he was waiting for me at the same airport along with an entourage of about 10 members of my extended family. I spent several glorious days with Aleksander in 1967 in his flat in Haifa reminiscing, weeping and rejoicing. His wife, Lola, had died in the early 1960s, and he later married a widow called Zosia. In Israel, he changed the spelling of his name to Biberstein, because the remnants of his family in Israel spelled it so (after all, there are no vowels in Hebrew, and to have two for one sound seemed like one too many).

In the 1970s, when Thomas Keneally was researching material for his book *Schindler's Ark,* Aleksander was one of the key people he interviewed. Motivated by Keneally's interest, Aleksander began to collate and type up his old memoir notes, making carbon copies for his son Edwin Opoczyński[9], who had remained in Poland. Edwin's son, Igor, remembers that at the time communication across the Iron Curtain was difficult, post between Poland and Israel took weeks, and each edited sheet had to be painstakingly copied on a noisy typewriter. Aleksander died in 1979 in Israel at the age of 90, without seeing his book in print, and it was Edwin with the help of the Polish journalist Mieczysław Kieta[10], who prepared the final draft for publication. The book, *Zagłada Żydów w Krakowie*[11], was finally published in 1985 and reissued in 2001; it became one of the most definitive books on the German Occupation of Kraków. The book is dedicated to Aleksander's mother (my great-grandmother), who died when he was a teenager, his brother Marek (my grandfather) who was 'tormented and killed in Płaszów Concentration Camp', and his wife, Lola, who died after the war.

In 2014 my husband and I went on a guided tour of Schindler's factory in Kraków, which is now a museum. My husband, who does not speak Polish, attached himself to a group of English-speaking Jewish Holocaust students and when the guide referred deferentially to Aleksander Bieberstein, the famous doctor, mentioned his definitive book and pointed out his name etched on the commemorative ceiling, my husband tapped the guide on the shoulder and told her that I was his great-niece. You can't imagine how amazed and thrilled they were to meet me – to my huge embarrassment.

Aleksander is survived by his grandsons Igor, in Kolobrzeg on the Baltic Sea, and Olek in Kraków, his granddaughter Krysia in Tel Aviv, and great grandchildren, nephews and nieces. In 2015 we held a birthday party for my nine-year-old grandson Freddie with Igor, Olek and their families at the chocolate factory in Kraków; they ordered a sumptuous cake for the occasion. It was a memorable way to re-establish precious family ties, which now in the internet age we joyfully maintain.

Notes

1. Stepanova, M., trans. Dugdale, S., *In Memory of Memory* (New York: New Directions Publishing Corporation, Translation edition, 2021).
2. Stone, L., He, D., Lehnstaedt, S. and Artzy-Randrup, Y., 'Extraordinary curtailment of massive typhus epidemic in the Warsaw ghetto', *Science Advances*, 6, 30, 2020.
3. Pankiewicz, T., *The Kraków Ghetto Pharmacy* (Kraków: Wydawnictwo Literackie, 2013), p. 68.
4. Ania Lichtarowicz tells the BBC: 'My grandfather helped ghetto Jews', *BBC News*, 24 January 2003, retrieved from: http://news.bbc.co.uk/1/hi/world/europe/2491107.stm (accessed 14 July 2021)
5. Benisch, P., *To Vanquish the Dragon* (New York: Fedheim Publishers, 1991).
6. Crowe, D., *Oscar Schindler: The Untold Story of His Life, Wartime Activities and the True Story Behind the List* (Boulder, Colorado: Westview Press, 2004).
7. 'GolleschauTradgedy', Jewishgen.org., retrieved from: https://www.jewishgen.org/yizkor/schindler/sch020.html (accessed 15 July 2021)
8. Crowe, *Oscar Schindler*; Aleksander Bieberstein's witness statement in transcript of Amon Göth's trial *Proces Ludobojczy Amona Leopolda Goetha*, p. 287 (available from the Wiener Library).
9. Edwin chose to use his mother's maiden name rather than Bieberstein, because it sounded more Polish. (Actually, surnames derived from names of towns – in this case Opoczyn – were Jewish anyway, but not as obviously Jewish as Bieberstein.)
10. Mieczysław Kieta was a Polish social and political journalist (born in 1920, died in 1984) from Kraków. He was instrumental in the publication of Aleksander's book, though he too died before the book came out in print. Kieta had been a prisoner of KL Auschwitz, Gross-Rosen and Litomierzyc. He was co-author of such titles as: *Echo*

Krakowa, Gazeta Krakowska (editor-in-chief from 1955 to 1957), President of the Kraków branch of the Polish Journalists Association, secretary of the International Organization of Journalists (1973-1978), secretary general of the International Auschwitz Committee, Editor-in-chief of *Dziennik Polski* (1969-1970) and *Przekrój* (1969-1973).

11. Bieberstein, A., *Zagłada Żydów w Krakowie* (Kraków: Wydawnictwo Literackie, 1985).

4

Ludwik

'Make peace with the past and look forward to the future'

Ludwik about 1950

Ludwik before the war

My father's elder brother, my uncle Ludwik (we called him Ludek), was born on 30 January 1910. For him, like for all the Jewish boys of my father's generation, there was not much option in the choice of career. If you were able, you chose medicine or law. He chose medicine and got his well-connected uncle Aleksander to use his influence to secure him a coveted place at the Jagiellonian University of Kraków. He graduated with an MD in 1935 and soon became promoted to assistant director of the department of obstetrics and gynaecology at the Kraków University Hospital.

My uncle was not much of a sportsman, but he often tested his logical, agile mind in a game of bridge. My friend Ewa Kalina, whose mother, Helena Landau, was Ludwik's childhood friend, told me that when they were all young before the war Ludwik used to host bridge parties, often hiding the cards from the eyes of his disapproving parents. Once they even wickedly played on the sacred day of Yom Kippur, behind drawn curtains while their parents were in shul.

Before war broke out, Ludwik had the good sense to leave Kraków, boarding a train for Budapest. He had heard that conditions for Jews are better there than in Poland and this indeed proved to be so, at least in the initial stages of the war. After Hungary he travelled to Romania, and then France and in 1941 he joined the Polish armed forces. The Anders' Army, as it was known, in recognition of its charismatic commander, was a force which for the next three years made an epic 9,000-mile journey through Siberia, central Asia, the Middle East and Africa, eventually to confront the Germans in Italy for one of the most crucial battles of the war. I don't know on how much of that gruelling route he was actually with them, but I know that he played the part of the Army doctor in the Second Corps (part of the British 8th Army) during the Italian campaign in Ancona on the Adriatic coast.

On 18 July 1944 Anders' unit won the strategic port of Ancona, breaking the northern German defence line and shortening lines of communication. Miraculously, the manoeuvres (based on surprise and radio deception) left the city unscathed, but there were many casualties. It must have been there and then over the beds of the wounded that Ludwik, the army doctor, and Jasia, the army nurse, met and fell in love.

After the war they both settled in London. He set up practice as an obstetrician and gynaecologist, serving both the NHS, and the private sector in Harley Street. He had many private patients visiting their house in Earl's Court, which had spacious consulting rooms, and of course a trained nurse on hand. His patients adored him for his kind, gentle, sincere

Ludwik and Jasia around 1950

'We are going to see the Queen.'

My great uncle Aleksander and uncle Ludwik in Haifa (1962), on one of Ludwik and Jasia's visits to Israel

Waving goodbye at Waverley Station, Edinburgh after one of their visits in 1964

and professional manner. They had no children, but were very good to me, their niece. When I first came to the UK at the age of 11, I remember being shown the sights of London. 'Now we are going to see the Queen', my uncle said, while driving up The Mall. I was quite disappointed when I found he had been joking. A visit to the Queen, I thought, was an entirely plausible suggestion, given how distinguished and well connected he was.

Later, when I was at University, Ludwik paid for my student accommodation. He knew that my parents were fighting, that I was caught in the crossfire, and that I needed to leave home in order to study in peace. I shall be for ever grateful to Ludwik for this.

For the last few years of his life my uncle suffered from chronic heart disease, and my aunt tried to protect him from all stress. When they went on a trip to Israel to meet relatives, the subject of the Holocaust inevitably came up, and my aunt was furious that the stress would be bad for him. Likewise, whenever I brought up the past I was promptly shushed. She was right, of course, because his heart finally failed when he was only 60. That November in 1970, when the news came of my uncle's death, and I went to stay with Jasia until the funeral, I remember fielding numerous phone calls from his crest-fallen patients. My aunt Jasia was not Jewish, but she had suffered her own traumas and deprivations during the war. Her brother was killed at Katyń, she was deported to Kazakhstan, but she was never keen to talk about old times, which was a pity because I so wanted to know. She was also not keen to remind her Polish friends that her husband was Jewish. Maybe she feared that they might be antisemitic; set in their old ways as many of them were. 'Child, you don't know what people are like', was one of her memorable sayings. A few years before she died, when I was already thinking about writing these family memoirs, I asked her if she had any old photos or letters. She said she had none. She did not like to dwell on these bad times, she said, and she had burnt them all.

PART II

The Reiners

5

Alfred and Kazimiera

'A dream is what makes people love life, even when it is painful.'
Theodore Zeldin[1]

My maternal grandfather, Alfred, survived the war to become the only grandparent I had. I simply adored him. No photographs of my grandmother Kazimiera exist, but I shall do my best to bring her out of the shadows.

Alfred was born on 12 August 1890 in Podgórze. He was one of 5 children of Daniel Reiner and Jentel Rubner. It is mildly interesting that Daniel and Jentel did not in fact marry until 1890 just a few days before Alfred was born, and their first two children, Anna and Celina, were born as Rubners. Could it be that Daniel was not their father? I don't think so. A much more likely explanation is that their original marriage was by religious ceremony only and was not therefore officially registered. The genealogist, Michael Tobias, whom we consulted about this discrepancy, assured us that this was extremely common. By 1890, the Austrian authorities ruled that marriages carried out by rabbis were invalid in the eyes of the law, so they would have hurried along to the registrar to ensure legitimacy for their about-to-be-born baby. After Alfred came two more boys, called Jacob and Juliusz Reiner. I don't know what became of them.

My great-aunt Celina, the second daughter of Daniel and Jentel, survived the war and played a large part in my life when I was growing up in post-war Poland. Her grandson Lucjan is now a dear cousin and a very good friend. Celina also played an important part in my mother's life when they were in hiding on false papers in Warsaw from 1942 to 1945.

As a young man Alfred was a peoples' person, he played bridge a lot, and had a great following among the young ladies of Kraków. Amazingly, I found his name on the database of graduates from the *Liceum Ogólnokształcące im. Króla Jana Sobieskiego* (King Jan Sobieski's General High School) in 1910.[2] Just looking at his classmates' names, I would think that between a third to a half were Jewish.

After school he enrolled at the Jagiellonian University in Kraków to study medicine, but with the outbreak of the First World War in 1914, he was mobilised into the Austro-Hungarian Army's Medical Corps. As an almost qualified doctor, he faced the grim reality of battlefield surgery – the amputations without anaesthetics, the smell, the blood and the gore. This so depressed him that as soon as war was over, he gave up all thoughts of becoming a doctor. However, he must have been an able soldier because he was quickly promoted to the rank of Cavalry Officer. It was there, no doubt that he learned to handle horses and be an excellent shot, skills which he later put to good use as a huntsman.

Alfred in his Austro-Hungarian officer uniform in the First World War

It must have been a year or so before his mobilisation that he would have met my grandmother Kazimiera (or Karolina, as she was known in official papers). She was four years older than my grandfather, born on 7 December 1886, née Grunberg. She was mature, beautiful, and a keen activist in the Polish independence movement. According to the registry records the marriage took place on 9 November 1914 and my mother was born on the 10 May 1915. It could be that they had a shot-gun wedding, as it must have taken place while he was on leave from the front. Or it could be that like in his parents' case, a religious ceremony would have preceded the formal registry office one. Like Alfred, Kazimiera was not a practising Jew, and did not bring my mother up to observe any of the rites or rituals of Judaism. Instead, the family venerated Polish culture of the Romantic period through poets (e.g. Mickiewicz), writers (e.g. Sienkiewicz) and composers (e.g. Chopin). Kazimiera was a voracious reader and loved opera and concerts.

Alfred missed Jadwiga's early years, which was a pity because I remember how good he was with me when I was a small child. When war ended, he re-qualified, this time as an engineer. Soon after he finished his studies, he entered a partnership with a much older Polish colleague, Jan Godzicki, to start up a building firm specialising in the fabrication and sale of construction materials. He had a good business head and the firm thrived. When old Godzicki died, leaving behind a beautiful widow called Stasia, my grandfather together with Stasia became the firm's joint owners and directors. Stasia, fondly known as Siasia, also became his lover.

My grandmother must have known about my grandfather's philandering, and probably chose to ignore it, but after my mother's birth became reclusive, agoraphobic, and given to psychosomatic illnesses. Her frailty may well have been aggravated by jealousy. Very few photographs remain of the Reiner family before the war (all salvaged from cousins or friends), and there are none of Kazimiera, so I try hard to visualise her. Sometimes her presence with a deliberately blurred face occupies my dreams.

In every other way Alfred was a good husband. The family spent their summers and winters in Zakopane, the mountain resort in the Polish Tatra mountains, where he built a house called Jagoda (pronounced Yagoda), meaning blueberry, named after my mother, Jaga (pronounced Yaga). They all loved that house, their spaniel dog Tusia and the horses in the nearby stable. Alfred enjoyed hunting and shooting, and the easy camaraderie of *górale*, the mountain people.

Jagoda, the Zakopane House that my grandfather built, photographed in 1995. We looked
for it again in 2015 but could not find it; we think it must have been taken down and
rebuilt. Our enquiries were met with hostility, probably because the locals thought we had
come to reclaim our repossessed property.

By August 1939, with Germany threatening invasion, Alfred was
mobilised yet again, this time by the Polish Army. With his laudable First
World War credentials, he was immediately recruited as an officer. When
war was declared at the beginning of September, he would have been with
his army unit defending the Polish/German border. Fearing imminent
bombardment of Kraków, Alfred sent word to his building firm colleagues
to collect his wife and daughter and with them to flee east away from the
German front. In the next chapter I describe my grandmother's and
mother's quick exit from Kraków in my grandfather's Tatra car, leaving
behind their home and their family dog Tusia in the care of their faithful
Catholic housekeeper, Zosia. None of them knew that they would never
return.

Sadly, the army's efforts to delay the advance of German troops from
the west and the Soviet troops from the east proved fruitless as the whole
of Poland was annexed by the end of October. Although the Molotov-
Ribbentrop pact, which was in fact just a pact between Hitler and Stalin,
was signed in August 1939, there was initially some confusion as to which
bits belonged to whom, and Alfred's regiment was caught in the crossfire.
He was imprisoned at Katyń (which was on the Soviet side) but managed
to escape in the winter of 1939 before they were all murdered in the
infamous Katyń Massacre the following spring. He jettisoned his Polish
officer uniform, acquired a peasant's coat and making his way stealthily
across the countryside, he turned southwards towards Lwów, where he

hoped to find his wife and daughter. How he found them in Lwów, after that 900km trek through the Russian winter of 1939/1940, was a mystery, although he probably used his ample guile and ready supply of contacts to good effect. By then Lwów was in Soviet hands.

I need to digress a bit to tell something of the history of this 'city of the lions' with the lion on its crest. It has been called Leopolis (in Latin), Lviv (in Ukrainian), Lvov (in Russian), Lwów (in Polish), Lemberg (in German) and Lemberik (in Yiddish), but it's all the same place. As Borowiec[3] put it most succinctly 'it has a quarrelsome history and a divorcee's list of known names'. I have to say that researching the history of the city under its various tyrannical occupations, which I have had to do because it has shaped my family's story, has been more difficult than researching Kraków or Warsaw. The process is furthermore hampered by the fact that Jewish, Polish and Ukrainian memories of the war contradict each other.[4]

Its name changed with the occupying forces, but I prefer to obstinately use its Polish name 'Lwów' throughout. This city, the capital of Eastern Galicia, which since medieval times became the melting pot of Ukrainian, Russian, Polish, German and Jewish cultures has been fought over, year after year. Ironically, its beautiful Italian, Austrian and Slavic architecture has survived, it is just the people that have not. Sadly, today battles have started to rage again, the pogroms are starting again, and its tiny remnant of Jewish diaspora is leaving. In June 2016, the Lwów ghetto memorial was vandalised.

Zordrager and Driebergen[5] in their emotive study-tour of the city bemoan the current lack of pointers to its Jewish past. There are a few modest memorials, mostly put up by a Jewish organisation, but no museum to commemorate the genocide. It did not surprise me to read that the Ukrainians memorialize the 1941 German invasion with patriotic speeches and songs. Stepan Bandera, the infamous Nazi collaborator, was just last year (2020) awarded the posthumous title of Hero of Ukraine. They say that the earlier overt antisemitism has now turned into indifference, as if Jews had simply disappeared from the collective memory of the place.

In 1931 about half the population was Polish, a third was Jewish and 15.9 per cent were Ukrainian.[6] However, the Ukrainians thought of the city as theirs and were fiercely antisemitic. The Poles did not much love the Ukrainians but were equally antisemitic. Simon Wiesenthal, the famous Nazi hunter and Lwów resident, who was born there and studied there, describes the antisemitic atmosphere of Lwów in his brilliant book *The Sunflower*.[7] When he was student in Lwów in the 1930s the Poles would hunt down anyone with a vaguely semitic appearance and attack them with razor blades fastened to the ends of sticks. They, with the full support of the academic staff, also instituted a 'day without Jews' at the university to coincide with examinations, which made it difficult for Jewish students to qualify. What he found incomprehensible was that 'at a time when Hitler was on Poland's western frontiers, poised to annex Polish territories, these Polish "patriots" could only think of one thing: the Jews and their hatred of them'.

These feelings intensified when in September 1939 the Jews from the West (the Reiner family among them) flocked into Lwów fleeing from the German invaders. After September the city swelled to 700,000 inhabitants, of which 180,000 were Jews. [8] By the time Alfred arrived there Lwów was a city where the Soviets ruled, but everyone was at each other's throats.

The Ukrainians disliked the Soviets, their memories raw with previous atrocities, but were glad to be liberated from the rule of bourgeois Poland. The common enemy of Poles, Jews and the Ukrainians at the time of the Soviets was the NKVD (The People's Commissariat for Internal Affairs). More commonly it is simply known as Stalin's secret police. After the war it underwent organisational changes and morphed into the dreaded KGB, which was on everyone's hushed lips while I was growing up in Stalin's post-war Poland. Both the NKVD and its successor, the KGB, were good at exploiting antagonisms in societies; they encouraged and thrived on denunciations.

Under the Soviets in 1940 private trade flourished with lots of black-market dealings and currency speculation. The rouble was the official monetary unit, but dollars were the currency of choice. I remember that a similar situation prevailed in post-war Poland in the Stalin years. Certainly, things were better for the Jews in Lwów under the Soviets than in Nazi-occupied Poland a mere 50km to the west, but life for the Reiner family was far from peaceful. Although ethnicity was not as much of an issue as class[9], everybody was firmly categorized, Jew versus Aryan, Polish versus Soviet, Polish versus Ukrainian, bourgeois versus working class. The Soviets abhorred anyone who had pretensions to the bourgeoisie or thought of themselves as belonging to the economic elite. My grandfather's Polish officer status made him especially at risk. Andrew Borowiec in his memoir[10] recounts a conversation he overheard at the time: 'Officers and policemen. That's who the Russians will go for first. Then it will be the rich shopkeepers and the lawyers. It's going to be fun to watch.' My mother was not a shopkeeper or a lawyer, but she had professional qualifications. Both my grandfather and mother would therefore have been seen as enemies of the people and would almost certainly have been on the NKVD's list for deportation to Siberia, so they were permanently 'on the run' from Stalin's cadres, who were so good at making people disappear.

The Soviet rule did not last long. In June 1941, the Red Army surrendered as Germany took control of the whole of Galicia. As the German tanks rolled in, the Ukrainian population cheered and threw flowers to the German soldiers. Young women dressed in Ukrainian folk costume embraced the marching Nazis. Some accounts talk of the Ukrainian Nationalists (UNO) marching side-by-side with the Germans as they entered the city. The UNO believed, wrongly as it turned out, that the Germans would join forces with them to rid the country of both its Jews and its Poles, and ultimately secure independence for themselves. Using the age-old proverb 'your enemy's enemy is your friend', they viewed the new red flags fluttering about town – this time with the swastika instead of the hammer and sickle, with friendly enthusiasm, adding some of their own. They almost succeeded in proclaiming an Independent Ukrainian State, allied with Nazi Germany, but this turned out to be done without pre-approval from the Germans and the group was disbanded and its organisers arrested. Despite this setback many Ukrainians still believed that they could only free Ukraine with German assistance and were only too willing to act as their lackeys and later became enthusiastic members of their murderous death squads.

On the day that the Germans marched in my grandfather and my mother were both imprisoned for their alleged involvement in the murder of Ukrainian prisoners but were later released. The reason for their arrest only became clear later when they found out that the Ukrainians accused the Jews (collectively) of helping the NKVD in the murder Ukrainian patriots. They were lucky to escape alive; 4,000 other Jews were killed in that first of many *Aktions*. The atmosphere in Lwów changed from the red terror of the Soviets to the black terror of the Nazis, but for Jews, the conditions got visibly worse.

As in Kraków a couple of years earlier, the antisemitic restrictions came in by degrees. Within a few weeks of the invasion all Jews had to wear a Star of David armband on the right arm. As in Kraków it was a white armband with a blue star carefully embroidered in blue silk. Kazimiera, who was skilful with a needle, would have embroidered several for all her family, but Alfred and Jadwiga never considered themselves Jewish and often risked going out without one. Public places became out of limits, trams were first segregated and then banned altogether; daily victimisation went on unpunished. The Ukrainian press took up the old propaganda slogan of 'Judeo-Communism' and accused the Jews of profiting from the

Soviet occupation, but they were just giving vent to years of pent-up hatred. At the same time the Poles accused the Jews of disloyalty to the Polish state and daily life was underpinned by an atmosphere of mutual hatred and distrust. As in Kraków a couple of years earlier antisemitic posters appeared glued to the walls within a few days of the German occupation: 'He who helps a Jew is worse than a Jew and will be killed on the spot'; pamphlets bearing caricatures and proclamations were given out, their content disseminated further by radio and in the legal Ukrainian press.[11]

I asked my mother whether my grandmother worked at the time, or whether she was still an agoraphobic invalid. My mother said she did 'jobs'. She took in washing and ironing and baby-sat for children of people who worked. My grandfather worked when he was not too ill to do so. I believe his work had something to do with changing the rail tracks to the German gauge. Work was important because people with a labour pass were freer to move about the city. What is more, men who were working for German firms, as my grandfather was, were entitled to specify one woman who would also receive *Ausweis* papers. With these in their possession, they perceived themselves to be immune from deportation.

On 11 December 1941, four days after Pearl Harbour, Adolf Hitler declared war on the United States and later that day the US, which had previously been neutral, retaliated with a declaration of war against Germany. With this new turn of events on the world political stage, the Jews of Lwów took new courage, believing that the Allies, now made so much mightier, would bring things to a swift conclusion.

It was about this time that my grandfather suffered his first heart attack. A doctor was called and prescribed pills and bed rest. I know bed rest is not what doctors prescribe now, but nor was he fit for hard physical labour. The day after the doctor's visit, a German (or maybe a Ukrainian) in hob-nailed boots came to the door, kicked him out of bed and ordered him to push a loaded hand cart up a steep hill. Amazingly he survived the ordeal.

I don't know whether my grandfather's heart attack was before or after November 1941 when Jews had to relocate to the *Judenviertel* (the Jewish Quarter). I write about the ghetto in greater detail in the next chapter, because it would have been my mother's accounts and written statements that I use to inform my impression of those times. The ghetto was 'open', that is without walls, unlike the enclosed space of the Kraków ghetto, but its small area (less than a quarter of a square mile) was occupied by 100,000 people. I describe their small half-room space in the next chapter. Earlier in the summer of 1942 my grandmother took under her wing a four-year-old orphan boy, Romek, whose parents had previously been shot or deported, but I don't know the circumstances of how he came to have been left behind. I believe that the four of them only had the one mattress between them in one half of a room.

What is for sure is that their life was lived on a knife edge. They would have constantly feared a knock on the door, or a round-up in the street. They would have been aware as Primo Levi[12] put it that 'outside the ghetto reign the lords of death, and that close by the train is waiting'.

The first deportations of the ghetto residents to Belzec took place between 16 March and 1 April 1942, when reputedly 15,000 were deported.[13] After that, new cards were issued for the workers. [14] These were red *Meldekarten* with a photograph and description. The workers '*Arbeiter*' had 'A' on their armbands, and each worker was allowed a special registration card for one named woman. The women '*Haushalt*' (Household-help) had 'H' on their armbands. So, I would assume that my mother and grandparents would both have had such *Meldekarten*; my mother's and grandfather's with an 'A' and my grandmother's with an 'H'. All three would have confidently believed that the cards would protect them from further deportations as each bore the words clearly stated, 'It is illegal to seize the owner of this card on the street'. In the event by August my mother's 'A' and my grandmother's 'H' must have carried no indemnity whatsoever.

My mother's story of how she was rounded up when on her way to work on 10 August 1943, imprisoned in Janowska camp, and herded onto a train but miraculously escaped, is told in detail in the next chapter. In the meantime, my grandfather and grandmother, having lost their daughter, (they presumed for ever), shut themselves in their ghetto room, too frightened to know what to do. Nowhere was safe, it was impossible to stay at home, impossible to go out. A few days later they experienced the expected hammering on the door. My grandfather met the young Gestapo men at the door with the words, 'I fought alongside your fathers. Can't you leave us alone?' He then offered to bribe them with everything they possessed. It was, however, to no avail. They took my grandmother and little Romek, and just kicked him aside.

My grandfather was destitute. He had no hope of seeing his wife again. His daughter was taken a few days before, and he did not expect her to be alive. He hid in the now almost empty ghetto apartment and wept. A few days later news reached him (I don't know how) that his daughter was alive and waiting for him in a house belonging to a Polish (or possibly Ukrainian) friend. As he walked there his heart sang at the thought that she was alive, while preparing himself for her inevitable question, 'Where is Mama?'

The attrition of the Jewish population in Lwów is summarised by Friedman.[15] In October 1941 there were 119,000 Jews; in July 1942 there were 82,000; by September 1942 there were 36,000; by December 1942 there were 24,000. Thereafter the *Judenrat* was disbanded, and no further figures are available.

Alfred and Jadwiga now had to decide what to do next. Staying in Lwów was not an option, because they would only be picked up again. The only option was to flee somewhere where they could mingle with the crowds and Warsaw seemed like the safest place to go. But how were they to get there, how should they go about getting Aryan papers? The people in the 'safe house' helped them again, particularly my mother's German factory director (more about him later). They got train tickets and embarked on a journey into what my mother called 'a life of illegality'.

When they arrived in Warsaw, they decided to split up so as to attract less attention. My grandfather went to seek out his sister Celina, who was already living as an Aryan, while my mother went to a village near Warsaw to hide with some friends. Their housekeeper Zosia scooped up the 'portable wealth' that she had salvaged from their Kraków flat and brought it to Warsaw. With these they bought new Aryan identities.

I was delighted to find my grandfather's *kennkarte* between my mother's papers. I enclose scans of the six sides of this original document here. It was issued in November 1942 under his new assumed name of Alfred Kwiatkowski who is said to have been born in Lemberg on 7 August 1886. Both his place of birth and his date of birth are fictitious. Thankfully, my grandfather had almost no grey hair, so he easily assumed the identity of someone six years his junior.

I then wondered if he would feature on the internet. He did, but (understandably) back to front:

Alfred Reiner (born Kwiatkowski), born 1890

Alfred Reiner (born Kwiatkowski) was born on *month day* 1890.
Alfred married Kazimiera Reiner (born Grunberg).
Kazimiera was born on December 8 1886, in Krakow.
They had one child.
Alfred passed away.
https://www.myheritage.com/names/alfred_kwiatkowski

The year of birth is right this time, but the names are the wrong way round. He was born Reiner, and 'bought' the name Władysław Kwiatkowski.

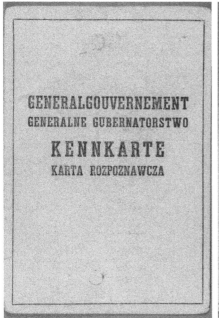
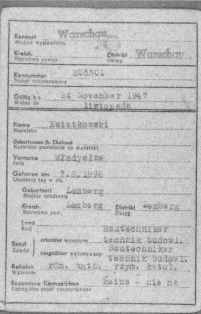
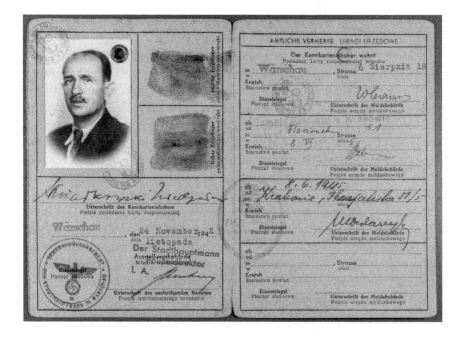

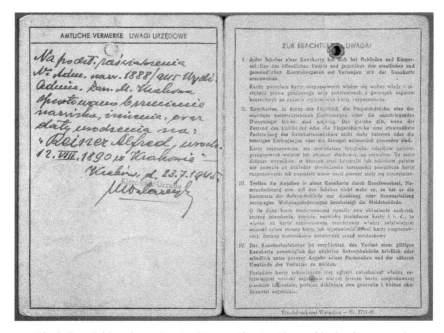

Alfred's 'bought' *kennkarte* showing his new identity. The card had to be stamped at frequent intervals. The penultimate page would have been filled in after peace was declared.

With these papers in his possession, my grandfather decided to go incognito, and where better to vanish than in plain sight in the very heart of the enemy. He had heard that the quasi-Nazi Organisation Todt (OT) were on a recruiting drive for engineers, so he presented himself at their offices in Warsaw and spun a plausible story. He told them he had been an officer in the First World War on the same side as them, he was a qualified engineer, but unfortunately, he had lost all his papers in an earlier bombing raid. He offered to sit an engineering exam if they wished to test his skills. Maybe they believed his story, or maybe they just wanted to believe it. Maybe they did test him; in any case they hired him on the spot.

I have researched this organisation (OT), so will offer a quick explanation. Fritz Todt, after whom the organisation is named, was a senior Nazi road builder and engineer with considerable drive and ability. He rose through the ranks to become the Reich minister for arms and ammunition. He founded the organisation in 1937 and expanded it to an army of half a million workers in 1941. He led it through various projects which included the construction of the 'West Wall', later renamed the Siegfried Line for the defence of the *Reich*. He died in an aircraft accident in 1942, but was succeeded by another Nazi, Albert Speer. Speer was sentenced in 1946 to 20 years' imprisonment for having headed this organisation and thus having sanctioned the illegal use of forced labour. My grandfather, however, was not employed as a forced labourer, he was there as a respected, skilled engineer who joined voluntarily.

Before the outbreak of the war the OT had been instrumental in building military fortifications and strategically important roads. Its workforce was initially German but later foreign-born workers and prisoners of war were recruited into its labour squads, including irresponsible adventurers, swashbucklers, crooks, self-seeking speculators and many enemies of the Reich.[16] Alfred, who was good at heel clicking and the kissing of ladies' hands, would have fitted right in. I was a bit worried when I first looked up the Organisation on the internet to see on Google images of OT engineers wearing khaki uniforms with a swastika on the sleeve. The thought of my grandfather dressed as a Nazi sent goose pimples down my spine, but when I read on, I found that only German engineers were thus attired, whereas employees of other nationalities wore civilian clothes.[17]

Shende in his book, *The Promise Hitler Kept*,[18] describes similar experiences of another Jew in hiding, one Adolf Folkmann, who like my grandfather, was hired in Warsaw at about the same time. Folkmann professed himself to be a carpenter, since he knew that carpenters were needed for active barrack building. He described sticking his private member in freezing cold water so as to shrink it prior to the obligatory medical examination.

My grandfather did not have to do that, because he had a good German boss – one of these 'Good Germans' who undoubtedly aided his survival. The two men got on well on their various engineering projects, the German always allowing Alfred privacy in the toilets, showers and bedrooms. Alfred thought that the man suspected that he was Jewish and took care to protect him from the scrutiny of less well-intentioned colleagues.

It could of course be that his boss simply valued Alfred's expertise in the fabrication and sale of construction materials because he took him on various sourcing ventures – round Germany and to German-occupied Norway. When I heard this, I worried about my grandfather's contribution to the German war effort, but I am sure that he himself had no such qualms of conscience, not then, nor ever. He was simply in hiding, trying to survive.

My grandfather was on placement in Germany when he heard of the Warsaw uprising. The news that at least 50 per cent of the city's civilians had perished would have filled him with dread. He only had two telephone numbers for Warsaw, his sister Celina's and my mother's friends' number in Milanówek. He was not too surprised that Celina's number did not work since the city was destroyed, but the Milanówek number did work. He was overjoyed to find that his daughter was safe and sound – at least for now. At the time when he made the call, he was stationed in Glatz, building barracks for the concentration camp and the AEG armaments factory. He persuaded my mother to join him, as he was planning another trip to Norway shortly. Escape to the West had always been his goal, and he thought that from Norway they could inveigle their way to the UK maybe, or even to the US. Of course, when she arrived in Glatz their father-daughter relationship had to be kept secret. He said she was a distant relative or a daughter of a friend, and even found her some temporary employment in the office. Some weeks later they set off for Berlin, and from there to the coast, with a view to boarding a passenger ship for Norway. Unfortunately, all was to no avail as the ship never sailed to Norway, having previously been terminally bombed. They returned to Berlin, and spent Christmas of 1944 each living separately, a few streets away from Adolf Hitler in his bunker.

My grandfather's last OT assignment was in Leipzig, and that is where they were on the day of its liberation in April 1945. Of course, peace was not officially declared until 8 May 1945, but Leipzig was freed earlier by the US army. It was from there that they made their plans to return to Kraków, the only home they knew.

Their arrival there is described in Part III. To start with Alfred and Jadwiga went to look for Zosia, their faithful housekeeper, who lived with her sister in the suburbs of Kraków. They were welcomed with open arms, not only by Zosia and her sister, but also joyfully by Tusia, the Reiners' beloved spaniel, the only member of the family to have survived the war unscathed. Their second port of call was Alfred's friend Hugo Haber, who immediately made a room available for them in his beautiful flat on Florianska 51 (that is the address he gives on the *kennkarte* above). It was soon after his return that he re-established contact with his previous lady-friend and building-firm partner, Stasia Godzicka. As true (not pretend) Aryans, Stasia and her two children had a relatively trouble-free war. Alfred and Stasia, now in their fifties, took up their old romance and were married a couple of years later. He moved in with Stasia into her apartment on Grodcka Street 32, but one of our three rooms in our flat was kept for him and the bed there was always for *Dziadziuś* (Granddaddy).

The building firm was re-established after the war, under the joint directorship of my grandfather and Stasia. In the evenings and weekends,

My grandfather with Tusia, winter 1945/1946. Amazingly the 'Jewish' dog survived the war unscathed, looked after by the Reiners' faithful housekeeper, Zosia.

Alfred and Stasia's wedding 1948 (left to right: Artur, Jadwiga, possibly Mrs Haber and Dr Haber, Stasia and Alfred, Stasia's elder son, Anna (her daughter-in-law), Janek (her younger son)

Alfred and me, 1948

Spring, 1951

he became the *bon-viveur* again, playing bridge, drinking coffee in Kraków's famous coffee houses and going on hunts. Hare was his favourite prey. I loved the way my nanny Nela served it in a delicious wild mushroom sauce. He also hunted fox and my mother had numerous fur coats and collars made. One such collar with the head complete used to give me the evil eye from its coat cupboard den. I was relieved when it finally succumbed to a cloud of moths – not so very many years ago.

My grandfather was without doubt my favourite person in the world when I was growing up. He was kind and fun, and the only person for whom I could do no wrong. He died on 28 October 1956 from a massive heart attack while walking home after a game of bridge. I still remember that phone call and the realisation, the first for me, that life doesn't just go on. He was buried on Rakowicki cemetery on 31 October 1956, on the day of my tenth birthday. I remember clutching the 'zloty' coin which he had

Alfred, 1955

given me a few days earlier and I kept it safe in my pocket like a talisman for months.

Stasia died in the 1970s, but Stasia's son Janek and his wife Anna remained good family friends and hosted us lavishly when we went to visit them in the 1990s.

Notes

1. Theodore Zeldin, 'A constitution penned by lawyers not poets', *The Guardian,* 29 May 2006.
2. *Liceum Ogólnoksztalcące im. Króla Jana Sobieskiego* retrieved from: http://www.sobieski.krakow.pl/historia/absolwenci-1883-1939/ (accessed 12 April 2021)
3. Borowiec, A., *The Warsaw Boy* (New York: Viking, 2014).
4. Mick, C., 'Incompatible Experiences: Poles, Ukrainians and Jews in Lviv under Soviet and German Occupation, 1939-44', *Journal of Contemporary History,* 46:2 (April 2011), pp. 336-363.
5. Zordrager, H., and Driebergen, M., *The Jews of Lemberg: a Journey to Empty Places* (London: Vallentine Mitchell, 2017).
6. Judah, T., *In Wartime: Stories from Ukraine* (London: Allen Lane, 2015).
7. Wiesenthal, S., *Sunflower* (New York: Schocken Books, 1998).
8. Philip Friedman, 'Extermination of Lvov Jews', *JewishGen* retrieved from: http://www.jewshgen.org/yizkor/lviv/lvi593.html (accessed 12 April 2021)
9. Mick, 'Incompatible Experiences', pp. 336-363.
10. Borowiec, *The Warsaw Boy.*
11. Mick, 'Incompatible Experiences', pp. 336-363.
12. Levi, P., *The Drowned and the Saved* (London: Abacus, 1989).
13. The figures in Friedman's timeline don't quite add up; (according to the above figures it was only 10,000).
14. Philip Friedman, 'Extermination of Lvov Jews', *JewishGen* retrieved from: http://www.jewishgen.org/yizkor/lviv/lvi593.html (accessed 12 April 2021)
15. Ibid.
16. Shende, S.,*The Promise Hitler Kept* (Whitefish, MT: Kessinger Publishing, 2010); this is a facsimile reprint of the original published in 1945.
17. US War Department, 'The Todt Organisation and affiliated services' *Tactical and Technical Trends* 30 (29 July 1943) retrieved from: https://www.lonesentry.com/articles/ttt/todt-organization-ww2.html (accessed 16 July 2021)
18. Shende, *The Promise Hitler Kept.*

6

Jadwiga

'I don't think of all the misery but of the beauty that still remains.' Anne Frank[1]

Early Life

My mother, Jadwiga, was born in Podgórze, a suburb of Kraków on 10 May 1915. According to registry records her parents Alfred and Kazimiera were married on 9 November, a mere six months before her birth. Was it a shotgun wedding? Probably, because my grandfather was known to be a ladies' man, but we will never know for sure, nor does it matter. She was a much-loved only child.

Alfred (Fredek) was a cavalry officer in the Austro-Hungarian Empire during the First World War, so would have been absent in the first few years of her life. In contrast to the extrovert, bon-vivant Alfred, my grandmother, Kazimiera, was a timid person, always apprehensive of the cold and fearful of drafts. She may have suffered from agoraphobia or maybe post-natal depression. My mother said that she rarely went out. I never knew my grandmother, and don't know what she looked like because no photographs of her remain.

My mother was a cheerful optimistic girl, with many friends. Her name was usually abbreviated to Jaga (pronounced Yaga), or the more diminutive form Jagusia. She attended a private girls' high school in Kraków, called *Gimnasium Królowej Jadwigi,*[2] near the Wawel Castle, where about a third of the pupils were Jewish.[3] Before the First World War, Jews formed about a quarter of Kraków's population. In Podgórze where she lived, the proportion may have been even higher. My mother's family was completely assimilated, and my mother did not feel at all Jewish. She did not know the customs, she did not speak Yiddish and she never attended the synagogue (not then nor at any other time in her life). She had vague memories of going to Friday night meals at her grandparents and the lighting of candles, but the significance of these rituals escaped her. My mother was keenly interested in Polish history and literature, and her cultural roots were firmly Polish, not Jewish. She learned German at school, as they all did, and spoke it fluently, which proved useful later. She played the piano as a girl, a pasttime she pursued when living alone in Edinburgh. I was always impressed by her ability to sight-read and play tolerably well, despite being largely self-taught. Not surprisingly, her favourite composer was Chopin.

Although the girls who formed her inner circle were mostly Jewish, she did have some good Catholic friends. Of course, the distinction she made was always between Catholics and Jews, not between Poles and Jews, because she, along with all the Jews of her acquaintance, felt fiercely and patriotically Polish. The religious distinction was an artificial one anyway, because none in her inner circle of friends were religiously observant. If somebody had asked her are you Polish or Jewish, or which comes first, she would say Polish without any hesitation. The trouble is, of course, that the Nazis never asked her. Nevertheless, since religious faith was down in black and white, one or the other, easily available from census lists, the Germans had access to a ready-made hit list. Religious faith still features as a question even in the last Scottish census of 2011, though thankfully now, you can elect to tick a box for 'no religion'. What they really should have is a box for 'I do not want to answer that question – religion is a private matter'.

My mother doted on her father and shared with him her love of horses and dogs. Summer and winter holidays were spent in the Tatras in their house Jagoda, which my grandfather had built. They all enjoyed the outdoors, and in the winter they skied. She still knew how to do it even in her eighties, when she took my son Tim on a skiing holiday to Switzerland. My grandparents had a faithful live-in servant called Zosia, who proved invaluable later. I remember visiting Zosia in the early 1950s in her cottage on the outskirts of Kraków. I was a picky eater when I was a child, but distinctly remember wolfing her mouth-watering fresh bread spread with creamy butter.

My mother's best subject at school was maths. I remember how easily she solved my algebra and trigonometry questions when I brought them home as a work-shy schoolgirl. I have her *Matura* certificate from 1933, with 'excellent' for maths. I wonder how on earth that flimsy piece of paper had survived. Did she keep it with her, even when she herself acquired a new identity? Or had it been safeguarded by Zosia? Since I only found it among her papers after her death, the answer to that question must remain a mystery. I should say that *Matura* in Poland was and still is much more than a school leaving certificate. You need it for entry into university, but it

One of the very few photographs to survive from before the war; this must have been around 1928. My mother looks about 13.

is also a rite of passage signifying adulthood and admission into a class of educated people. What my mother really yearned to do at university was architecture, but the subject was not taught in Kraków. Reluctant to leave her frail mother for studies elsewhere, she chose to study chemistry and qualified with an MSc (*Magister*) in chemistry in 1938 from the Jagiellonian University in Kraków. In the last couple of years of her degree course, my mother had to sit at the back of the class with the other Jewish students, because by then the University had adopted a 'seating ghetto' policy that required segregation in the classroom. I remember her telling me that several of her Catholic friends chose to sit with her out of solidarity.

At some time during her student years, the family moved from Podgórze to the intellectual centre of Kraków to occupy a beautiful apartment on Mikołajska Street 32. I have passed it many times on my tourist trips to Kraków and tried to imagine her there. The 1932 census lists a building firm at that address; this was probably my grandfather's office.

Despite her 'posh' address my mother's peer group consisted of her old Podgórze friends. Her best friend since early childhood was Irena (Irka) Oberleder, a sporty girl, very good at tennis and a champion skier, but not very diligent in her schoolwork. One of my favourite stories when I was growing up was how Irka, having come to school unprepared, set about copying from my mother's test paper, starting with my mother's name at the top. Later, when they were all students, Irka became my father's first girlfriend. Both were frequent visitors at my mother's central Kraków flat, which was near the University. My grandmother thought Artur was wonderful, a fact which my mother later interpreted as a sort of blessing from beyond the grave. She was much less keen on my mother's beau of the day, a boy called Tolek, calling him *kurdupel* (runty wee guy). Tolek survived the war, wrote her beautiful poetic letters, and my mother often said she might have done better if she had stuck with him.

Politically, my mother leaned to the left, supported Josef Piłsudski until his death in 1935, and remained a Socialist till the day she died. In the *interbellum* she was too steeped in Polish culture to have any time for

Jadwiga in the early 1930s

Zionism. Poland was her motherland, and she did not like the Zionists' militant stance against the Arabs, not then and not later.

Alfred was called up into the Polish army one week before the Germans marched into Kraków. On 6 September my mother heard for the first time in her life the rattle of guns and the blast of bombs falling on the outskirts of the city. There were rumours of imminent bombardment and gas attacks. Though himself on the front-line, my grandfather must have been worried about his family in Kraków, so he sent word from his army hide-out to his firm's office to send a car. My mother wrote of this day in a memoir she once thought to publish.

> Early in September 1939 there is a ring at the doorbell and in front of the house stands my father's small 'Tatra' car with the firm's driver in the driving seat. In the back seat sits the professor of musicology, Zdzisław Jachimecki[4], and his wife (also an academic – a linguist) and crammed between them is my grandfather's building firm co-owner Stanisława Godzicka (Stasia).

Stasia, as explained in a previous chapter, was by then my grandfather's mistress. Stasia, I should add, was Polish, not Jewish. There was just enough space in the front seat for my mother and grandmother, but absolutely no room for baggage or any memorabilia – such as photographs. My mother took only one thing – a new umbrella. (To her dying day she hated umbrellas.) My grandmother, who as I said was a bit of a recluse, had never met my grandfather's mistress before, but she certainly knew of her existence. So, you can imagine the dynamic in that car.

I am sure that at that moment it had not crossed my mother's mind that she would never return home again. Their flight to the East was merely to avoid the threat of imminent bombardment and they fully expected to be back within a month. After all, even before they left, Neville Chamberlain had officially announced on 3 September that Britain and France were at war with Germany. Surely it would make sense to wait out the current unpleasantness in the relative safety of the still Polish East. Then the Allies would invade, and it would all be over.

Lwów under the Soviets (Lvov)

The car drove across the Wisła (Vistula) away from the German front, eastwards towards Lwów. The journey of 330km, which nowadays would take less than four hours, was fraught with danger and probably took several days as the roads were constantly bombed by German planes. William Brand recalls, 'The roads out of town were blocked by the crush of cars, trucks, and carts piled high with people's belongings. It looked like a village fair on a vast scale'.[5] They arrived in Lwów safely but by the time they got there they realised that their flight was in vain; the Germans were already on the outskirts of the town, raining bombs and shells onto the most thickly-populated areas. So, my mother and frail grandmother were suddenly dumped in an alien mixed-up city under threat of imminent bombardment, with nowhere to live and no friends to call on. Everyone was sheltering in over-crowded basements and cellars and did not welcome intruders. My grandmother's distant relative who lived there, was not prepared to give them shelter. The Polish professor, his wife and Stasia found rooms with relations (and later returned to Kraków), but my mother and grandmother were homeless. The town was teeming with fugitives, all with nowhere to go, sleeping under arches, in doorways, in public buildings, schools and churches.[6] But luck was with them. My mother told and retold me the story of how the pair of them stood looking distressed and lost when they saw leaning against a doorway a handsome Jewish boy. Mietek Raher, as he introduced himself, gave them food, shelter in his cellar, and later found them lodgings with his friends.

The siege, sometimes called the Battle of Lwów, lasted two weeks, with the German Wehrmacht at one stage breaking through to the city centre, only to be repulsed by the Polish infantry. Then on 19 September the Soviets appeared and linked with the German army besieging Lwów from the west. On 22 September, the Germans withdrew leaving the city to the Soviets. To celebrate the victory the Soviets bedecked the city (now called Lvov) with red Soviet flags, and larger-than-life portraits of Lenin, Stalin, and other Soviet leaders. Streamers across streets proclaimed slogans in Polish, Ukrainian and Yiddish.[7]

To find food at the time when all the shops were shut was no mean task, requiring jumping over walls to find clandestine butchers and bakers. My mother was rightly impressed by Mietek's ability of negotiate life under difficult circumstances, and she fell in love with him. In her reminiscences she always added, 'But I Did Not Lose My Virginity' – probably to protect my virtue. Sadly, their relationship did not last. She said that he was too young at 19, to her 24, and 'he did not belong to the educated class'. She had met his family and was appalled to see 'no toilet in their house, only one on the porch, accessible only by a key hidden in the kitchen'. He survived the war, and they corresponded briefly after they were both married to other people. She later rather regretted her class-based decision, particularly when she heard that his wife was the wealthiest and most desirable woman, who chose him above numerous other suitors.

Slowly my mother and grandmother settled and survived doing odd jobs to pay for food and lodgings. It was at this time that my grandfather came searching for them. The Polish army capitulated in the winter of 1939 and grandfather was imprisoned by the Soviets at Katyń. He escaped and tramped for weeks through snowy forests, stealing food and hiding in hayricks by day. My mother often recounted the moment of his arrival – he was sporting a beard, looked like a tramp, and she did not recognise him. The family was happy to be reunited, but their life in Lwów was fraught with difficulties amid pogroms and cruel persecution by the Ukrainians.

Under Soviet rule Lwów, swollen from the numbers of Jewish exiles from the West, was in the meantime undergoing attrition of its population as convoys of them were sent off to Gulags. Among those evicted at the time was my aunt Jasia, and her London friend Irenka Starzecka, exiled in separate transports to Kazakhstan and Siberia. They were Polish, not Jewish. However, it would be wrong to imply that Jews were 'safe'. They were similarly hunted, and according to Friedman,[8] 10,000 Jews were exiled together with the Poles and the Ukrainians to the depths of Asian parts of the USSR. Particularly at risk from the NKVD (Communist Secret Police) were officers, like Alfred, and professional people, like my mother. In one of my mother's letters, she told a friend 'most of the time I was on the run from the NKVD'.

Trying to eke out a living under these circumstances made life very difficult, but nothing compared with what was to come.

Lwów under the Germans (Lemberg)

At the end of June 1940, the Soviet rule came to an end when the Germans marched in.[9] As Hitler reneged on the Molotov-Ribbentrop pact, the Polish and Ukrainian residents cheered. The Ukrainians in particular saw the Germans as liberators, who would ultimately help them establish a Ukrainian free state. The Jewish population, however, were under no illusions. The situation was made worse by a rumour spread by the Germans and the Ukrainians that the Jews had taken part in the execution of Ukrainian political prisoners whose bodies had been discovered in the dungeons of the NKVD. This particular propaganda item fitted well with the image nurtured by the Ukrainians of treacherous Jews, hand-in-glove with the communists. *Żydokomuna* (Judeo-Communism) was an idea that started in the nineteenth century and persisted until well after the war in Poland, Ukraine and Lithuania. In Ukraine it persists still.

On the day after the Germans entered the city, Jadwiga and her father were thrown in the Brygidki Prison. Jews were accused of the murders, and so Jews were rounded up to pay the price. In one of my mother's hand-written testimonies, she wrote 'I witnessed massacres in the jail', then 'we were by a miracle liberated'. They were lucky. In four days of rioting, ending on 3 July 1941, 4,000 Jews were murdered.[10] From July 25 to 27 the Ukrainians again went on the rampage, murdering 2,000 more Jews.[11] It was the first *Aktion* against the Jews that my mother experienced.

The scenes of the time are corroborated by historians. Friedman[12] quotes the testimony and personal experiences of the Lwów attorney Dr Isidor Eliasha Lan:

> It started in the streets with chasing of Jewish men. Lvov Jews, stricken by panic and fear, predominantly stayed indoors. The majority of them hid in their apartments, in various shelters or in basements and attics. The Ukrainian police and Germans, dissatisfied with a meagre catch in the streets, began to comb Jewish apartments in search of their victims. They took away men and sometimes entire families under the pretext of needing to clear Lvov prisons of corpses. Several thousand Jews were thus rounded up and sent to the prisons...all the while being thrashed and jeered by the mob. In the 'Brigidka' prison, they trapped a mob of several thousand Jews in the prison courtyard and assaulted them mercilessly. The walls of prison around the court were covered with blood...

At the very same time the marching Germans presented themselves as Hitler's Christian Soldiers, with the words *Gott Mit Uns* inscribed on their belt buckles. [13] No wonder the Poles and the Ukrainians cheered. These Christian soldiers were finally going to solve their twin problems of the Christ killing Jews and the Bolsheviks all in one. All over the city gold and blue Ukrainian flags fluttered next to the red, white and black swastikas, while notices appeared proclaiming 'Smash the Jews and the Communists. Long live Stepan Bandera',[14] and 'long live Adolf Hitler'.[15] The notices were made by the Organisation of the Ukrainian Nationalists (OUN) who tried to ingratiate themselves with the German occupiers. In the event, the OUN were sold up-river, and their leader, Bandera was imprisoned, while the Germans reneged on their initial promise to save Ukraine for the

Ukrainians. But in the meantime, the Germans were quick to capitalise on the sympathy of the Ukrainians at the expense of both Poles and Jews. Like in Kraków two years earlier a hierarchy quickly established itself. The Germans were better than the Ukrainians which were better than Poles, which were better than Jews.

Within two weeks of the German take-over all adult Jews had to identify themselves with a Star of David. The atmosphere of constant threat continued, especially now that the targets were easily discernible. A Jew identified with an armband would have to hurriedly step off the pavement if they saw a German approaching. Whoever did not move fast enough would be beaten or even shot. There would be no peace in the lodgings, either. To her end my mother would be scared witless of any loud knocks, remembering the Gestapo's (or their Ukrainian henchmen's) hammering followed by guttural shouts – *Alle Jude Heraus*. Once in the last few years of her life my mother had inadvertently bolted herself in the house, so I banged on the door to be let in. She was seriously petrified when she eventually opened the door.

In Lwów, as in Kraków, a *Judenrat* was formed to facilitate the fulfilment of German orders. My mother did not know any of them, but it would have made no difference anyway. Within a month of the *Judenrat*'s formation it had to oversee a wave of expropriation of Jewish goods and valuables. 'Sometimes, they demanded hundreds of furniture sets. Another time, they demanded so many hundreds of Persian rugs, large quantities of coffee or cocoa, sardines, several hundred meters of original carpet runners, gold, diamonds, expensive tableware, bed linens, etc. Their demands were based on the belief that all property belonged to them.'[16]

I need to digress here from the flow of the Lwów timeline to tell of what happened in the meantime to my mother's apartment and possessions in Kraków. This is relevant as it affects the rest of the story. When my mother and grandmother fled East at the beginning of September 1939, they left for the last time their beautiful apartment in the affluent central area of the city. Their faithful Catholic housekeeper, Zosia, was left as a caretaker of their jewels, pictures, Persian rugs, antique furniture, as well as their dog Tusia. They thought at the time that their flight to the East would be temporary, and that they would soon return to find it all unchanged. That is of course not what happened. Within a couple of weeks, still in September 1939, the apartment was requisitioned by high-ranking German officers. Luckily Zosia had the presence of mind to move the jewels to her sister's house in the country, but the rest of the valuables were relinquished when she handed over the keys.

Within a few weeks of the German invasion, Lwów, like the whole of *Generalgouvernement* (GG), was plastered with antisemitic posters, which made clear to the rest of the civilians that the Jews were out-with the limits of the law. You would have thought that the malicious humiliation of the Jews would inspire some compassion among the resident population. Sadly, it only served to confirm their image as pariahs. My aunt Jasia, as a young Polish woman in Lwów, overheard a conversation between two Poles on a tram. 'It's a good thing that the Jews are now segregated, as I would really hate to sit in a place just vacated by a smelly Jewish arse.' And that was just a mild expression of disdain. The hoodlums of society would have had serious fun with their easy prey.

'*Divide et impera* (divide and rule) policy was introduced, with the city's rich tapestry of religions, languages and cultures being cut up into ethnic regions. First to be segregated were the Germans, requisitioning the most well-to-do district of Lwów in the area surrounding the Stryjsky Park. The assimilated and cultured Jewish inhabitants who lived there were evicted with only a few hours' notice.[17] My mother's family did not of course live anywhere as affluent as that. Their lodgings in Lwów were modest and unadorned.

The Jewish ghetto *Judenviertel* (the Jewish Quarter) was created in the slum areas of Zamarstynov and Kleparov in the northern part of the city in November 1941, with a view to separating the scum of the earth from the rest of society. The only way into the ghetto was along Peltevna Street, which passed under a railway bridge – named the 'bridge of death' by the inhabitants. Friedman describes the scene[18]:

> Under the bridge, the Ukrainian and German guards thoroughly checked the innumerable masses of Jews continuously flowing into the future ghetto area. Using carts, wheelbarrows, children's carriages, with bags in their arms and trunks on their backs, the Jews transferred their property into their new places of residence in the ghetto. The crowd of these hapless creatures was carefully controlled by the German and Ukrainian guards. If someone did not please them, they were taken inside the barracks, while ordered to leave their possessions outside. Those who appeared poor, sick, exhausted or incapable of work, as well as those who could not produce work certificate, in general women and children, were invited into the old barracks. They were greeted by beatings by the dregs of the Jewish community, which the Germans caught and forced to perform this function. Germans and Ukrainians supplemented the rest. In the

evening, thus assembled victims were sent to the Lonzky prison. There, they were stripped naked, thrown onto the trucks and carried into the forest to be executed. This 'bridge of death' absorbed in November and December of 1941 several thousand victims, predominantly women. This was the first vast German action against the Jewish women of Lvov.

The above description concurs exactly with my mother's description in a letter to a Polish attorney in 1966. She says:

> The bridge of death…led to Zamarstynowska Street, where the SS picked off scores of Jews who were relocating to the ghetto district… , 'playing with them' in a most awful way. There they beat children in front of mothers, and mothers in front of children. Nobody then taken came out alive.

In her memoir she says she witnessed many what she called 'Dante-esque scenes'. Except that in Dante's inferno the punishment was usually deserved.

While the atrocities under the bridge were taking place the population of Lwów jeered and hurled abuse at the victims. 'Throughout the period it [the move to the ghetto] was treated as one of the town's most amusing spectacles'.[19] With a tremendous thrill the Poles said, *Ale biją Żydków* ('see how they are beating the Yids') and their eyes glowed with happiness.[20] Kahane[21] believed that 'the main beneficiaries of the *Aktion* under the bridge were the Ukrainian policemen. Under the pretext of looking for the elderly, they would burst into Jewish homes at night, extorting large sums of money from the residents.' This concurs exactly with my mother's account. One day the Ukrainian henchmen of the SS came to her lodgings to conduct a search and took away everybody's valuables. This sort of legitimised robbery was an everyday occurrence. Some people kept their diamonds hidden in a condom shoved up their anus;[22] others swallowed them and tried to recover them later.[23] My mother's portable wealth (though she did not have much) was sewn into the hem of her dress.

Eventually, between 110,000 and 120,000 Jews were forced into the new ghetto. In my mother's reminiscences the district designated to be the ghetto was the poorest district of Lwów, and was mostly lived in by Ukrainians, who wanted to extort huge rents from the Jewish incomers. She continues in her letter to the attorney:

The overcrowding and the high rents made finding a place to live very difficult and took a long time, necessitating repeated journeys over the bridge of death. Then when people had handed over their savings to the Ukrainians to secure a place to live, the edict changed. They moved the Jewish district from the centre of Zamarystynowa to the previous Jewish quarter, including the Jachowicza Street. From the spring of 1942 nobody could live out-with that area, and nobody did. In fact, the district was not closed off, it's just that anyone who left the area risked death. Prowling SS-men patrolled the streets looking for Jews, who were then told to dig their own grave at the side of the road and shot into them. This was a daily sight that I encountered. Passing under the bridge of death continued to be risky...It was difficult to find lodgings and I went from house to house looking for somewhere for my family to live, every day in danger of my life, witnessing people being thrown out of windows, murders in the street, house searches by SS-men, the deportation of people to work from which nobody ever returned. Since March when I lived there, there was not a day without grief for a murdered child, or an elderly person, or a young person deported for 'resettlement'... Because it [the ghetto] was 'open', if you were lucky enough not to meet a policeman, you could move to the Polish side, but the movement was connected with huge risks. In other ghettos, for example in Kraków, Jews were only taken in *Aktions*. In Lwów, murder on a large scale was a daily occurrence. Once when, in the early days I went to buy bread with my armband, I was taken by a Ukrainian to his house where his wife forced me to clean, wash clothes etc. He stood at the door and watched that I carried out these tasks dutifully. I carried on working all day and at night he took me and whipped me mercilessly. He could have killed me, but I came out alive...My cousin who was a soloist in the Polish Philharmonia at the age of 20, had to dig his own grave at the side of the street and jump into it. He was then shot.

The last item in the above testimony relates to her cousin Jakub (Kuba) Weissman, born in 1918. She often told me about the boy's prodigious talent for the piano. Aged only 20, he was the principal soloist with the Lwów Philharmonia (1939-1941). I have devoted a small chapter to him, so as not to detract from the flow of my mother's story.

Shootings continued throughout that summer of 1941, probably about the time when Kuba was killed. The mass *Aktions* and deportations came later, but these were not half as much fun for the sadistic occupants. Maria Jordan, a Polish biologist who corresponded with my father, recalled that near her home-town of Stanisławów, there was wood called the Black Forest where shootings took place. 'I happened to be on the street when a convoy of young Gestapo boys were returning "from their work"; I was shocked by their laughter and mimicry of their victims falling to their deaths.' In Stanisławów the shooting gallery was the Black Forest, in Kraków it was *Hujowa Gora*, but in Lwów it was *Piaski*, a mountain of sand in Janowska camp, where the ground was soft, and the victims were often made to dig their own graves.

Interestingly, Janowska camp still exists, not as a museum or a memorial, but a fully operational Ukrainian State Prison still surrounded by barbed wire. According to Zorgrader and Driebergen[24] there is no memorial. The only signs to explain what this once was are the swastikas defacing its outer walls. They confirm that the locals do know what this is, have no regrets, and are clearly still intent on inciting antisemitic hatred. The gate with the words *Arbeit macht frei* has been taken down, but the rails are still there, leading to nowhere. The sands themselves ('*piaski*') were until recently used as a training terrain for police dogs. Now it's a grassy area with a pool. Lwów's tiny Jewish community refer to them as Lwów's Babi Yar.

My mother must have heard of reports of what happened in Babi Yar in Kiev (500km east), where all Jews were given this instruction: 'All Yids of the city of Kiev and its vicinity must appear on Monday, 29 September [1941], by 8 o'clock in the morning at the corner of Mel'nikova and Dorohozhytska streets...Bring documents, money and valuables, and also warm clothing, linen, etc. Any Yids who do not follow this order and are found elsewhere will be shot.'[25] They were shot anyway, all 33,771 of them, between 29 and 30 September 1941. Led undressed into a ravine 150 metres long and 30 metres wide, 15 metres deep, they were shot one after the other while standing on layers of corpses.

And maybe she would have heard reports of what happened in July 1941 in the village of Jedwabne (500km north) when in a village of 1,600 inhabitants, half of whom were Polish and the other half Jewish, the Polish villagers massacred their Jewish neighbours; one mass of humanity against another. Maybe reports of these atrocities would have left her less surprised by the sadism raging around her.

She knew that the infirm, the useless and the unemployed were the first to be seized for deportation, so her most important immediate aim was to find work. Without it she would not have the all-important

Jews assembling for deportation in the courtyard of the Sobieski School in Lwów (Source: Chris Webb Private Archive)

certificate of employment *Ausweis* or *Arbeitskarte*. Not far from where she lived was a glass factory, and that is where she went to look for work. She told me how she stood in a long queue which snaked right around the corner of Zamarstynowska Street where the factory was located, everyone waiting for their turn to be interviewed. When she got to the head of the queue, she was pleasantly surprised by the manner with which she was treated. She immediately felt that the German director was what she called a 'good man'. When he interviewed her, he shook her hand warmly and apologised for only being able to offer her manual work despite her chemistry qualifications. This was the beginning of a rapport that later served her well.

I asked my mother where she lived at the time, and the address she remembers was Tarnowskiego Street 66, which I am told was situated far from the ghetto. Anyway, the ghetto borders changed over time several times, so I am not sure whether this was her address before her move to the ghetto, or after the ghetto boundaries changed and she had to relocate yet again. As she said in another testimony, 'she was always on the run'. Philippe Sands[26] refers to the ghetto's seven districts in which all Lwów's Jews lived, so she may have lived within the ghetto as it was defined at that time. She said that her route to work passed under the 'bridge of death', which gives a bit more information. However, she did describe the final Lwów home (wherever that was) to me one night in the final years of her life, during one of her talkative spells. The flat her family lived in contained several rooms, each housing at least one family. Their room was divided into two by a washing line strung with a sheet, so that it housed two families, their side of it also serving as a corridor between two other rooms. Towards the end of their time in that half-room, my mother's family of three (her mother, her father and her) was increased with the addition of a little four-year-old orphan boy called Romek, whose parents had been taken in a previous *Aktion*. It was a difficult situation, offering little privacy. She also described how the other family, the one on the other side of the washing line, shared a single bed with a small baby. The baby died of cot-death, though my mother believed it had been smothered.

The rather fluid perimeter of the ghetto, and its 'open' nature subsequently prevented my mother from gaining any reparation payments from the Germans. The refusal letter clearly said that she was not eligible because at no stage was she in an enclosed ghetto. Her subsequent experiences also seemed to count for nothing. The lack of a defined boundary to the Jewish district is confirmed in other memoirs. Reder[27], whose memoirs I shall draw on extensively in the next few pages, says, 'there was no separate ghetto in Lvov. A few streets were designated for Jews only and thus formed a Jewish district...Here we lived deprived of peace and under constant harassment.' In between the *Aktions* snatching people for the camps never ceased. According to Friedman[28] 50-100 Jews disappeared daily without a trace.

In contrast to the grim housing situation, the glass factory offered good working conditions. She sorted through recycled glass and painted the ceramic and glass utensils which the factory produced. The German director continued to treat her well, maybe because he was a good man, but it must also have had a lot to do with her. She worked hard, spent her meagre money generously and she was smartly dressed, young and pretty. She continued to work there for about a year until August 1942. In her diary she described how lorries used to drive up to the glassworks demanding Jewish workers, and how her colleagues would hide her in some crates behind packing cases. The German director, Dr Bauer (or Bauman – my mother was never any good with names), who my mother said was a *Volksdeutsche*, and his Ukrainian manager Dr Jan Fierl were both extremely helpful in keeping her safe. Much, much later, just a few years before my mother died, she asked me to try to find out whether the internet might not yield some details about the glass factory and Dr Bauer (Bauman) in particular, with a view to posthumously honouring the good man.

My researches yielded details of the glass factory in the accounts of Adolf Folkmann published by the Hungarian journalist Stefan Shende in 1944, even before peace was declared.[29] I was lucky to find the first edition of this book in the National Library of Scotland. Folkmann, a Polish Jew from Kraków, survived first in the Lwów ghetto and later disguised as an Aryan working, like my grandfather, for the Organisation Todt. Although Folkmann's (or maybe it is Shende's) version of the execution method used in Belzec is so fanciful that his book was at one time banned or burned, his testimony about the glass factory is likely to be accurate. There were two glass factories in Lwów at the time. One employed 500 and the other employed 200 people. The larger factory where Folkmann worked manufactured glass bottles for the wine and spirits industry. Being a glass engineer by profession, Folkmann was its business manager in the early part of the German occupation, but then the Germans dismissed him and most of the rest of the staff, and installed a *Volksdeutsche* as director, 'a *Sturmabteilung* [SA] man who apparently enjoyed even better connections with the Gestapo than G. [the previous director] had'. Folkmann does not give the *Volksdeutsche's* name, but that would probably have been my mother's German director. If he had good connections with the Gestapo, he would have been in a position to help Jews. Folkmann, once dismissed, found other work as a salvage collector, but maybe had he been kept on, he too may have benefitted from the beneficence of this good German boss. In the meantime, my mother and presumably some others in that waiting queue had the good fortune to be hired as part of the factory's restructured workforce.

I was further helped in my researches on this topic by the BBC in 2019 who wondered whether my family's story might form part of their Holocaust series 'My Family, the Holocaust and Me'. In the event, they decided not to air my story (probably because I am not very telegenic) but not before they put some of their skilful researchers onto the case. They identified both the glass factories and the 'Good *Volksdeutsche* German' Dr Bauer (not Bauman). He was, apparently the industrial chief of both the factories, which at the start of the German occupation kept their pre-war names of 'Leopolis', for the larger one, and 'Lwów', for the smaller. When the Germans took over the factories, the numbers of workers were slimmed down to 175 and 125 workers in the two factories respectively. It is likely that my mother worked in 'Leopolis', because its address[30] was closer to Zamarstynowska and the bridge of death, which she passed daily on her way to work.

According to my mother's memories not many Jews were employed there, or she may even have been the only one. On one occasion one of her co-workers said about her, 'look a Jew who speaks perfect Polish'. Apparently, the Jews she had usually came across were laughable people who only spoke Yiddish.

By the summer of 1942 Jewish people of Lwów already knew what 'resettlement' meant. One or two prisoners had escaped due to the guards' lucrative past-time of 'Jew dealing' or extorting money from the victims' relatives in return for their release,[31] and one of the Ukrainians had told his girlfriend what was going on. These people spread the word, and the Jewish inhabitants of Lwów were scared. However, the word Bełżec was not yet on everyone's lips. My mother and grandmother were not yet then aware of the destination of these one-way journeys. Reder[32] wrote, 'two weeks before the resettlement, news of the impending calamity was already circulating'. The workers of a few chosen factories had been issued with work stamps, presumably to seek extra protection from deportations. My mother certainly had a work permit, and may or may not have had a special stamp, but by August 1942 the German Employment office was closed down, and the responsibility for the Jews was transferred entirely to the German police and the SS. According to Shende[33] even 'the best papers were not sufficient to save a man'.

Hans Frank the governor of the GG visited Lwów on 1 August 1942. A great rally was organised in the opera house to mark the anniversary of Galicia's incorporation into the GG. It included a Hitler Youth fanfare, a performance of a 15,000-strong choir and an oft-quoted speech from Frank (cited by Sands[34]).

> We appreciate what the Fuhrer has given us with his gift of Galicia, and I am not talking here about its Jews. Yes, we still have some of them around, but I will take care of that. Incidentally, I don't seem to have any of that trash hanging around here today. What's going on? They tell me that there were thousands and thousands of those flat-footed primitives in this city once upon a time – but there hasn't been a single one to be seen since I arrived. [Here the audience erupted into applause]…Don't tell me that you have been treating them badly [great hilarity].

Frank was speaking a few hundred metres from the ghetto, and he knew well that there were still 76,000 Jews alive in Lwów. The news of his speech, though given behind closed doors, spread like wild-fire around the Jewish residents and everyone was fearful. On 9 August 1942 'no one in the Jewish quarter slept the night…Everybody who had good papers had to go to work every day throughout the period of the *Aktion*. We had to pass through SS cordons with raised hands holding the precious stamped labour card… [Those apprehended] shouted, "Tell our boss…Tell him to save us".'[35] Frank was as good as his word. In the 'Great *Aktion*' between 10 and 23 August he duly 'took care' of 50,000 Jews.[36]

My mother was rounded up on the first day of the *Aktion*. (The date she told me was 10 August 1942.) Reder[37] described the scene, just as she had described it to me: 'Early in the morning the guards blocked all the streets leading out of the Jewish district. Squads of four or five Gestapo, SS and *Sonderdienst* [special paramilitary services] spread out every couple of metres…anyone putting up resistance got a bullet in the head'. She was whipped and herded onto a lorry, but not before she had thrust a hand-written note along with some money into the hand of a passing Ukrainian boy. The note was for the attention of her German boss, the payment was for the messenger. The packed lorry was driven to the courtyard of Kazimierzowska prison where SS-men beat her and repeatedly kicked her in the stomach. From there she was taken to Janowska camp. She tried to escape through the electrified barbed wire fence but was caught, beaten some more, this time with a board studded with nails until she bled. The whole purpose of the Janowska camp interlude was to assess her ability to work, but after all the beatings she had received she probably did not look her best. After roll call the next day she was 'selected' for 'resettlement'.

But even then, she was not resigned to her fate. She thrust another note for the German director into the hand of a kindly-looking Ukrainian policeman. In the evening along with all those who had 'failed' the selection process she was marched out in rows of 4 or 5 from Janowska camp to the Kleparów railway station (it was early evening by then), where a cattle train 50 wagons long was waiting. Lining the sides of this trail of human misery was a cordon of Ukrainian guards, arms linked forming a human chain, and on the inside Gestapo men with rubber truncheons and guns. While she waited to be propelled onto the train, she did what she was always good at – she 'read' the guards' faces. There were two of them, she thought, who looked more kindly than the others. She smiled at them and she thought she detected a flicker of response. She was almost on the steps of the train when a cart full of skeleton-like prisoners drew up. As the guards started to load this human cargo onto the train, the attention of the Gestapo men was diverted and in the commotion that followed the guards, unintentionally or maybe intentionally, let her slip through. Unnoticed, her Star of David torn and discarded, she walked feigning confidence, across the platform and slipped into the station cafeteria. But she was not entirely unobserved, because standing at the door was an elderly waitress, who said to her softly in Polish, 'I know where you have come from.' Discreetly she led my mother into a dark corner of the café, placed a cup of coffee before her and a cigarette between her fingers. Then lifting from her own neck a chain with the medallion of the Virgin Mary and the baby, she hung it on my mother's neck. 'Hold on to her tight', she said, 'She will save you.' So, when the Gestapo came in, there she was – a 'saved' Christian girl, a friend of the waitress.

This pivotal moment in my mother's life was one she told to all those whom she considered to be her friends. Indeed, I used to measure her acquaintances' position on the friendship ladder by asking her 'Well have you told her *the story* yet?' What was it that saved her? Was it the Virgin Mary? She certainly venerated the icon as a symbol of mother love, and a statuette of the Virgin Mary went with her to her grave. Yes, she had a deep faith in the power of human love. But above all, she was resourceful, brave, canny and plucky. She was not and would never be a victim.

The view from the café was grim. In the August heat the victims were packed into the cattle trucks, 100 people per wagon, each wagon intended for 6 cows. Their terrified faces at the grilled window cried out for 'water, water, water'. The Gestapo guards patrolled the platform jeering, 'They will be wanting toothpaste next'. This scene is described almost identically by a Jewish policeman, Ben Z. Redner,[38] who was at the very same station on that very day and at that time. According to his account the jeering words were 'What? You want water? Why not beer? Hallo, bring some beer!' The jibe was maybe uttered by a different guard, but the sense of atmosphere is uncannily similar. The policeman saw a girl break free and run from the thronging victims, their guards and the train. Then he heard a shot and saw her limp body and smashed skull. This alternative ending sent shivers down my spine. What a good thing that my mother had not read those words. Redner[39] also described the moment when the cartful of skeleton-like prisoners was brought to the station:

> Lastly, the sick and the paralysed were brought on wagons from the camp, they were thrown on the grass where they lay motionless, moaning and whimpering. Some bodies were half-dead and others monstrously swollen, naked, with shocking facial expressions. We were ordered to grab them by the hands and throw them into the

train cars among the healthy, one on top of the other. They emitted a terrible stench.

This might have been the commotion, or one like it, which helped her to escape.

It was while she was still in the café that my mother saw her German boss, Dr Bauer, with his German uniform emblazoned with Nazi insignia, walking the length of the train. One of the messengers had clearly delivered the note, and the director came, just as she had hoped he would. She sent her waitress friend out to fetch him and he was truly delighted to find her. She returned the precious chain and said goodbye to the waitress. She never knew her name and never saw her again.

The empathetic acts of the waitress and the German director have stayed in my mother's mind and also mine, as an affirmation that goodness can and does exist even in the midst of hell. Both these brave, honourable people could have paid for their actions with their lives. Neither is celebrated as a 'Righteous Gentile'.

Now at Kleparów train station a modest plaque exists to commemorate the half a million Jews who passed through it to be loaded onto cargo trucks and sent to their deaths. The station is still operational but serves for the transport of goods.

The 'safe house' to which the German Director took my mother on their return to Lwów was the home of his humble Polish servant – yet another of these uncelebrated selfless people. There is unfortunately a truly tragic ending to this survival story, for when she returned to Lwów and was reunited with her father, she found out that her mother and little Romek had been rounded up from the ghetto earlier that day. That's when the realisation sunk in that they were probably on that very same train from which she had escaped. It was the start of 'survivor' guilt which never left her.

Plaque at Kleparov Station, Lviv, 2006 (Photo: Samuel D. Gruber)

My grandfather wept as he described how the Gestapo came to the door. According to the German law, all Jews aged from 14 to 60 years old were required to work. Romek was only 4, and therefore useless, but my grandmother was only 56. Her occupation was merely 'housewife'. Since neither could be considered an 'essential worker', they were expendable. My grandfather remonstrated flashing his credentials from the First World War. It was all to no avail, but maybe they were just a tiny bit impressed, because after all they left him behind.

Friedland[40] described the *Aktion* that took place on 10 August. The details concur completely with my mother's account.

> On Monday, August 10th, at dawn, the new 'action' began. This was the largest one to date in the City of Lvov. It was prepared in advance by the German military and political specialists. Plans were made to blockade certain areas and whole streets, to 'clear' entire city blocks, and remove the victims, and this plan was followed to a tee. Special SS brigades…as well as Ukrainian police participated in the 'action'. In good summer weather, surrounded by flowering and blooming nature, the Germans assisted by their 'helpers' were implementing their 'action' coolly, quietly and with attention to every detail. Every day, several thousand Jews were brought to Yanovsky (Janowski) camp. Accompanied by brutal beatings, they were sorted there: women, elderly and children as well as those appearing unhealthy were sent to their death in Belzec.

Another website[41] provides the names of those responsible:

> The second mass deportation of the Jews of Lvov commenced on 10 August 1942 and it continued until 23 August 1942, this 'Aktion' was directed and supervised by the SS and Police Leader of the Lvov district *SS-Gruppenführer* Fritz Katzmann along with his subordinate Erich Engels. Thousands of Jews were arrested every day and taken to Janowska camp, where SS officers under the command of Ernst Inquart performed selections and sent the vast majority to Belzec death camp, in cattle cars from the Kleparow railway station.

Belzec (in Polish Bełżec)

My mother lived and relived her mother's journey in her mind repeatedly, as I do now. There are many accounts of it in literature, and now on the internet. Wisława Szymborska's poem *Jeszcze* (meaning 'Still') resonated with her, when she imagined her mother on that final train journey, and she even translated the poem herself before there was an official English version. This is how she translated the end of it:

> That's how it is: into the forest without a sky
> That's how it is; with no-one to hear them cry
> That's how it is; awakening in the night I sense
> That's how it is; voices cutting silence into silence.

But this is how it would really have been:[42]

> A transport numbering 40-60 rail trucks…would arrive at Belzec station. It would be divided into two or three smaller convoys which would be pushed into the camp. The Jews would then be rapidly disembarked onto the platform where they were assured that they had arrived at a transit camp. They were told that before being assigned to labor duties elsewhere they would be disinfected and showered. Men were separated from women and children and marched off to large huts where they undressed. Women had their hair shaven off. They were then brutally pushed to 'the tube' and into the gas chambers which were disguised as 'showers'. The brutalized and disoriented Jews, often weak from hours or days spent in cattle trucks, had barely any time to evaluate their fate or react defensively.

Somewhere my mother had read about homicidal mobile vans or freight cars lined with quicklime which burns the flesh on contact. I believe these were in use, but earlier in 1942 before the gas chambers were perfected. These vans or carriages in sidings, where people were locked in and took much longer to die, often plagued her dreams. When the book by Pankiewicz[43] came out in 1947 (I still have my parents' first edition) she would have read of 'secret stations without a name, with dead-end rails where freight carriages full of people stood for days on end without water or food, before becoming forever lost in dense dark forests surrounded by barbed wire, from which nobody could hear them'.

Mobile gas vans are known to have been used in Chelmno, but not at Belzec at that time. We are now almost certain that my grandmother was one of the 50,000 or so victims transported from Lwów to Belzec in August 1942.[44]

I need to introduce Belzec with the benefit of hindsight, but I don't suppose that my grandmother would have known where she was going. Nevertheless, she would almost certainly have been aware that the journey was going to be one way. The name Belzec seems to be relatively unfamiliar to my friends, hardly any of whom had ever heard of it. The few nights my father spent in Auschwitz never fail to impress, but when I tell people of my grandmother's death in Belzec their eyes glaze over with incomprehension. One of the reasons for Belzec's obscurity is because almost no-one survived to tell the tale; another reason might be because it was never liberated by the British. Along with Chelmno, Sobibor and Treblinka, Belzec was liberated by the Soviets in the summer of 1944, but by then there was nothing much left to liberate. The 500,000 Jews it had processed were dead and the killing machinery had already been dismantled.

In the early days of the war Belzec had been a work camp for the Jews of Lublin, and although it had ceased to function as a work camp by the autumn of 1940, the infrastructure was already there to convert it into an extermination camp. It thus became the first *Aktion Reinhard* extermination camp, a template for others that followed at Sobibor and Treblinka. It is believed that the order to build it came from Himmler to Globocnik (an associate of Eichmann) in October 1941, and that construction began a month later. Belzec was in a good location, on the main Lwów to Lublin line, also easily accessible from Kraków. The commandant of the camp was Christian Wirth, whose nicknames included Christian the Terrible and Wild Christian, known for 'his iron hardness, unconditional obedience, belief in the *Führer*, absolute heartlessness and ruthlessness'.[45] Trained in the *Aktion T4* (German involuntary euthanasia programme of the sick and disabled), he became habituated to murder, and well-honed in ruthlessness.

The first deportations to Belzec started in March 1942, though they were temporarily halted in the middle of June to facilitate the construction of newer and larger gas chambers. They then resumed again in July 1942, just a few weeks before my grandmother was taken.[46] Belzec, Sobibor and Treblinka were in fact not camps at all; they were 'killing centres'.[47] As Hilberg[48] puts it, 'there was no prototype, no administrative ancestor... Never in history had people been killed on an assembly line basis'. The plans for these death factories were hatched in secret at the Wannsee Conference in January 1942 (where incidentally seven of the fifteen participants had law degrees). Some historians call them Globocnik camps after Himmler's obsequious follower. They relied on a 'combination of deception, speed, threats and violence'.[49] They also depended on a policy of concealment and the Nazis took many precautions to swear all the personnel to secrecy. The first verbal camouflage which they utilised was to collectively call all the killing centres 'The East'. According to Hilberg,[50] even Hans Frank did not know what was going on there. The idea was to fool the victims into thinking that they were being deported to ghettos or labour camps in the East, when in reality they were all, except for the death squads, swiftly and ruthlessly gassed.[51] The members of the death squads were gassed too, but only after they had served a few months. They would have been replaced regularly just in case any of them got too wise and rebelled or got to know the terrain and its guards so that they might find a way to escape. The three killing centres came under a different authority, were staffed by 'euthanasia' programme personnel and their only goal was the implementation of 'The Final Solution'.

Of course, many people died in Auschwitz and Majdanek, but these were also slave labour camps; people spent time there and not everybody died. Wachsmann[52] calls Auschwitz and Majdanek 'hybrid' camps as they served both as labour camps and also later as death camps.

The other difference between these and the 'hybrid' camps was the timings when selection was carried out. In the former, selections were carried out before the deportation began, whereas in the latter selections were made on arrival. My mother and grandmother had already been selected for death and knew what their fate would be.

I have now read and compared the death machine protocol in the killing centres of Belzec[53], Treblinka[54] and Sobibor[55], and it is uncannily the same. In all music played, in all there were flowers. The commandants were different, but there must have been some collusion between them, or an order from above. Were these details discussed at Wannsee?

Though the existence of these camps and what went on there was a Nazi secret, the more savvy Jews knew that once they entered the cattle truck there would be no escape, even if they did not know precisely where the trains were headed, what extermination methods were to be used, or what the final tally in the mathematics of murder would be. *Aktion Reinhard* was the code name the Nazis used for the extermination of Polish Jewry and it was applied to both the 'hybrid' and the 'killing centre' ones. The name Reinhard was conceived later to honour Reinhard Heydrich, the coordinator of the Final Solution, who was killed in Prague in May 1942.

At Belzec there were no striped uniforms and no roll call (except for the death squad). There was no need for either as most of the victims were only there about 2 hours.[56] As the plan on page 162 shows there were very few barracks because this was not a camp where people slept. Estimates of the number of victims of Belzec are discussed objectively by Webb.[57] They vary from 434,508[58] to 550,000[59]; to 800,000[60], and have been hotly debated by historians, but the consensus is about 500,000-600,000.[61] The first of these figures comes from a recovered telegram sent by Operation Reinhard's Chief of Staff from Belzec to Berlin in January 1943.[62] It may indeed be the exact figure, or it could be that more people were murdered before or after the counting took place. It is of course impossible to know because all records were destroyed in the autumn of 1943, but whichever figure you accept as most accurate the number of people is in the region of the population of Edinburgh, and all this happened quickly over a period of about 9 months. Doing a quick back of the envelope calculation, over 270 days, 2,222 people died per day, or 222 per daylight hour; that's more than 3 per minute.

Incidentally, I have just realised that the number of people murdered at Belzec (and Belzec only), is more than the number of characters (letters, I mean not words) in the text I am writing. It is a sobering thought.

Of all those hundreds of thousands annihilated, only seven survived,[63] and of these only two left testimonies. They were called Rudolf Reder (whose testimony I have already drawn on) and Chaim Hirszman.[64] Both these men avoided instant death because they were trained metal workers – useful for servicing the gas chambers. Otherwise, their job was to 'process' the victims. Hirszman presented his testimony to the Jewish Historical District Commission in 1946, a couple of months before he was murdered by antisemitic Polish Nationalists.[65] That same year Reder, who may well have had the job of dragging out my grandmother's lifeless body, testified before the Central Commission for Investigation of German Crimes. He told of his time in the camp even before peace was declared and published it in 1946 in his book *Bełżec*. It was reprinted in 1999 by the Auschwitz-Birkenau State Museum, but the edition I read was Forstater's,[66] a beautiful, but harrowing book, a memoir within a memoir. I read it in one sitting with a mounting feeling of horror, thankful that my mother had not come across it before she died.

Reder's testimony starts with 10 August 1942 in Lwów, the very day and place that my mother was taken. In Reder's freight car in which there were 100 people, 'no one spoke, but everyone knew that they were to be killed'. Once in the camp he had to 'sort the Jews' belongings, cut, and collect the women's hair before gassing, to drag corpses from the gas chambers to the burial pits...to dig the graves for the corpses'.[67] Hirszman's task was much the same, except that he also had to 'process' the bodies of his wife and child.[68] The two managed to escape to tell the world of the atrocities being committed. Reder slipped away when he was taken to Lwów to collect sheet metal and his guard fell asleep, whilst Hirszman escaped from the last train out of the camp to Sobibor.[69]

Five thousand people were deported per transport, three trains a day[70]; nobody lingered in the camp for long. The ramps at Belzec were too short to accommodate lengthy trains, so transports were backed into the compound to be unloaded a few cars at a time.[71] I can imagine what it would have felt like to be left in a siding for hours without food or water, waiting, waiting, waiting…for death.

I think my grandmother would have perished in one of the 'Phase 2' gas chambers, built of brick and mortar, and airtight, with a hand-painted sign on the entrance *Stiftung Hackenholt*, named after the SS-man who designed it.

Sources based on Reder's testimony describe the building as:

> …low and wide, grey concrete, with a flat roof covered in tar paper, and above that another roof of netting covered with foliage. From the yard three steps a meter wide, and without railings, led up to this building. A big vase full of different coloured flowers stood in front of the building. On the wall it was clearly and legibly written *Bade und Inhalationsräume* (bath and inhalation rooms). The stairs led to a dark corridor, a metre and a half wide but very long. It was

Gas chamber at Belzec
(Image drawn by William 'Billy' Rutherford; Chris Webb Private Archive)

completely empty, four concrete walls. The doors to the chambers opened to the left and the right.[72]

Christian Wirth stood on a podium and said, 'First you bathe and then you will be sent to work.' Some people clapped, believing that despite the rumours they still had a future. I don't know whether my grandmother would have been taken in by these few words of comfort, the sign 'bath house' and the flowers. I can't help hoping that she would have been.

Among the archaeological remains found on the site is a plaque which greeted new transports with instructions for undressing, and numerous numbered concrete discs, which are thought to have been given out to victims as tokens for the handover of their valuables.[73] This administrative detail must have been invented to give the victims hope, for if they were meant to reclaim their clothes after the shower, then maybe the bathhouse sign was genuine. Then 750 people were counted into each gas chamber, and the doors were shut. Only when all six chambers were filled were the engines switched on. Reder, who witnessed maybe 100,000 go to their deaths in the four months he was there, described how he 'could tell precisely at which moment they would all realise what was awaiting them and the fear, the despair, the cries and the terrible moans that mingled with the notes of the orchestra'.[74]

I first heard of the orchestra in Reder's memoir, and its eerie theatricality was chilling. Six musicians on violins, flutes and an accordion, their instruments salvaged from the dead, were positioned between the gas chamber and the graves. 'Everything passes, everything goes by' was appropriately enough one of the tunes they played. The victims would only have heard it played once, but Reder, the slave gas chamber worker, and the perpetrators must have carried the tune in their heads like an earworm until the day they died.

Hilberg[75] also describes the orchestra, which he says was made up of ten inmate musicians and singers. Making musicians play mechanically in these circumstances sends shivers down my spine, but the idea of inmates being made to sing is macabre. The orchestra and the singers were apparently used to greet the new arrivals, as well as later when they filed into the gas chamber. Hilberg also reports violence inflicted by the guards, with screaming women prodded with whips and bayonets. Gitta Sereny's telling interview with Franz Stangl,[76] the ex-commandant of Treblinka (while he was awaiting trial in 1971) describes what it must have felt like to be faced with all that 'cargo':

Q: There were so many children, did they ever make you think of
your children, of how you would feel in the position of those parents?
A: No...I can't say I ever thought that way...you see, I rarely saw
them as individuals. It was always a huge mass. I sometimes stood
on the wall and saw them in the tube [the passage leading to the gas
chamber area]. But – how can I explain it – they were naked, packed
together, running, being driven with whips like...
Q: Could you not have changed that?...In your position, could you
not have stopped the nakedness, the whips, the horror of the cattle
pens?
A: No, no, no. This was the system. Wirth had invented it. It worked.
And because it worked, it was irreversible.

Carbon monoxide was the preferred killing gas at Belzec. Wirth decided
against cyanide B since it was produced by private firms and its extensive
use would have aroused suspicion. He also decided against bottles of
carbon monoxide that he had earlier seen used at the euthanasia
institutions, perceiving them to be too obvious, so he opted for a self-made
gassing operation. The mobile killing vans which used self-made exhaust
fumes worked well in Chelmno, so he decided to upscale them. A diesel
engine was mounted outside the gas chamber and the carbon monoxide
belching forth from its exhaust was piped in.[77] That way, many more could
be 'processed' at the turn of a key. The asphyxiation process would have
taken 20-30 minutes. At Auschwitz, the homicidal 'showers' spouted
cyanide gas, which would have been generated from crystals of Zyclon B
exposed to air. Theirs was a slightly quicker death. At Belzec the bodies
were dragged out of the gas chambers and inspected by a dentist, who
removed finger-rings and gold teeth, while someone else searched the
body orifices for hidden valuables. After this procedure, the corpses were
thrown into a big pit.[78] The corpses would have been buried, not cremated,
for at Belzec there were no crematoria. However, some burning must have
taken place as there are several written reports of the smell of burning
flesh.

The above facts, most from Reder's testimony, are almost completely
corroborated by Kurt Gerstein, an SS *Obersturmführer* (lieutenant) and gas
expert who in 1942 witnessed the gassings of Jews at Belzec. His
testimony[79], so harrowing that it carries a warning '*Note: this document
contains graphic and potentially disturbing information*'. Here are some
extracts from it:

Then the procession started to move. With a lovely young girl at the front, they all walked along the path, all naked, men, women and children, without their artificial limbs.

I stood with Hauptmann Wirth up on the ramp between the chambers. Mothers with their babies at the breast came up, hesitated, and entered the death chambers. A sturdy SS man stood in the corner and told the wretched people in a clerical tone of voice: 'Nothing at all is going to happen to you! You must take a deep breath in the chambers. That expands the lungs. This inhalation is necessary because of illnesses and infection.' When asked what was going to happen to them, he answered: 'Well, of course, the men must work, building houses and roads, but the women don't have to work. Only if they want to, they can help with the housework or in the kitchen.'…

The chambers filled. Cram them well in, Hauptmann Wirth had ordered. People were standing on each other's feet. 700-800 on 25 square metres, in 45 cubic metres! The SS forced as many in together as was physically possible. The doors closed. Meanwhile the others were waiting outside in the open air, naked…

After 28 minutes only a few were still alive. At last, after 32 minutes everyone was dead.

Hilberg[80] quotes a different fragment of memory, presumably also from the perpetrators: 'At Belzec, where *Oberscharführer* Hackenholt was in charge of the motor, a German visitor, Professor Pfannenstiel, wanted to know what was going on inside. He is said to have put his ear to the wall and, listening, to have remarked: "Just like in a synagogue".'

The hair was packed and sent off to Budapest[81] or 'put to some special use on U-boats, caulking or something like that',[82] the gold was melted into gold bars. Before the collected clothes were washed and packed, they were inspected carefully for hidden money, and any found was distributed round the SS supervisors, always the same team.[83]

Each side of the camp measured 886 feet[84] and the outer fence was camouflaged with tree branches. The plan on page 162 shows two main areas: Administration and Reception Area, and an Extermination Area. The mass murder area was cunningly hidden from view of the victims waiting in the reception area, and the two were connected by a narrow, enclosed path, called 'the tube' or 'the sluice'. Note that there were a few barracks for prisoners. They would probably have belonged to the 'death squad': the gas chamber operators and those whose job it was to dig enormous ditches. Reder and other gas chamber operators would probably have slept in the barrack labelled 29. The 100 or so Ukrainian guards who manned the

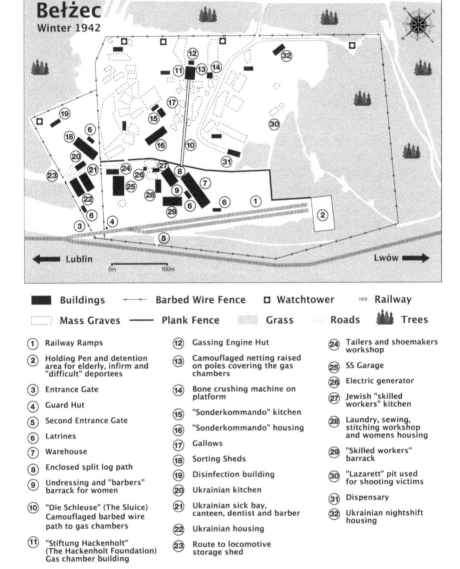

Bełżec
Winter 1942

Buildings	Barbed Wire Fence	▫ Watchtower ⅲ Railway
Mass Graves	Plank Fence	Grass Roads 🌲 Trees

① Railway Ramps

② Holding Pen and detention area for elderly, infirm and "difficult" deportees

③ Entrance Gate

④ Guard Hut

⑤ Second Entrance Gate

⑥ Latrines

⑦ Warehouse

⑧ Enclosed split log path

⑨ Undressing and "barbers" barrack for women

⑩ "Die Schleuse" (The Sluice) Camouflaged barbed wire path to gas chambers

⑪ "Stiftung Hackenholt" (The Hackenholt Foundation) Gas chamber building

⑫ Gassing Engine Hut

⑬ Camouflaged netting raised on poles covering the gas chambers

⑭ Bone crushing machine on platform

⑮ "Sonderkommando" kitchen

⑯ "Sonderkommando" housing

⑰ Gallows

⑱ Sorting Sheds

⑲ Disinfection building

⑳ Ukrainian kitchen

㉑ Ukrainian sick bay, canteen, dentist and barber

㉒ Ukrainian housing

㉓ Route to locomotive storage shed

㉔ Tailers and shoemakers workshop

㉕ SS Garage

㉖ Electric generator

㉗ Jewish "skilled workers" kitchen

㉘ Laundry, sewing, stitching workshop and womens housing

㉙ "Skilled workers" barrack

㉚ "Lazarett" pit used for shooting victims

㉛ Dispensary

㉜ Ukrainian nightshift housing

Belzec, winter 1942. Map adapted by Andy Quinn of Emma Quinn Design from an original by William 'Billy' Rutherford, from Chris Webb's book, *Belzec*.

watchtowers and the perimeter of the camp and assisted the SS-men in the initial unloading and processing of the victims probably all slept in the barracks labelled 22 on the map.

Some references cite an even larger capacity for murder than the 2,222 per day, cited earlier. Rubenstein and Roth[85] give the figure of 15,000 per day for the maximum capacity of the six gas chambers shown (labelled 11 on the map). This number of 15,000 people is equivalent to two thirds of all undergraduates at Edinburgh University per day.

My grandmother's death certificate, lodged in a Kraków registry office, gives the date 30 August 1942 in Belzec, but how they should know the exact date is a mystery to me, because no lists of the exterminated exist. Probably the date was a guess, and her death certificate details would have been surmised by my grandfather in 1946. Strangely enough, there is a testimony relating to that very day. Wilhelm Cornides,[86] a German officer, quotes from his diary of that very date 'that trains filled with Jews pass almost daily through the shunting yards, are dispatched immediately on their way and return swept clean, most often the same evening'. Wallach[87] goes on to divulge more details; after the corpses were buried the remains often swelled in the heat as a result of putrefaction and the escape of gases. The surface layer of soil split. Later, when they found that burying so many in a small space did not work, the bodies were exhumed, placed on pyres made from railway tracks and burned. Franz Stangl, the commandant of Sobibor and later Treblinka, after a visit to Belzec remembers, 'the smell… Oh God the smell'.[88] Finally, the larger tell-tale bones were collected and crushed. The concealment plan was so successful that archaeological studies carried out recently show a relative dearth of human remains, a fact that convinced some holocaust deniers such as Carlo Mattogno.[89]

Hilberg[90] compares the different body disposal procedures at the different camps and killing centres. At Belzec in the first half of 1943 they built firing grids which were capable of destroying 2,000 bodies a day. At that rate it would have taken them about a year to complete the task. Belzec was evacuated in the autumn of 1943, and pine trees were planted. In fact, they can't have finished the burning task because after the war a Polish investigator had found that the locals had been digging up the camp, searching for valuables, which the Germans might have missed, leaving hands, bones and flesh exposed.

Killing centres could be hidden through secrecy, but I would like to ask those holocaust deniers who still propagate their ill-founded views, where is my grandmother? How have all these vibrant Jewish communities with their humour and song vanished? Where have they gone to?

I asked my mother whether she at any time thought that there might be a chance that her mother might have survived the deportation. 'Not for a minute', she said, 'nobody ever survived'. So, I am sure too that my grandmother would not have been one to be taken in by the 'Bath House' sign. Maybe she tried to comfort little Romek on that train journey through the dark forest telling him how they were going to see his parents. Maybe they died separately, maybe together. I prefer to think that she lulled them both into eternal sleep with a lullaby.

'Is there a way to describe the last journey in sealed cattle cars, the last voyage into the unknown?', writes Elie Wiesel[91] in his seminal book *Night*. An incredibly sad poem originally written in Hebrew by Dan Pagis[92] probably does it best – entitled 'Written in Pencil in the Sealed Railway-Car':

> here in this carload
> i am eve
> with abel my son
> if you see my other son
> cain son of man
> tell him i

The poem is deliberately unfinished. One imagines the scratched message that could have been written on the wood inside the cattle wagon or on a scrap of paper trampled by many feet.

I tried repeatedly to enter my grandmother's name into the Belzec database. I tried with Karolina, I tried with Kazimeria, I tried with Reinerowa. All names gave the same response:

> *No records were found for* **LAST NAME: REINER; ACCURACY: EXACT; FIRST NAME: KAZIMIERA; ACCURACY: EXACT; MAIDEN NAME: GRUNBERG; ACCURACY: EXACT; YEAR OF BIRTH: 1886; ACCURACY: EXACT; YEAR OF DEATH: 1942; ACCURACY: EXACT; NATIONALITY: POLISH JEWISH**

Maybe she did not even feature in the statistics; her name is not written down. By January 1945, all remaining records of prisoners, past and present were blown up or burnt by SS men desperately trying to conceal the evidence, to eradicate from the history books the worst mass murder that had ever existed. This was happening at Belzec, and also in camps all over the Reich.

It has been claimed that 'The World' knew nothing before the Allies liberated the concentration camps in 1945. Some newly-unlocked files confirm that the world knew well long before then, and that the Allied powers did very little about it. Bruno Bettleheim, in a lecture he gave in 1985, said, 'above all it was the silence that condemned Jews to death'. As Goran Rosenberg puts it, 'people say they heard and saw nothing and in any case they had nothing to do with it and then they say they opposed what they neither saw nor heard'. There are surely lessons to be learned for present-day atrocities when knowing what is going on is so much easier. Yet still refugees (lumped together with other immigrants) are restricted, feared and unwelcome. In 2017 the British government reduced the number of unaccompanied minors fleeing persecution from Syria and other conflict zones (the Dubs scheme) from its original pledge of 3,000 to 350. No good reason was given.

My mother, unlike me, was not keen on holocaust literature because not surprisingly it brought on terrible nightmares. *Mamo, Mamo* (Mummy, Mummy), she would scream. The last such nightmare was in the final few months of her life when I was her carer one weekend. I came and sat on her bed to comfort her while she said, as she always said, 'If I had not run away, I could have saved her'. Like in Wisława Szymborska's poem *Still*, 'awakened in the night she could hear the rattle of the train and their voices cutting into silence'. I would hold her and reassure her that it would all have been in vain. It was her courage that saved her – and me, and her grandsons and great-grandchildren.

Warsaw

Mother and Grandfather knew that they could not now return to their apartment, and that they must leave Lwów to escape further round-ups. They decided to go to Warsaw, where they hoped to mingle in the crowd and effectively disappear. It was the German director, yet again, who stepped in to help. He wrote a very plausible official-looking, SS-stamped letter, to say that Mr and Miss Reiner were on their way to fulfil a mission to benefit the GG, and they were not to be stopped from accomplishing it. Then he went to the train station and bought two tickets for Warsaw. My grandfather, in the meantime, took out his First World War insignia and stuck them conspicuously on the lapel of his suit. Luckily, the journey passed uneventfully.

The only story that remains from that particular train journey is of a child who screamed and screamed, as children do, particularly when they are hungry. My mother's blouse had a breast pocket in which she had hidden a sugar cube. She took it out and offered it to the hungry child. I remember that story, because that's how she was – kind, always generous, always giving. My son, Martin, when he read this bit in draft form said, 'yes, of course, now I understand; that's why she always stole a few sugar cubes from café sugar bowls and stored them away for later'.

On arrival, they assessed their options. They knew that joining the ghetto was only a half-way house to the gas chambers, so they both decided to go underground under an Aryan identity. Proper false papers were hard to come by, as you had to know who to ask, and very expensive to buy. Obviously, they had no money with them, but some Reiner family valuables had been left in Kraków, entrusted into the safekeeping of Zosia, their old servant friend. They contacted Zosia and asked her to deliver these to Warsaw as soon as she could. But in the meantime, they were hungry, moneyless, paperless and homeless. I don't know why at that point they decided to split up; maybe two crooked noses were more of a give-away than one. Alfred's sister, Celina, was in Warsaw, and he wanted to find out if she was alive and safe. My mother, on the other hand, headed for Milanówek, a small town about 30km from Warsaw, where she thought she might find her old schoolfriend Irka Oberleder (the same one who had once been Artur's girlfriend).

Milanówek is now a suburb of Warsaw, but it was then a small resort town for wealthy residents. She made her way there at night following the railway track, so as not to lose her way. (She, like me, had an atrocious sense of direction). She found her old Jewish friend, now Irka Piekarzewska, with her mother Tosia and sister Wisia (all with newly-bought Aryan identities) in a flat consisting of two rooms, a kitchen and a windowless loft, but no bathroom. Her friends were overjoyed to see her alive and said, 'you can stay as long as you like, we can hide you'. My mother remembered being washed in carbolic at the kitchen sink to free her of the lice, fleas and bedbugs which had been her constant companions. While she was being washed, her friend commented on the weals on her back, which must have been acquired several days previously from the whippings and beatings she had received. After all that had happened, she was completely unaware of her wounds. Clothed in fresh pajamas, she was hoisted into the loft space and left to sleep. Irka and her family (I remember them well), were always full of jokes and fun. Once there was a knock on the door and my mother's legs were still dangling from the ceiling. Luckily, it was a friend, not a foe, so there was much laughter. She often reminisced about the family's generous hospitality and good humour.

In the meantime, Grandfather, who had remained in Warsaw, waited patiently for Zosia to bring the jewels and money which she had thankfully managed to hide from the Germans. Once these were delivered my mother and grandfather bought false papers and baptismal certificates. My mother became Miss Danuta Majewska and my grandfather became Mr Władyslaw Kwiatkowski, a name he kept to the end. His subsequent adventures are recounted in the previous chapter.

I need to explain in a bit more detail how false papers are obtained. First of all, you have to know someone who knows someone, who knows someone who does them for a diamond each (at least). The forger has to find the obsolete papers of someone who has recently died. The relatives of the deceased also have to know someone, who knows someone, who wants to buy them. However, if they are really deceitful and clever (they know the name after all), they can subsequently make loads more money by extorting a ransom from the recipients. As Kaplan[93] put it, getting fake documents is 'harder than parting the Red Sea'. Another source, other than adapting the papers of a deceased person, is to obtain blank passports through the agency of some corruptible civil servant. The false information can then be written into the clean passport, and an official can be bribed to stamp it with a pre-war seal. Some priests could also be trusted to help Jews, usually upon receipt of a generous bribe. A priest 'could simply write out a birth certificate stating that So-an-so is an Aryan from a long line of Aryans. The priests made fortunes. The certificates are assumed to be genuine, and no one disputes their veracity.'[94] I don't know which of these methods my mother and grandfather used to obtain their fake documents.

In addition to fake identity documents, each fake Aryan would also require a fake baptismal certificate. My mother's friends in Milanówek knew a friendly priest, who had helped many Jews in different ways. It was he who had performed a Catholic wedding ceremony on my mother's friend Irka Oberleder and her husband-to-be, Julek Djament (both living under false Polish names – hers was Piekarzewska, his was Rutkowski), saying, 'the sin is mine, and mine alone.'[95] It is possible that my mother and grandfather would have gone to him for help, and maybe offered a 'donation'. No wonder that when I was born, I was immediately baptised. 'Why not – it was free.'

David Kahane, a rabbi who survived the occupation years hidden by the Ukrainian archbishop of the Uniate Catholic Church, reflected in his *Lvov Ghetto Diary:*[96]

> I doubt whether anyone is capable of understanding the feelings of these phony Aryans or those hiding in mouse burrows waiting for the defeat of Hitler. A passing car, a stir, a suspicious noise sent shivers down their spines, their hearts would start thumping, their imaginations would go wild, and their limbs go numb.

So, feeling rather insecure, Danuta Majewska and Alfred Kwiatkowski set off separately into an unknown city with their newly-purchased Catholic identities. Of course, being in a place where they would not be recognised was a huge advantage. Hiding in Kraków would have been no use whatsoever. What was not so good was that with different names, my mother and grandfather could no longer introduce themselves as father and daughter. They decided it would be safer to live at separate addresses but managed to meet up from time to time, often making rendezvous in churches, rather like the fictitious hero of Louis Begley's excellent little semi-autobiographical novel, *Wartime Lies.*[97] There they could communicate kneeling together as if mumbling prayers. Throughout this time my mother became well acquainted with Catholic liturgy, and could when challenged recite great tracts like a true Catholic. It came easily to her as she always had a good memory for poetry, verse and songs. She also had to remember to cross herself before eating a meal with Catholic friends or whenever she came across a church or cemetery or any sort of accident. Strangely, she said, she never recalled seeing Catholics cross themselves when Jews were being shot.

I asked her whether she ever over-heard antisemitic remarks. 'Of course', she said, 'all the time'. Another Jew in hiding in Warsaw at the same time published his memoirs in a fascinating book *The Warsaw Diary.*[98] His antisemitic landlord said to him, 'You see God is powerful. He has given the Jews their due.' After the ghetto uprising, he overheard the conversation two Poles were having with one another, '[When it's all over] Warsaw would be rid of its Jews, who had poisoned the atmosphere for far too long.' That seems to sum up what many Poles thought at the time.

Despite this, she made many Polish friends, who never suspected that she was Jewish. They called her Danusia, the diminutive of her Aryan 'Christian' name. She continued to correspond with at least one friend from those Warsaw days after our emigration, as in her bundles of letters I found some addressed to 'Dear Danusia'.

Unfortunately, the false papers she had bought were flawed. Despite the high price she paid for them, her new identity had a give-away error: the address given on the document was of a house which had been demolished in a bombing raid two years earlier. Anyone who knew Warsaw would smell a rat and see extortion potential. Life was hard and there was ready money to be made from denouncing Jews in hiding. If anyone even had a faint suspicion of her false identity, they would threaten to betray her. Since she had little money to give away, she would promise to deliver the money and then flee to another part of Warsaw, where other lodgings would have to be found and rent negotiated. She had to relocate like this several times. However, she could not live without work, and she could not work without a *kennkarte*. She finally plucked up her courage to apply for one. Luckily the official in the Kennkarte office did not notice the error and she was issued with one probably in November 1942. I don't have her *kennkarte* from that time, but I do have my grandfather's, which I scanned in the previous chapter.

Her miscellaneous writings mention one address, Lwowska 10, where she lived longer than in other places. Once when the Police came to that address looking for Jews, she hid in the house of a German lady, whose Polish servant provided shelter for her and several others. To make ends meet she picked up work wherever she could, including one as a laundress to the Gestapo. She was then, as always, resourceful. As a chemist, she knew how to make soap from raw ingredients, and sold it for profit. She even experimented with colours, once disastrously making a pretty yellow tablet, which dyed the skin of its hapless user bright yellow. She knew how to make meals from scraps of food, and how to knit using wool unravelled from old jumpers. There were no patterns in those days, but she had a good design sense, and she made some money by selling many of her knitted creations.

The knitting projects would no doubt have been encouraged by her aunt Celina Wajtzman, who was living on false papers as Celina Wrońska, a name she kept to the end. Celina's *kennkarte* states her occupation as a tricotière (knitter). Celina's *kennkarte* lists at least 4 different addresses during 1943 and 1944. I wondered whether my mother might have lived with Celina some of the time, but her grandson, Lucjan Wroński, told me that though they met regularly they never lived together. He remembers his grandmother telling him that they never even told each other of their addresses – in case either of them was interrogated under torture. He also told me of how my mother had reminisced to him that at one stage she had shared an apartment with a distinguished-looking stranger with a kindly face. She found out later that he was in fact a resistance leader with the

Polish Home Army (AK), and he too was in hiding, but at the time neither knew of each other's true identity.

Extortionists were called *'szmalcownicy'*, who blackmailed both the hiding Jews and Poles who helped the Jews. (The word comes from the Yiddish word 'shmalts' or grease and is also a slang word for money.) They sometimes got triple income, my mother said, one from the victim, another from whoever was involved in hiding her, and then from the *Generalgouvernement* (GG) when they turned them in anyway. The ransom paid by the victim would have been either in the form of money or jewellery. Those were the people she feared most while on false papers in Warsaw, because by then her supplies of money and portable wealth had been used up.

On one such flight from extortionists she took shelter with her Reiner cousin (I think her name was Freida[99]), who was surviving on false papers as a mistress of a German officer. The cousin hid my mother in a servant's pantry and assured her that she would be safe there overnight. Later in the evening she heard a commotion in the street and peeped out of the window to see a gang of Germans lining Jews against a wall. Having fired their shots, they holstered their guns and raucously entered the house where she was hiding. She did not stay the night, but fled, terrified. It might have been then or on countless other nights that she spent the night in a sewer. She would eventually emerge from hiding, and look for new lodgings in a different neighbourhood, in a cat-and-mouse game to evade her extortionists.

One place she avoided was the ghetto, fearing she might be recognised, or in some way become 'sucked in'. Nevertheless, in April 1943 she alternately cheered and wept when the sky went red as the ghetto burned. She, better than anyone else, knew that those who died in the Ghetto Uprising were at least spared the gas chambers of Majdanek.

My mother, along with many residents of Warsaw at the time, looked towards the Red Army as saviours. So, on 1 August 1944 when the Soviet troops approached and amassed on the easternmost margins of the city (along the line of the river Vistula), the Polish Resistance movement (AK) launched their heroic bid for freedom. In the event, the Soviets did not respond to the Polish Resistance Army's pleas for help and stayed outside the city boundaries. The Warsaw Uprising lasted only 63 days during which a quarter of a million people died, and the city was razed to the ground.

There is much discussion among historians as to why the Soviets failed to support the uprising. Some say the Red Army did try but having encountered fierce German opposition, were exhausted in strength and supplies. Others say that Stalin considered the insurgents to be just a band of criminals; according to yet another theory the lack of support from the Soviets was a deliberate tactic intended to weaken any control of the Polish government in Exile. Yet another theory that is popular now is that Stalin did it deliberately in order to weaken Polish resistance to Soviet occupation, laying the ground for a Communist future.

My mother knew nothing of the background political situation, but remembered the battles in the streets, the barricades and the marching Polish soldiers singing. These tunes with perfectly-remembered words were often on her lips a few days before her death, as if she too were marching to war. Even though her mind was slipping, the words of the Polish marching songs were etched on her mind. I have very crackly recording of her singing this one recorded on her carer's (Grażyna's) phone. I struggled with the translation for a bit, but then found one on a website.[100]

Wojenko, wojenko, cóżeś ty za pani,	War, the little war, what kind of lady are you?
Że za tobą idą, że za tobą idą	That you attract, that you attract
Chłopcy malowani?	These most handsome boys?
Chłopcy malowani, sami wybierani,	Handsome boys, by choice,
Wojenko, wojenko, wojenko, wojenko,	Little war, Little war, Little war, Little war,
Cóżeś ty za pani?	What kind of lady are you?
Na wojence ładnie, kto Boga uprosi,	On the war, who asks the God nicely,
Żołnierze strzelają, żołnierze strzelają,	Soldiers are shooting, soldiers are shooting,
Pan Bóg kule nosi.	the Lord is carrying bullets.
Maszeruje wiara, pot się krwawy leje,	Guys are marching, bloody sweat is pouring,
Raz dwa stąpaj bracie, raz dwa	One, two step my bro, one, two step my bro,
stąpaj bracie,	'Cause Poland is heating like that.
Bo tak Polska grzeje.	
Wojenko, wojenko, co za moc jest w tobie?	War, the little war, what kind of power is in you?
Kogo ty pokochasz, kogo ty pokochasz	Whoever you love, whoever you love,
W zimnym leży grobie.	He lies in the cold grave.
Ten już w grobie leży z dala od rodziny,	This one lies in grave far from family,
A za nim pozostał, a za nim pozostał	He left behind, he left behind,
Cichy płacz dziewczyny.	Silent girlish cry

When my mother visited Warsaw with my son, Martin, in 1994, she took him to the place where she had then lived and showed him the roof from where she had observed the running battles in the streets and the city on fire. A similar roof-top scene is described by Louis Begley.[101] Like everyone else at the time, she had been filled with patriotic pride and, as it turned out, unfounded optimism that the days of the occupation were numbered.

Following Himmler's orders to suppress the uprising, squads of SS-men used terror tactics against Polish civilians, Jews and insurrectionists, women and children, making no distinction between them. In the wake of this unprecedented, planned destruction and ethnic cleansing, by 1944 around 200,000 civilians were killed, or over half of the population of Warsaw.

My mother found herself in the middle of a massacre in the Factory *Ursus* in the Wola District of Warsaw, where 6,000 people were murdered in one day (5 August 1944). Then the factory was set on fire. I was there a couple of years ago and saw the small plaque at the site commemorating those 6,000 who were rounded up and killed in its yard. A witness says, 'Imagine the scene: executions here, houses ablaze there – and then they burnt the bodies. You don't forget a smell like that.'[102]

Again, she was lucky to be one of survivors. She wrote in one of her statements to the attorneys that after *Ursus* she was captured, imprisoned and held in a forced labour camp for several weeks, though she never offered any details of her experiences of her time there. She was finally released in early October when the Polish Army capitulated. With nowhere to go, I believe that she made her way to her friends in Milanówek again.

The two-roomed flat in Milanówek where the Oberleder family lived all under assumed names was a hub for displaced persons. At this point in the war, it was seriously over-crowded. There were underground activists, patients recovering from operations and Jews hiding from blackmailers. The father of the family, who had joined them after all sorts of adventures, had a different assumed name from the mother, so he became 'the lover', causing much hilarity. There were two bedrooms but no bathroom in the flat. They were supposed to use the neighbours' bathroom but were reluctant to do so because the neighbours were fiercely antisemitic, and anyway they traded in butcher meat and often kept their stock in the bath.

I have Wisia Oberleder-Haran's accounts of their time in Milanówek; I don't know if they are published anywhere, but they make fascinating reading. When I stayed with Wisia in Jerusalem in 1967, and again in 1994 (she was in Tel-Aviv then), she recounted many of the stories to me first-hand. She was an excellent raconteur.

Although my mother was aware that she should not abuse that generous family's hospitality for too long, she went there because Milanówek was the one address that my grandfather would have had, the one place where he might call to find her.

While listening to her reminiscences, the question I asked, was, 'how did people communicate?' 'Yes', she said, 'it was easy; the telephones were working even then. Telephones were mostly accessible to me, except on the odd occasion when I was imprisoned.' She always did love the telephone.

Alfred, in the meantime was abroad in Norway and Berlin building bridges for the Nazis (see previous chapter). He did indeed contact her in Milanówek sending instructions to meet him so that together they could go to Norway and thence escape to the West. At that moment, however, he was working in Glatz (Klodzko in Polish), which was then in the GG, and now in Polish Lower Silesia. He said that she should meet him there. My grandfather, with his good relations within the Organisation Todt, had no trouble securing a secretarial position for 'a distant relative'. He met her at the Glatz station, took her to the office and introduced her to his colleagues. If they suspected something, nobody said. Anyway, the job in hand was to build barracks for the factory AEG, and since the factory's product was armaments for the Reich, the more hands-on-deck the better. Glatz was also a concentration camp, where my father would have stopped on his gruelling foot-march. My mother and grandfather, however, were privileged as civilian workers to live in relative freedom.

As usual with an eye to escape, my mother and grandfather yearned for the West. At that moment, an opportunity came up for a trip to Norway, which my grandfather had already visited on a previous mission (to build something or to requisition specialist supplies). How my grandfather managed to hatch and negotiate such an ingenious plan for both of them I will never know. It could be that he was highly respected as a builder and engineer and was good at stating his terms, or it could be that some diamonds were used up in the process. And it all so nearly worked. They travelled to Berlin and from there to the port of Kiel. Except that when they reached Kiel to embark for Norway, they found that the boat that they were expecting to board had fallen victim to a bombing attack. Any further crossings across the Baltic, at least for passengers, were thereafter suspended because of the heavy allied bombardment in the course of the 1944 Baltic Sea Campaigns.

Back in Berlin, during Christmas 1944, my mother lodged with a German family and remembers the Christmas festivities, singing *Stille Nacht*, and having to 'Heil Hitler' before the start of the Christmas meal. Of course, although they were both in Berlin, my mother and grandfather were there as unrelated individuals. They met up in secret, and lodged separately, not far from Hitler in his bunker. The last trip of the war took them to Leipzig. I am not sure what she did there, though in one of her letters she claimed she was in a forced labour camp. The likelihood is that, as one of the Polish civilian workers, she was housed in barracks and lived under prisoner-like conditions. And that is where they were when peace was declared. The Holocaust Encyclopaedia entry for Leipzig states that the camp, which was a sub-camp of Buchenwald, was liberated by the 69th Infantry Division (an American Army division) on 19 April.[103]

How did they feel on the day of liberation? 'Jubilant', she said, 'but disorientated, because what were we to do now?' The road to the West was a possibility, though not without problems. The UK was not keen to take in refugees (was it ever?), and anyway they knew nobody and did not speak the language. And 'when did you hear of the death of Hitler?' I asked. 'Almost immediately', she said. 'He died at the end of April, when Leipzig was already free. We were still there, but his death gave us "permission" to return".' Like my father, a few weeks later, they decided to go to back to Kraków, the only home they knew. In a letter to a friend in 1995 she wrote: 'Your roots remain in the place where you spent your childhood, schooldays and youth, where you culturally belong – that is "home".'

So, they bought train tickets and arrived back in Kraków in May 1945 after a six-year absence.

Notes

1. Frank, A., *The Diary of Anne Frank* (London: Pan, 1955).
2. This roughly translates as *Queen Jadwiga's High School*.
3. Sean Martin, 2004 in his book, *Jewish Life in Kraków*, gives the figure of 28% Jewish girls for that school in 1937.
4. Professor Zdisław Jachimecki was Stasia's brother-in-law. He unwisely returned to Kraków from Lwów as he was subsequently arrested in the *Sonderaktion Krakau* in November 1939. He spent four months in various prisons before being released. To my knowledge he was not Jewish. After the war he was a frequent visitor in my parents' house. The following website offers a full biography of his musicological career: http://www.malopolskawiiwojnie.pl/index.php?title=Jachimecki_Zdzis%C5%82aw (accessed 22 July 2021)
5. William Brand, 'September 1939 Remembered', *The Kraków Post*, retrieved from:http://www.krakowpost.com/1531/2009/09 (accessed 17 March 2021)
6. Shende, S., *The Promise Hitler Kept* (Whitefish MT: Kessinger Publishing, 2010); this is a facsimile reprint of the original published in 1945.
7. Ibid.
8. Philip Friedman, 'Extermination of Lvov Jews', *JewishGen* retrieved from: http://www.jewishgen.org/yizkor/lviv/lvi593.html (accessed 12 April 2021)
9. The last Russian troops left Lvov on the night of 28 June 1941, and the first Germans entered the city on 29 June at about 11am.
10. Yones, E., *Smoke in the Sand* (Jerusalem: Gefen Publishing House, 2004).
11. These pogroms became known as the Petliura days named after Simon Petliura, who had organised anti-Jewish pogroms in Ukraine after the First World War.

12. Friedman, 'Extermination of Lvov Jews'.
13. Borowiec, A., *Warsaw Boy: A Memoir of a Wartime Childhood* (London: Viking, 2014).
14. Stepan Bandera was a Ukrainian nationalist, independence activist and supporter of Adolf Hitler.
15. Yones, *Smoke in the Sand*.
16. Friedman, 'Extermination of Lvov Jews'.
17. Ibid.
18. Ibid.
19. Shende, *The Promise Hitler Kept*.
20. Yones, *Smoke in the Sand*.
21. Kahane, D., *The Lvov Ghetto Diary* (Amherst MA: University of Massachusetts Press, 1990).
22. Crowe, D., *Oscar Schindler: The Untold Story of His Life, Wartime Activities and the True Story Behind the List* (Boulder, Colorado: Westview Press, 2004).
23. Bau, J., *Dear God, Have you Ever Gone Hungry* (New York: Arcade Publishing, 1998).
24. Zordrager, H. and Driebergen, M., *The Jews of Lemberg: A Journey to Empty Places* (London: Vallentine Mitchell, 2017).
25. 'The Holocaust in Kiev: Babi Yar', retrieved from: https://www.yadvashem.org/education/educational-materials/learning-environment/babi-yar/historical-background3.html (accessed 22 July 2021)
26. Sands, P., *East West Street* (London: Weidenfeld and Nicholson, 2016).
27. Reder, R. and Forstater, M., *I survived a Nazi Extermination Camp* (Hove, East Sussex: Psychology News Press, 2015).
28. Friedman, P., 'The Destruction of the Jews of Lwow 1941-1944', in Ada June Friedman (ed.), *Roads to Extinction: Essays on the Holocaust* (Philadelphia. Jewish Society of America, 1980), pp.244-321.
29. Shende, *The Promise Hitler Kept*.
30. The address of the factory was at 106 Khmelnytskoho St – now 'Almazinstrument', in the district called Nowe Zniesienie.
31. Karski, J., *The Story of a Secret State* (Boston:Houghton Mifflin Company,1944).
32. Reder and Forstater, *I survived a Nazi Extermination Camp*.
33. Shende, *The Promise Hitler Kept*.
34. Sands, *East West Street*.
35. Shende, *The Promise Hitler Kept*.
36. Spector, S. and Wigoder, G. (eds), *The Encyclopaedia of Jewish Life Before and During the Holocaust Vol.II* (New York: New York University Press, 2001).
37. Reder and Forstater, *I survived a Nazi Extermination Camp*.
38. Redner, B. Z., *A Jewish policeman In Lwów : an early account, 1941-1943*, translated from Polish by Jerzy Michalowicz.(Jerusalem, Yad Vashem: The International Institute for Holocaust Research, 2015), pp.201-205.
39. Ibid., p.206.
40. Friedman, 'Extermination of Lvov Jews'.
41. 'Lvov (Lemberg)' (Holocaust Historical Society, 2014), retrieved from: https://www.holocausthistoricalsociety.org.uk/contents/ghettosj-r/lvov.html (accessed 23 July 2021)

42. 'Belzec Concentration Camp: History and Overview' (American-Israeli Cooperative Enterprise, 1998-2021), retrieved from: https://www.jewishvirtuallibrary.org/history-and-overview-of-belzec-concentration-camp (accessed 23 July 2021)

43. Pankiewicz, T., *Apteka w Getcie Krakowskim* (Kraków: Nakladem Instytutu Wydawniczego, 1st edn, 1947).

44. 'The Belzec Remembrance Project' retrieved from: http://chelm.freeyellow.com/belzec.html (accessed 23 July 2021)

45. 'Christian Wirth', Aktion Reinhard Camps, retrieved from: http://www.deathcamps.org/reinhard/wirth.html.

46. Gribetz, J., Greenstein, E.L. and Stein, R., *The Timetables of Jewish History* (New York: Simon and Schuster, 1993).

47. Hilberg, R., *The Destruction of the European Jews* (Boulder CO: Lynne Rienner Publishers, 1985); Mayer, A., *Why Did the Heavens not Darken: The Final Solution in History* (New York: Pantheon Books, 1988); Sereny, G., *Into That Darkness* (New York: McGraw Hill, 1974).

48. Hilberg, *The Destruction of the European Jews.*

49. Wachsmann, N., *KL: A History of the Nazi Concentration Camps* (New York, London: Farrar, Straus and Giroux, Reprint edition, 2015).

50. Hilberg, *The Destruction of the European Jews.*

51. Arad, Y., *Belzek, Sobibor, Treblinka* (Bloomington IND: Indiana University Press, 1987).

52. Wachsmann, *KL: A History of the Nazi Concentration Camps.*

53. Reder and Forstater, *I survived a Nazi Extermination Camp*; this is Forstater's translation of Reder's memoir from 1944.

54. Rajchman, C., *Treblinka, a Survivor's Memory* (London: MacLehose Press, 2011).

55. Rashke, R., *Escape from Sobibor* (Champaign IL: University of Illinois Press, 1995).

56. Reder and Forstater, *I survived a Nazi Extermination Camp.*

57. Webb, C., *The Belzec Death Camp* (Stuttgart: Ibidem-Verlag, 2016).

58. Witte, P. and Tyas, S., 'A New Document on the Deportation and Murder of Jews during "Einsatz Reinhardt" 1942', *Holocaust and Genocide Studies,* 15, 3 (Winter 2001), p.472.

59. Hilberg, *The Destruction of the European Jews.*

60. Robin O'Neil, 'Belzec: Stepping Stone to Genocide', JewishGen, 2009 retrieved from: https://www.jewishgen.org/yizkor/belzec1/belzec1.html (accessed 23 July 2021)

61. Gilbert, M., *The Holocaust* (London: Collins, 1986); Pohl, D. and Witte, P., 'The number of victims of Belzec concentration camp, a faulty reassessment', *East European Jewish Affairs,* 31, 1 (2001), pp.15-25.

62. Hoefle Telegram, National Archives, Kew, HW 16/32: retrieved from: https://www.nationalarchives.gov.uk/education/resources/holocaust/hoefle-telegram/ (accessed 23 July 2021)

63. 'Belzec Camp History' retrieved from: https://web.archive.org/web/20051225034440/http://www.deathcamps.org/belzec/belzec.html (accessed 23 July 2021)

64. Gilbert, *The Holocaust.*

65. Millet, K., *The Victims of Slavery, Colonisation and the Holocaust* (London: Bloomsbury, 2017).

66. Reder and Forstater, *I survived a Nazi Extermination Camp.*

67. Millet, *The Victims of Slavery, Colonisation and the Holocaust.*

68. Gilbert, *The Holocaust*.
69. Winstone, Martin, *The Holocaust Sites of Europe: An Historical Guide*. (London, New York: I.B. Tauris, 2010).
70. Reder and Forstater, *I survived a Nazi Extermination Camp*.
71. Hilberg, *The Destruction of the European Jews*, p.245.
72. Chris Webb and Carmelo Lisciotto, 'The Gas Chambers at Belzec, Sobibor and Treblinka' (H.E.A.R.T., 2009), retrieved from: http://www.holocaustresearchproject.org/ar/argaschambers.html (accessed 23 July 2021)
73. Winstone, *The Holocaust Sites of Europe: An Historical Guide*.
74. Reder and Forstater, *I survived a Nazi Extermination Camp*.
75. Hilberg, *The Destruction of the European Jews*.
76. Sereny, *Into That Darkness*.
77. 'The Belzec Remembrance Project' retrieved from: https://chelm.freeyellow.com/belzec.html (accessed 23 July 2011); Crowe, *Oscar Schindler*.
78. Webb and Lisciotto, 'The Gas Chambers at Belzec, Sobibor and Treblinka'.
79. 'An eyewitness to gassings at Belzec', (Alpha History, 2020), retrieved from: http://alphahistory.com/holocaust/an-eyewitness-to-gassings-at-belzec-1942/ (accessed 23 July 2021)
80. Hilberg, *The Destruction of the European Jews*.
81. Reder and Forstater, *I survived a Nazi Extermination Camp*.
82. 'An eyewitness to gassings at Belzec'.
83. Reder and Forstater, *I survived a Nazi Extermination Camp*.
84. 'Belzec', Holocaust Encyclopaedia.
85. Rubenstein, R. and Roth, J., *Approaches to Auschwitz: The Holocaust and Its Legacy* (West Lafayette, IND: Purdue University Press, 1987).
86. 'Wilhelm Cornides Report' (Holocaust Historical Society, 2014), retrieved from: https://www.holocausthistoricalsociety.org.uk/contents/belzec/gaschambers.html (accessed 23 July 2021)
87. Wallach, K.L., *Man's Inhumanity to Man* (Lulu.com, 2020), available on Googlebooks.
88. Sereny, *Into That Darkness*.
89. Mattogno, C., *Belzec in Propaganda, Testimonies, Archaeological Research and History* (Theses & Dissertations Press, 2004), p.87.
90. Hilberg, *The Destruction of the European Jews*.
91. Wiesel, E., *Night* (London: Penguin Books, 1985).
92. Pagis, D., *Written in Pencil in the Sealed Railway Car* (1981), retrieved from: https://www.ronnowpoetry.com/contents/pagis/WritteninPencil.html (accessed 23 July 2021)
93. Kaplan, C., A., *Scroll of Agony, The Warsaw Diary of Chaim A. Kaplan* (London: Hamish Hamilton, 1966).
94. Ibid., p.229.
95. Testimony of Wisia Oberleder-Haran (in my possession).
96. Kahane, *The Lvov Ghetto Diary*.
97. Bagley, L., *Wartime Lies* (London: Penguin, 2007).
98. Zylberberg, M., *Warsaw Diary* (London: Vallentine Mitchell, 1969).
99. Freida had previously escaped from the ghetto, after losing her baby twins in the *Grossaktion* of July 1942.

100. The translation of the song is retrieved from: https://lyricstranslate.com/en/wojenka-little-war.html (accessed 22 July 2021)
101. Bagley, *Wartime Lies*.
102. 'Firsthand accounts of the 1944 Poland Uprising', Poland Gallery, retrieved from: http://polandgallery.tumblr.com/post/148303686337/first-hand-accounts-of-the-1944-warsaw-uprising (accessed 23 July 2021)
103. 'The 69th Infantry Division during World War II', Holocaust Encyclopaedia, retrieved from: https://www.ushmm.org/wlc/en/article.php?ModuleId=10006167 (accessed 23 July 2021)

7

Jakub Weissman

'I tell my piano the things I used to tell you.' Frederyk Chopin[1]

His name was Jakob Weissman, but in Poland a name can be altered to reflect your mood. So, Jakob (on his birth certificate of 9 September 1918) was Jakub (Polish version)), Kuba (abbreviation) or Kubek (boyish) or Kubuś (affectionate). Later as I will reveal, he inexplicably became known as Marek. He was my mother's cousin, friend and soul mate.

Kuba in 1933. I found this photo in my mother's papers. It may have been sent to her by Stanisław Frenkiel.

As I grew up, Kuba became one of my childhood heroes. I was told of his prodigious talent on the piano, and how Arthur Rubinstein on hearing him play had reputedly said, 'child, you have a talent greater than mine'. I knew that he had been the principal pianist in the Lwów Philharmonic in 1940, and that he died aged just 23, grabbed from his flat, forced to dig his own grave and shot into it. I resolved to find out more.

On the family trees which I drew up with my mother's help in 2001, there appeared to be no twig for Kuba, so I was unsure how they were related. However, the Grunberg family genealogy page[2] which I found on the internet resolved this. The relationship comes from my maternal grandmother's side. My grandmother, Kazimiera (Karolina) and Kuba's mother Helena Grunberg were first cousins, so my mother and Kuba, who was three years younger, were second cousins. Kuba, who had two older sisters, was the adored baby of his family.

One of my first sources of information about Kuba was a stack of letters between my mother and Stanisław Frenkiel (the painter of the portrait, which is shown below) from the early 2000s. Frenkiel was a well-known expressionist artist (in the manner of George Grosz and Stanley Spencer), who had a wide following in the artistic circles in Poland and London. He was also a relative of both Kuba and my mother (a second cousin on her maternal side). The correspondence was fascinating, redolent of a vibrant world in dark times. They spoke of the need to resurrect and honour Kuba's memory, but sadly they both died before they managed to achieve this. I thought that Frenkiel's daughter Olenka[3] might be interested in the letters, so I contacted her having found her email address on the internet. We met in London, and I must thank the ghost of Kuba for having initiated a new friendship. Stanisław Frenkiel (known as Staszek) had in fact written a memoir, a digital copy of which Olenka shared with me. It is currently unpublished, so I cite it sparingly, as she hopes to make it publicly available soon.

Kuba's talent as a pianist was recognised from an early age, and fostered by Egon Petri, the legendary Dutch pianist who conducted master classes in Zakopane, for selected young piano students.[4] In one of my mother's letters to Frenkiel she describes a holiday with the Weissmans in the Reiners' holiday villa,[5] when Kuba was 14 and my mother 17. 'We developed a friendship and could talk about everything openly and sincerely; I don't think I have ever had a better soul mate…he had an innate ability to penetrate into the depths of one's soul.' I don't know if this was one of the occasions when Kuba attended the master classes; perhaps it was just a holiday. In Frenkiel's memoirs he also talks of bonding with Kuba in

Zakopane 'under the common umbrella of symbolism and expression'. He continues, 'It was Kuba's influence which contributed to the aesthetic maturation and to a more subtle discernment in art, music and literature.' Both would have been in their teens at the time, and my mother three years older.

Another teenage friend was the Polish and Israeli author Leo Lipski (born Lipshutz). Lipski's best-known works include *Day and Night* and *Little Peter*, but it is his lesser known, posthumously published work, *Paryż Ze Złota*[6], that includes his reminiscences of Kuba. Leo recounts how they first met in a downpour while they were walking home from school. Leo's home was nearby, so Leo asked Kuba to come in to shelter from the rain. Leo sat down at his piano to show his new friend that he could play. Kuba listened quietly to Leo's halting rendition of a Chopin *Mazurka* and then, after some hesitation, went to the piano and played the same piece in C-sharp minor. Leo's mother came out of the kitchen and they both listened open-mouthed. From then on, the two boys spent a much of their time in each other's houses. Leo read, and Kuba practised, each infecting the other with their enthusiasms for literature and music. Leo remembers Kuba as 'one of these people blessed with the spirit of God, and also something elusively different, alarming, insinuating'. He adds, 'We were in love in that typically boyishly youthful way.' Later, as Lipski published his writings, Kuba, who was exceptionally well-read in classical literature, became his severest critic. Leo often accompanied Kuba on his visits to my mother's flat on Mikołajska in Kraków, where they discussed books and Kuba played on the Reiners' piano. A downside to this friendship was that it caused my mother to cease her piano lessons because she felt she was no good (though this revelation was crossed out in the first draft of her letter).

Another contemporary and distant relative of both Kuba and my mother was Juliusz Eisenberg. He may be one of the young men in the group photograph reproduced here. His father, who became a Professor of Microbiology in Lwów, was later deposed from his post and offered employment as 'louse feeder' for the Nazis' immunology experiments, mentioned on page 195 of this book.

Kuba studied piano at the Kraków Conservatory under the tutelage of the pianist and musicologist Jan Hoffman.[7] When my mother met Jan Hoffman after the war, he spoke of Kuba with tears in his eyes, saying 'his sort of talent is rare, maybe one in 100 or 200 years in the whole world, and that never in his musical career had he found anyone to match him'. As a student Kuba played as a soloist at various venues. He is mentioned in the April 1939 issue of the Polish Newspaper *Nowy Dziennik*[8] as a participant in a ceremonial Passover seder, and in the June issue of the same newspaper[9] as a participant at an 'Artistic Evening' in Kraków. This latter event had a charitable aim of raising financial help for refugees from Czechoslovakia.

With the start of the war in September 1939, Kuba, like my mother but independently from my mother, fled eastwards to Lwów. The city was in Soviet hands at the time and refugees from Western Poland were flooding in. Surprisingly, in the midst of all this chaos, the music scene flourished, and Kuba was immediately hired as a soloist and accompanist by the Lwów Philharmonic Orchestra. He rented a handsome flat (on Ujejskiego) and when his Kraków friends made it to Lwów a few months later, he shared it with five of them.[10] Kuba, with his relatively well-paid job, subsidised them and often brought good food. Leo Lipski[11] recalls how, in a typical wartime manner, the six friends shared three beds. Their flat became a hive of intellectuals, attracting other interesting people some of whom stayed for a night or longer. Afterwards Leo Lipski related with regret that 'Kuba left our circle to go and live with Tadeusz (Tadek) and through him became slowly drawn into a life of homosexuality'. Frenkiel's memoirs provide further revelations. Apparently, his relationship with Kuba deteriorated – they had an argument, and Kuba packed his bags and left the flat. The result of this was that the two suffered different fates. Frenkiel was arrested by the NKVD and transported to a gulag in Russia for forced work (but survived), while Kuba perished at the hands of the Germans.

I was intrigued to find out more about the music scene in Lwów under the Soviets. All the survivors' statements concur on how the intellectuals, both Poles and Jews, were permanently on the run from the NKVD. Given this situation, how was it possible for the music scene to flourish? Yet it did; the theatres, music halls and opera houses were open and busy. The existence of a rich literary and musical scene in Lwów under the Soviets is confirmed in the accounts of Joanna Chłosta in her book *Polskie Życie Literackie we Lwowie w Latach 1939-1941* (*Polish Literary Life in Lwów in 1939-1941*).[12] There was even a literary magazine *Nowe Widnokręgi* (*New Horizons*). This magazine, which started circulating in January 1941, invited all 'writers, poets, critics, researchers of literature and drama to openly reveal their thoughts'. At the same time *Czerwony Sztandar* (the Red Banner), published in Polish by the Soviet Occupation authorities, carried overt propaganda against the Second Polish Republic, while at the same time advertising theatre events and concerts, including a Chopin event in which J. Weis(s)man played, and Jadwiga Hennert sang.[13] In a recent obituary[14] of the Polish composer and conductor Stanisław Skrowaczewski, who played in the Lwów Philharmonic in 1940, are quoted his reminiscences of Lwów under the Soviets and how 'life was dangerous, but the influx of Jewish musicians enriched cultural life'. How sad that it is now too late to ask him whether he remembered Kuba.

I found another mention of Kuba among my mother's papers in two photocopied pages (pp.34-35) from a book, but unfortunately, I don't know which book:

> Apart from musical talents he was distinguished by a formidable intelligence and great beauty. His portrait painted by the artist Stiebert-Obrebska, was owned by his mother who was in hiding on the outskirts of Lwów. They were both killed by the Nazis. Marek [Kuba] lived with his friend Tadek on Lackiego Street in Lwów. A Ukrainian policeman, in the service of the Nazis, came to his house and he [Kuba] was led out, ostensibly for forced work. Despite the protestations of his friend, Tadeusz Wojciechowski, Marek was shot.
> [Mentions of 'Marek' in Schultz's second letter relate to Kuba.]

I had heard of Bruno Schultz but could not recall how or where. The internet quickly provided an answer. Bruno Schultz had been a famous Polish writer, artist and art critic, and was killed by the Nazis in November 1942. Schultz's work has recently been brought to public attention following the rediscovery in 2001 of a mural by him that had been painted over and forgotten. The mural was taken to Jerusalem in fragments and painstakingly restored; after touring Poland, it now resides in the Bruno Schulz Museum in Drohobych (Schultz's home town) in Ukraine. Schultz's writings are included in a Penguin short story collection[15], and his most famous collection *Street of Crocodiles* has been dramatized.

To find out more, I googled Schultz's and Wojciechowski's names together and struck lucky. I found Schulz's (second) letter, the one mentioned in the above pages, published and available on the internet – but in Spanish. The services of Google Translate revealed the gist of the correspondence. In the letter Schultz talks about projects, paintings and prizes, but also mentions Kuba (whom he refers to as Marek) as 'a very kind, intelligent and exuberant man…seductive for his taste and artistic sensibility'. He ends the letter with 'Send my friendship to Marek too'.

My mother in her letter to Staszek Frenkiel remembers:

> In the first two years of the war, we were together in Lwów. After the German occupation Kuba came to see me frequently and told me

about a very complicated love affair he was having with someone
who was a Polish count. Apparently, this person adored Kuba and
was in love with his music. A day or two after Kuba's last visit, I found
out that during my absence someone came to see me to tell me about
Kuba's death, that he was apprehended by the Gestapo, that he was
told to dig his own grave and he was shot into it. I don't know who
it was who came to see me. And who denounced him? Was it some
(jealous) friend of the count? A question mark hangs over the end
of such a fantastic person and formidable talent.

From Bruno Schultz's letter to Tadeusz Wojciechowski, and the excerpt
from the two photocopies pages, I had assumed that Wojciechowski was
Kuba's boyfriend, but according to Frenkiel's memoir it was another
Tadeusz, who was called Tadeusz Żakiej. Both these Tadeuszes were Polish,
not Jewish, both were gay and both have Wikipedia entries. Maybe both
were his boyfriends? And who was the Polish count?

Tadeusz Wojciechowski[16] was an artist and belonged to an avant-garde
group 'Artes' formed in Lwów in 1929. In later years he was famous for his
stained-glass work and ecclesiastical art. He would have been some 16 years
older than Kuba. Tadeusz Żakiej was a musicologist and composer, and
later also a food writer. [17] He was born in 1915, so would have been only 3
years older than Kuba. Is it significant that Żakiej took on the name Tadeusz
Marek after the war?

Frenkiel's memoirs describe a drunken and debauched New Year party
of 1940/41 at the Tadeuszes'; it was teeming with gay men, including a
transvestite called Countess Leonora. Frenkiel and Lipski, as straight men,
were both a bit shocked, and left early, which was just as well, as according
to Kuba's later admissions to Frenkiel, the party turned into an orgy. Was
Kuba circumcised? I presume so, though I don't know, but some of the party
revellers might have had an opportunity to find out. Jewishness was not
much of an issue under the Soviets, but Kuba's Jewishness may well have
been noted and later used by informers.

As Frenkiel was deported to Russia before the Germans invaded, his
memoirs of Lwów only span the period of Soviet occupation. After the
Germans took over, all Jews were required to wear the Star of David.
According to my mother, Kuba did not register himself as a Jew and did
not wear the Star armband. 'Someone must therefore have denounced him',
she said. Had he been living openly as a Jew, he may have been summarily
shot or deported to Belzec, but no denouncement would have been
necessary. His crime was therefore most likely to have been that of a Jew in

hiding. It is likely that he was taken into the Janowska camp and told to dig a grave in the 'mountain of sand' behind the camp, a fate that befell thousands.

In one of the letters my mother confirmed that Kuba had said to her that his friends sometimes called him Marek. We don't know why. Nor do we know why Żakiej later replaced his surname Żakiej with Marek. Was it to honour his friend? Or was Kuba in love with the other Tadeusz or even the transvestite Countess Leonora? As to who denounced him, we will never know, but there is no shortage of potentially jealous people from whom to choose.

His listing in the Lwów Philharmonic records laconically, 'Pianist and accompanist…it was predicted that he would have a great future in music… murdered by the Nazis'.[18]

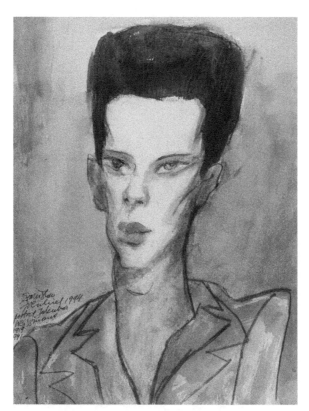

A sensuous and vulnerable Kuba, painted posthumously by Stanisław Frenkiel (1990s) – a gift from the painter to my mother. It now hangs in my study.

Kuba (standing) with friends before the war

The famous Polish composer Karol Szymanowski with a very young Tadeusz Żakiej, 1934.
http://drwilliamhughes.blogspot.co.uk/2014/03/tadeusz-zakiej-tadeusz-marek-karol.html[19]

Notes

1. Chopin, F. and Voynich, E.L. (eds), *Chopin's Letters* (New York: Dover Publication, 1988).
2. Dan Hirschberg, 'Grunberg families', retrieved from: https://www.ics.uci.edu/~dan/genealogy/Krakow/Families/Grunberg.html (accessed 3 August 2021).
3. Olenka Frenkiel worked as an award-winning and long serving BBC journalist.
4. Egon Petri actually lived in Zakopane, according to https://en.wikipedia.org/wiki/Egon_Petri (accessed 20 April 2021)
5. This is Jagoda, the house that my grandfather built, described in Chapter 5.
6. Lipski, L., *Paryż Ze Złota* (Paris of Gold) (Swiat Literacki, 2002). Not translated as far as I know.
7. 'Jan Hoffman', retrieved from: https://en.wikipedia.org/wiki/Jan_Hoffman (accessed 20 April 2021)
8. *Nowy Dziennik,* R22, nr 92, (2 April 1939), retrieved from: https://polona.pl/item/nowy-dziennik-r-22-nr-92-2-kwietnia-1939,NDc5MjcyMzM/16/#info:search:%22jakub%20weissman%22 (accessed 20 April 2021)
9. *Nowy Dziennik,* R22, nr 163, (16 April 1939), retrieved from: https://polona.pl/item/nowy-dziennik-r-22-nr-163-16-czerwca-1939,NDc5MjczNDg/14/#info:search:%22jakub%20weissman%22(accessed 20 April 2021)
10. Staszek Frenkiel was there, Staszek's girlfried Lotka (Anna), Leo Lipski, his brother Staś, and a girl called Ziuta (or Liuta), who considered herself to be Kuba's fiancée (apparently a beautiful and clever girl, but an indifferent pianist).
11. Lipski, *Paryż Ze Złota* (Paris of Gold).
12. Chłosta J., *Polskie życie literackie we Lwowie w latach1939-1941 w świetle oficjalnej prasy polskojęzycznej* (Wydawn. Uniw. Warmińsko-Mazurskiego, 2000).
13. *Czerwony Sztandar* (1940) 349, p.6.
14. Obituary of Stanisław Skrowaczewski, *Guardian,* 11 March 2017.
15. Roth, P. (ed.), *Writers from the Other Europe* (London: Penguin, 1977).
16. 'Tadeusz Wojciechowski (malarz)', retrieved from: https://pl.wikipedia.org/wiki/Tadeusz_Wojciechowski_(malarz) (accessed 2 August 2021)
17. William Hughes, 'Tadeusz Żakiej (Tadeusz Marek): 'Karol Szymanowski' ('Sygnały', nr.13, 1934), retrieved from: http://drwilliamhughes.blogspot.co.uk/2014/03/tadeusz-zakiej-tadeusz-marek-karol.html (accessed 3 August 2021)
18. Retrieved from: https://www.jewishgen.org/yizkor/musicians/mus247.html#Page278 (accessed 3 August 2021)
19. Hughes, 'Tadeusz Żakiej (Tadeusz Marek): 'Karol Szymanowski' ('Sygnały', nr.13, 1934).

PART III

Living with the Past

8

How was it Possible?

'Perhaps one cannot, what is more one must not, understand what happened, because to understand is almost to justify.' Primo Levi, 1987, in the Afterword to *If This is a Man*.[1]

The Holocaust, a word which defines the catastrophic destruction of Europe's Jews, took place over four years between 1940 and 1945, but its historical roots began in biblical times. Ever since Pharaoh, Haman, the Romans, the Black Death and the Crusaders, Jews were always treated as the scapegoats and outsiders. Their history has seen a sliding scale of three fundamental policies: conversion, expulsion and annihilation. The missionaries of Christianity had said, 'You have no right to live among us as Jews.' The secular rulers followed with: 'You have no right to live among us.' However, it was the Nazis who exacted the final decree: 'You have no right to live.'

In 1930s Germany, where the Nazi soldiers were groomed, there were not many Jews, merely about half a million which was less than 1 per cent of the German population. Nevertheless, this tiny minority was blamed for losing the First World War, Germany's subsequent economic collapse – in short, everything that was wrong in their world. Many of the German Nazis had never really encountered a Jew first-hand and were thus able to accept the antisemitic propaganda without applying it to anyone they knew. Films like *Jud Süss* (*Suss, the Jew*) and *Der Ewige Jude* (*The Eternal Jew*), which were screened in the early days of the war, confirmed their belief that Jews were dishonest moneylenders, corrupters of the world, carriers of disease and by a strange logic both Bolsheviks and unscrupulous capitalists at the same time.

German children were brain-washed from a very early age. They learned to count using a commercially produced board game called *Juden Raus* (*Jews Out*) in which, at the roll of a dice, they could collect wooden pawns with caricature faces and pointy hats to proudly expel them outside the city walls. The player who had captured the most Jews won. *Die Juden sind unser unglück* (the Jews are our misfortune), read the caption on the antisemitic cartoon on the front page of the weekly newspaper *Der Stürmer* lying on their breakfast table. Pre-school age children would have honed their reading skills on this. At elementary school 97 per cent of the teachers belonged to the Nazi Teachers' Association and more than 30 per cent were members of the Nazi party itself. Any teachers who were suspected of having Jewish sympathies were fired.[2] It is not therefore surprising that German boys and girls learned what the Nazis wanted them to know.

The front page of *Der Stürmer*. My mother-in-law brought this one from Germany in 1935.

A recent study showed that Nazi indoctrination was so successful that its effects have persisted until the present day.[3] The researchers asked the German population a host of questions about attitudes towards Jews, comparing antisemitic responses of Germans born in different decades of the twentieth century. The data showed that Germans born in the1920s and 1930s, were much more antisemitic than those born before or after that period, suggesting that it was indoctrination received at school, at a young age, which was the most effective. The results of the study are currently being used to address the issue of radicalisations of youngsters by Islamic militants.

Derek Niemann, the author of *A Nazi in the Family*, made an interesting observation in a recent zoom lecture. I asked him whether his grandfather (who had been a pen-pusher Nazi) raised his children to be antisemitic. Yes, he replied, but the strength of the prejudice waned with their position in the family. His aunt, the eldest, who had been schooled in Germany before and after the war, was shamelessly antisemitic all her life, his father, who was quite still quite young when the war ended may have said things that smacked of it, but the youngest, who had been a baby, has never expressed any antisemitism at all.

While exposing children to indoctrination at school had the most lasting consequences, the social environment, and extra-curricular activities such as Hitler Youth, also had an effect. Membership of the *Hitler Jugend* became compulsory for all German Aryans after 1939, even if the parents objected. For the young participants, the organisation promised privilege and fun. They offered uniforms, camps and sports competitions, hiking, calisthenics and rousing songs. I know what fun such an organisation can be from my own experience of the Red Pioneers. It's just that I swore allegiance to the Communist Party while the *Hitler Jugend* swore allegiance to the Nationalist Socialist German Workers' Party. For a child it was the activity that mattered more than the ideology, but the brain-washing received would have been delivered smoothly and thoroughly, straight into the child's psyche.

It is thus easy to see the Jews through a German youth's eyes. They were clearly subhuman, *Untermenschen,* not to be compared with *Herrmenschen.* They were not even the same species as themselves. Hofer[4] in 1935 defined *Untermenschen* as:

> ...biologically apparently our equal with hands, feet, and a sort of brain, with eyes and mouth – yet an utterly different, abominable creature, only a sketch of a human being, with humanoid features,

but intellectually and spiritually lower than any animal. Within this being, a barbarous chaos of wild, unbridled passions, a nameless destructive will, the most primitive cravings, the most naked bestialities. He is and will remain nothing but an *Untermensch*.

In a totalitarian state there is only one Truth. The German population, as also the Polish population under the Germans, were not able to compare the views of different political parties and choose what to believe. Foreign radio stations were jammed, books which deviated from the Truth were banned and burned, those in possession of such punished by jail or death.

What is more the church as an institution did nothing to counteract the public's perception of the official Truth. Undoubtedly isolated priests or pastors risked their own lives to help or save individual people, but the church simply chose to cherry-pick the antisemitic bits of the New Testament to affirm its belief that Jews, not just these Jews, but all Jews, are to blame for Christ's death. The antisemitism of the New Testament is still there of course. I heard it quoted just a couple of years ago at a Catholic funeral in Edinburgh:

> The Jews, who have both killed the Lord Jesus, and their own prophets, and have persecuted us; and they please not God and are contrary to all men: forbidding us to speak to the Gentiles that they might be saved, to fill up their sins always: for the wrath is come upon them to the uttermost. (1st Thessalonians 2:14-6)

Nor is the Protestant message any more merciful. Martin Luther, the founder of Protestantism, talks of the Jews as 'thirsty bloodhounds and murderers of all Christendom…they had poisoned water and wells, stolen children, and torn and hacked them apart, in order to cool their temper secretly with Christian blood'.[5] These Bible-founded accusations turned into full-blown racism in Germany long before the Nazis came to power. They were already there in the second half of the seventeenth century. By the nineteenth century the Germans were fond of quoting the jingle 'never mind to whom he prays/the rotten mess is in the race', and seeing how well it translates into English, the Brits were probably fond of it too. Well before that in 1290 Edward I of England expelled the entire Jewish population of England, and they were not legally allowed back until 1656. Then there are the horrors of the Inquisition in Spain under Ferdinand and Isabella in late fifteenth century. The list goes on.

In the Nazi ideology the Jews became (rather un-biologically) both 'blood-suckers' and 'cholera germs'. They have also been variously described as 'beasts of prey', 'imbued with satanical power', 'hostile, criminal and parasitic'.[6] The Nazi ideology was probably founded on the writings and speeches of Hermann Ahlwardt, who gained a seat in the Reichstag in 1893. Two years later in a speech to the German Parliament he 'cited the irreconcilable differences between the racial traits of the Jews and the Teutons and claimed that studies have shown that the innate racial characteristics of the Jews, acquired over thousands of years, have made it impossible for the Jews to change their nature'.[7] Even in 1943, by which time most of the six million were already dead, the Nazi press warned, 'do not overestimate the power of the Jews', and later in 1944 when the job was almost done Himmler defended himself saying, 'We had the moral right vis-a-vis our people to annihilate this people which wanted to annihilate us.' [8]

Then there was the health issue. The Germans convinced themselves, based on some dubious immunological evidence, that the Jews harboured typhus (transmitted by body lice), and were a medical risk to the Aryan population. Walbaum, the Chief Health Officer of the *Generalgouvernement* (GG), wrote in 1941: 'We sentence the Jews in the ghetto by hunger or we shoot them even if in the end the result is the same, the latter is more intimidating, we have one and only one responsibility, that the German people are not infected and endangered by these parasites, for that any means must be right.'[9] One of my distant relatives, Filip Pinkus Eisenberg, after being dismissed from his professorship in bacteriology in Lwów, was given the supposedly life-saving job of 'feeder of lice'[10] in Dr Weigl's famous (infamous) typhus vaccine laboratory. He escaped to Kraków but was caught and perished in the gas chambers of Belzec.[11]

Underlying this idea of eliminating the undesirables, was the (then) completely respectable concept of eugenics. Eugenics was not a German invention. It began here in the UK at the end of the nineteenth century instigated by Sir Francis Galton, a cousin of Darwin's. Darwin, my hero, of course started the ball rolling in 1859, by subtitling his *Origin of Species* the 'Preservation of Favoured Races in the Struggle for Life'. Darwin's theory was based on years of painstaking research on plants and animals, so he did not express judgement on the human species, while noting that the 'differences between the races of man are so strongly marked'. He also wrote a follow-up book called *Descent of Man*, but took care to maintain that 'all men were fellow creatures of one God', while warning that 'the civilised races of man will almost certainly exterminate, and replace, the savage races'. But it was his cousin Dalton, who a couple of decades later reinterpreted Darwin's ideas in a social, human context and coined the word 'eugenics'. This idea of improving the human species like one would a breed of cattle for beef, was enthusiastically taken up in the UK, US and the mainland of Europe in the first half of the twentieth century. It gave the Nazis an academically founded excuse for cleaning out the *Untermenschen*, to nobly populate the world with a fitter class of person. Surprisingly, despite the horrors of the Holocaust, the vile idea of eugenics persisted; my husband was still taught it by his professor, C.D. Darlington, in Oxford in the early 1960s.

Of course, the Nazis were not the first to commit genocide. The destruction of another people, their culture and religion, while dismissing them as barbarians goes back to Ancient Greece and beyond. Reasons for atrocities to these 'barbarians' may be any of the following: fear of those different from oneself; religious intolerance; the political need for a scapegoat; fear for one's own community's existence or financial exploitation. From the sixteenth century onwards, dominant states in the world expanded their empires, crushing the indigenous populations as they went. From the American West to the Australian Outback and the 'Belgian' Congo, native peoples were enslaved, their lands appropriated, their culture dismissed, their artefacts stolen, their religions descried, and their very lives only considered valuable in the monetary value to their owners. These Native Americans, Aborigines, Caribs, Indians to Africans and many, many others, were seen to be standing in the way of 'progress' (or profit?) and therefore expendable. From the Spanish, the Dutch, the British, and yes, the Germans, there was an 'us' and a 'them' past. The First World War had taken away Germany's Empire, but not that attitude. And along with the horrors of modern warfare, the First World War also saw the start of eight years of victimising, scape-goating, deporting and massacring the Christian Armenian minority in Turkey – Germany's ally in the war. This resulted in the death on one-and-a-half million Armenians, which Turkey to this day denies was genocide.

So, to view the Germans' intentions from a distance of eighty years, gives us a distorted view of how things were at the time. The genocide that they were planning follows on from others that took place in other parts of the world in the living memories of the older German perpetrators. It's not that I am excusing the Germans; their Holocaust was and always will remain the deepest scar to have defaced humankind, but it has to be viewed through the lens of history as it was being played out at the time.

It is with that in mind that I turn to the Germans as perpetrators. A brilliant book by Laurent Binet called *HHhH*[12] about the assassination of

Reinhard Heydrich, the architect of the Holocaust, shows up the farce and burlesque of the scene set in Berlin and Prague upon which the decisions to annihilate 90 per cent of Europe's Jews were made. While Hitler, Heydrich and Himmler walked the corridors of power clanking their medals, their subordinates – arraigned in a strict hierarchy of ranks – enacted their orders. At least 200,000 of them were directly engaged in the killings, while millions more were mere cogs in the wheel of the system. Less than 1 per cent of those directly responsible were convicted.[13]

And how many of them were sorry? Well, they were sorry they had lost the war, but were they really sorry for what they had done? Hitler, Himmler and Göring committed suicide and Heydrich was assassinated, but I doubt that any one of them was sorry. When Göth was put into pre-trial detention and presented with the indictment he is said to have turned to the last page and looked over the list of witnesses (my father among them). 'What, so many Jews?' he said, 'and they always told us not a single one of the pricks would be left'.[14] Most pleaded not guilty and exonerated themselves, claiming that they were only carrying out the orders of their superiors. Mietek Pemper, who participated as a witness or interpreter at numerous war crime trials, 'never heard any of the defendants utter a single word of regret or display any honest remorse'.[15]

One of the Nazi criminals, Dr Hans Munch, a camp physician of Auschwitz, was acquitted following his trial and extradited to Germany. Much later in the 1990s he is reported to have said that Eastern European Jews were *Untermenschen*, vermin, animals. He also said that he was an admirer of Josef Mengele.[16] It seems that the only way that the Nazi criminals could live with themselves, if they were allowed to do so, was to continue in their hatred of the Jews.

It is easy to see that filled with hatred and fuelled by venom the Nazis strived for complete annihilation, but why were the perpetrators driven to perform acts of wanton vandalism and humiliation? Why build a ghetto wall in the shape of Jewish tombstones? It's quite decorative, but really – it would have been cheaper and easier to build it straight. Why pave the roads most used by Jews with their ancestors' tombstones? They did this in Płaszów and Majdanek and Wabrzezno. Why gravel the paths of the SS-village at Auschwitz with human ash, including teeth and vertebrae? Was it really for practical purposes, or was it so they could trample their victims daily in an act of ultimate defilation? Why did they have orchestras playing as the children were being taken out of Płaszów, and as cohorts were being led into the gas chambers at Belzec? The role of music in death camps is explored in several memoirs and historical works. Some historians think that the music was partly for the entertainment of the SS-men, acting rather like musak on a factory floor, which various studies have shown can raise morale and increase productivity, especially where tasks are clearly defined and often repeated. That seems plausible given that this was a factory, and death was its product. However, the choice of the pieces for example 'everything passes' and 'Mamma songs' for orphaned children seems to me to be like pure *schadenfreude*.

My father said in his witness statement that Amon Göth normally flogged his victims first and then he shot them. Why go to the trouble of flogging? Gitta Sereny[17], the British investigative journalist, put this question to Franz Stangl, the ex-commandant of Sobibor and Treblinka, while serving his life sentence in jail in 1971, 'considering you were going to kill them all…what was the point of the humiliations, the cruelties?' He replied, 'to condition those who were to be the material executors of the operations'. Primo Levi[18], who reports on this interview, concludes that the aim was to physically degrade the victims to such an extent that they are no longer human, so that the murderer will be less burdened by guilt. Later in the interview Stangl says of the dead victims 'pits full of blue-black corpses. It had nothing to do with humanity, it couldn't have; it was a mass – a mass of rotting flesh.'

When Göth randomly shot people on the *Appellplatz,* he was scarily near to my father, close enough for my father to smell the drink on his breath. *Podchmielony* (beery) was the word my father used in his witness statement. Stangl's testimony to Gitta Sereny also confirms that the perpetrators were often drunk to anaesthetise them to the cruelties they were committing. Stangl at his trial confessed that, 'In the end, the only way to deal with it was to drink. I took a large glass of brandy to bed with me each night and I drank.'[19] This interview, which forms the basis for Sereny's fascinating book, is one of the best expositions of what makes a perpetrator. Stangl, apparently a nice man, a devoted family man, kind of fell into the role of commandant of Treblinka, presenting a convincing line-up of 'no-choices' which led to him being put in this invidious position. Survival, pure survival of himself and his family was his only motivation at every step in his progression through the ranks. Like countless other perpetrators he denied responsibility, 'My conscience is clear. I was only doing my duty.' What the interview exposes and what interested me most, was how this perfectly ordinary man managed to repress his moral scruples. At the end of the interview (and Sereny's book), he admits to guilt, but only the guilt of his own survival. Stangl died of heart failure nineteen hours after the interview ended.

Eichmann's tipple of choice was schnapps. 'I had to drink schnapps like water', he wrote in an autobiographical text from prison; he drank to anaesthetise himself against the sights he saw (and the horrors he perpetrated).[20] Hannah Arendt, who covered his trial in Jerusalem in 1962, saw Eichmann as 'intelligently stupid'.[21] The Greeks called this 'amathia', a concept used to explain why otherwise intelligent people believe and do stupid or evil things – it is not an inability to understand, but a refusal to understand.

Christian Wirth, who was the commandant of Belzec, and therefore ultimately responsible for my grandmother's death, died in May 1944 at the hands of Yugoslav partisans, so no interviews with him exist. Like Stangl, he was 'trained' in the T4 Euthanasia programme, gassing disabled patients. I say 'trained' because that was where their scruples were numbed.

The psychologist, Françoise Sironi, who treats twenty-first century torturers and victims, believes that true torturers such as Duch, the Khmer Rouge leader, and Pascal Simbikangwa, who was responsible for the Rwandan genocide, are what she calls 'man-systems'. These are people who have opted out of their own identity in favour of the ideological system they espouse. She once asked Duch, 'What happened to your conscience?' He replied he didn't understand the question.[22] The very same could apply to Amon Göth, Christian Wirth and Heinrich Himmler. Their consciences were not their own, they were the collective consciences of the system they espoused.

Himmler confirms this in the speech he gave to a group of SS-men in Poznań in October 1943: 'Most of you will know what it means when 100 bodies lie together, when there are 500, or when there are 1000…But altogether we can say: "We have carried out this most difficult task for the love of our people. And we have taken on no defect within us, in our soul, or in our character".'

Himmler, the man-system, espoused the identity of the totalitarian state. The fact that the SS did not find murder easy proved that they were 'decent human beings', who did not allow 'human weakness' to get in the way of the job in hand. Nevertheless, he concludes with a collective soul, a collective character.

There was one personal experience which made me realise how easy it is to become habituated to committing atrocities. As an undergraduate student in Edinburgh University in the 1960s, I took a course in Genetics, which required students to learn how to kill mice 'humanely'. The process involved lifting the mouse by its tail and then laying it on the table in front of you, and then whacking it across its neck vertebrae sharply with the side of the hand. If you hit the right spot the mouse died instantly. Three was the required number, they said, and three times we queued awaiting our turn. As I stood in the queue for the first mouse, I had serious misgivings. Should I go to the toilet hoping nobody would miss me, should I just skip to the end and pretend I had done it, or maybe I should leave the course? I did none of these things. I killed my first mouse and joined the end of the queue. The second time was a bit easier. By the third mouse I was doing fine. In other words, if you commit a sin again and again, eventually it does not feel like a sin anymore. I was even congratulating myself that I was improving because the mouse died quicker each time. (I must reassure all current and prospective Edinburgh University Biology students that this exercise is no longer practised.)

I wondered what the Nazis felt like when they were wielding their whips (made of dried-up bulls' genitalia). Did it give them satisfaction to aim their gun and shatter the victim's head in one shot? Precision was considered good not because it caused the victim less pain, but because it was economical. Or were they simply habituated, like I was becoming in the mouse killing exercise? Then off they went without a flicker or a flinch home to their families and their churches and slept soundly in their beds at night. Or did they?

The most likely answer to this worrying question is to be found in group, mob and squad mentality. When I took part in that mouse killing exercise, I was part of a class, and I did what the others did and what was expected of me. The SS-men, the Gestapo, the *Wehrmacht* in their group uniforms with their identical insignia and haircuts, did what they did not because they were evil, but because they did what was expected of them. They were in fact no longer themselves – they were de-individualised. So, when a mob set on a killing spree, they could kill individuals because the mob was able to yield its collective conscience to the norm of the group, however amoral that happened to be. Thus 'in the world Hitler imagined, the killers felt no responsibility for what they did'.[23] Wachsmann[24] adds another valid point, that I totally concur with, based on my own experience from that mouse killing exercise: 'participation in extreme violence can probably be explained by group pressure…men who stepped outside their comrades' circle of complicity were shunned and excluded from rewards and promotions'.

At the same time, a second de-individualisation triangle mirroring the first was happening, which enabled a single pen-pusher (Gitta Sereny calls them 'desk murderers') in Berlin to commit wide-scale genocide by considering the Jews to be a shapeless, anonymous amorphous mass. Such an act would simply be a bureaucratic stroke of the pen, ridding the pure and noble German nation of any risk of contamination by *Untermenschen*, be this by disease, or – God forbid – by interbreeding. As Hilberg[25] put it, 'bureaucrats composed memoranda, drew up blueprints, signed correspondence, talked on the telephone, and participated in conferences. They could destroy a whole people by sitting at their desks.' They never saw the victims which their actions affected, and this 'psychological distancing' facilitated their participation.

So 'Triangle One' is when a mob sets upon an individual, and 'Triangle Two' is when a single person orders the elimination of a mass. Both work through a process of de-individualisation. I can understand how both these de-individualisation triangles absolved the consciences of the perpetrators, what I cannot understand is how single individuals, ordinary people, even if they were acting on orders from above, could murder single defenceless victims. Killing of individuals by individuals must have awakened some feelings of compassion. Maybe what they needed was to be tanked up with alcohol, which my father could smell on Göth's breath. (That is indeed the view of Browning[26] and Westermann[27].) My father, had I asked him, would no doubt have contradicted that theory, believing Göth incapable of compassion drunk or sober. But for those perpetrators who did have something resembling a heart, would they not have looked at the faces of the dead and wondered what their names were or 'what it sounded like when they sang'.[28] Maybe that is why they elected to strip the victims of their dignity first; they made them face the wall or told them to run before they shot them, not out of respect for the victim, but out of respect for themselves, so that they would not have to meet their eyes. When dealing with them individually, they called them *stücke* (items or things), and branded them with eight-digit numbers. It was a way of protecting their consciences from any familiarity with the victims.

Another way of looking at Holocaust crime is presented by the human rights lawyer Philippe Sands in his excellent book *East West Street*.[29] The question which has been plaguing Sands is whether it matters in law that you are acting as 'an individual or because of the group of which you happen to be a member'. He discusses the different approaches of the two prosecuting counsels who both acted at the Nuremberg trials. Their names are Lauterpacht and Lemkin, and at least half the book is devoted to their different views on the same problem. Lauterpacht's principle is that the state and its leaders should be held accountable for crimes against humanity; this allowed the leaders, who were in the dock to be charged, convicted and executed at Nuremberg. Lemkin's new notion of genocide had a broader scope and emphasis on the attempt to eradicate groups of people such as Jews, Armenians, Slavs and others – it was not focused on acts against individuals. It was used more sparingly at Nuremberg, but both concepts have since been embedded in international law.

In the early days of the annihilation plan, mass murder of Jews was delivered by the *Einsatzgruppen* or paramilitary death squads which were made up of several hundred men. Historians call it 'holocaust by bullets'[30] to distinguish it from what took place later. Even though the men were in a group, all buoyed up by peer pressure and the promise of promotion, they often suffered from nervous breakdowns, depression and alcoholism. Suicides were common. According to Rubenstein and Roth[31] it was to protect the killers that 'a better way of killing had to be found'. They suggest that the 'Final Solution' by mass gassings evolved so as to further de-personalise the killing operations.

According to Hilberg[32] the Germans 'sought to avoid damage to "the soul" [by] the prohibition of unauthorised killings, making a distinction between killings pursuant to order and killings induced by desire'. They obviously discouraged the latter in Płaszów after it became a concentration camp, requiring the perpetrators to apply for permission to Berlin-Oranienburg by making them fill in forms in triplicate. That is what probably saved my father in his second face-to-face meeting with Göth. It does however seem bizarre that at a time when mass gassings were going on in Auschwitz, suddenly a new law should come out that an SS officer could be charged, convicted and even executed for the unauthorised murder of individual Jews. Was it to cleanse the image of the regime and give an impression of legality and order? Or maybe the killing of individuals by individuals was banned to protect the scruples of individual SS-men.

Rape, the ultimate one-on-one conflict, was luckily rare in the Germans' war against the Jews. Jewish women, young girls and even boys were saved from defilation by none other than the Nuremberg laws which forbad any sexual relations between Aryans and Jews. Any such couplings whether through love or force were considered as *Rassenschande,* bringing to the perpetrator 'racial shame' and 'racial pollution'. In contrast the Soviets after they entered Germany raped and pillaged without a scruple. Similarly, recent conflicts and genocides in Bangladesh, Cambodia, Ivory Coast, Cyprus, the former Yugoslavia, East Timor, Haiti, Liberia, and Uganda frequently report sexual terror as an instrument of war and domination.

The Nuremberg laws said nothing about murder of course, and despite 'damage to the soul', killings of individuals by individuals, also pogroms of masses by masses continued. In the infamous village of Jedwabne in northeast Poland, a mass of Polish villagers set upon and massacred a mass of their Jewish neighbours. De-individualisation did not come into it in this case; the perpetrators knew their victims by name. While the Jews were stoned, knifed, gutted and burned, it was the Germans who were the bystanders; they stood, watched, and photographed.

This issue of what motivated ordinary people to become brutal face-to-face killers, and therefore out-with what I call 'the two de-individualisation triangles' has been debated vehemently by two social historians, Browning[33] and Goldhagen[34]. Basing their argument on the same case study of a battalion who shot their victims at point-blank range (Reserve Police Battalion 101 in Józefów), they come to diametrically opposed conclusions. Goldhagen believes that these ordinary Germans actually wanted to be willing genocidal executioners, they slaked their Jewish blood-lust, they killed for pleasure because they were fuelled by an innate hatred of the Jews, which was historically inspired by Luther's polemics in the sixteenth century. Browning, on the other hand, believes that innate antisemitism was only one of many causes, which include peer pressure, alcoholism and general habituation to the acts of barbarity. The more they killed the more banal these acts became.

The Browning/Goldhagen argument is often used in undergraduate social science and psychology teaching, so has been extensively discussed in the literature. I read both texts now with great interest, though had not been aware of them or the debate they inspired when my parents were alive. Though they read neither text, I can guess what they would have said. My parents, particularly my father, would have been vehemently in support of Goldhagen's thesis, whereas I, who had not experienced the Holocaust, am in favour of Browning. Like Goldhagen, both my parents, I am sorry to say, were capable of indicting the entire German culture in the same way that the Germans indicted the entirety of the Jews.

Philosophers argue against the idea of collective guilt (and therefore collective pardon), but there is such a thing as collective responsibility because little acts of turning away, averting one's eyes from atrocity, make inhumanity possible. My father believed that the Germans must shoulder the blame collectively, for even those who were not perpetrators themselves were guilty of being bystanders. My father did not however mete out the same blame to those Jews who were required to commit perfidy on behalf of the Germans, such as OD-men (Jewish Policemen) or *Kapos*. He himself was never in that position, nor was my mother, but he did not condemn them. It was always the Germans he blamed.

I worried about that when I was growing up, but having now had time to delve into history, analyse and assess, I find my father's collective guilt standpoint more understandable. For the perpetrators he was once part of an amorphous mass of Jews, faceless and un-named. He survived by deliberately avoiding eye contact with them as individuals, so these murderers and even their descendants must simply figure as a de-individualised mass and in his mind they must remain forever guilty.

Notes

1. Levi, P., *If This is a Man* (New York: Abacus, 1987). The book was first published in 1947.
2. Rubenstein, R.L. and Roth, J.K., *Approaches to Auschwitz: The Holocaust and its Legacy* (Atlanta: John Knox Press, 1987).
3. Voigtlander, N. and Voth, H-J., 'Nazi indoctrination and anti-Semitic beliefs in Germany', *PNAS* 112 (June 2015), pp.7931-7936.
4. This definition of *Der Untermenschen* comes from Hofer, W.(ed.), *From the SS main office. Doc. 157b. Der Untermensch* (1957, p.280), originally published Berlin in 1935. Cited by Pemper, M., trans. D. Dollenmayer, *The Road to the Rescue* (New York: Other Press, 2008), p.106.
5. Cited in Hilberg, R., *The Destruction of the European Jews*, student edition (Boulder CO: Lynne Rienner Publishers, 1985), p.14.
6. Koenigsberg, R. A., *Hitler's Ideology: Embodied Metaphor, Fantasy and History* (Charlotte NC: Information Age Publishing, 2007).
7. Brustein, W.I., *Roots of Hate* (Cambridge: Cambridge University Press, 2003).
8. Hilberg, *The Destruction of the European Jews*.
9. Stone, L., He, D., Lehnstaed, S. and Artzy-Randrup, Y., 'Extraordinary curtailment of massive typhus epidemic in the Warsaw Ghetto', *Science Advances* 6 (24 July 2020), pp.1-8, retrieved from: https://advances.sciencemag.org/content/6/30/eabc0927 (accessed 3 August 2021)
10. 'Louse feeders' were people, who were deliberately infected with typhus carrying lice to produce a vaccine against the disease. Dr Rudolf Weigl, an ethnic German in charge of the experiments tried to give Filip Eisenberg this potentially life-saving job. Eisenberg declined – to his cost. The story of 'louse feeders' is recounted by Arthur Allen, *The Fantastic Laboratory of Dr. Weigl: How Two Brave Scientists Battled Typhus and Sabotaged the Nazis* (London: W.W. Norton & Company, 2015).
11. Filip Eisenberg', retrieved from: https://en.m.wikipedia.org/wiki/Filip_Eisenberg (accessed 4 August 2021)
12. Binet, L., *HHhH* (New York: Vintage, 2013).
13. Fulbrook, M., *Dissonant Lives* (Oxford: Oxford University Press 2007).
14. Cited by Pemper, M., trans. D. Dollenmayer, *The Road to Rescue*, p.173.
15. Ibid., p.188.
16. Ibid., p.183
17. Sereny, G., *Into That Darkness: From Mercy Killing to Mass Murder* (New York: Random House, 1974), p.100.

18. Levi, P., *The Drowned and the Saved* (Abacus Books, 1989).
19. Sereny, *Into That Darkness*.
20. Sadler, G., 'The Banality of Philosophy: A Response to Massimo Pigliucci by Kevin Kennedy', *Modern Stoicism* (5 January 2019), retrieved from: https://modernstoicism. com/the-banality-of-philosophy-a-response-to-massimo-pigliucci-by-kevin-kennedy/ (accessed 5 August 2021)
21. Arendt, H., *Eichmann in Jerusalem* (London: Faber, 1963).
22. Laura Spinney, 'Why help a torturer come to terms with their past?', *New Scientist*, July 2017.
23. Snyder, T., *Black Earth* (London: Bodley Head, 2015).
24. Wachsmann, N., *KL: A History of the Nazi Concentration Camps,* Reprint edition (New York: Farrar, Straus and Giroux, 2016).
25. Hilberg, *The Destruction of the European Jews*, p. 288.
26. Browning, C., *Ordinary Men: Reserve Police Battalion 101 and the Final Solution in Poland* (New York: HarperCollins, 1992).
27. Westermann, E.B., 'Stone-Cold Killers or Drunk with Murder? Alcohol and Atrocity during the Holocaust', *Holocaust and Genocide Studies*, Vol. 30, Issue 1 (Spring 2016), pp.1-19.
28. Savit, G., *Anna and the Swallow Man* (Vancouver: Ember Random House, 2017).
29. Sands, P., *East West Street* (London: Weidenfeld and Nicholson, 2016).
30. 'Holocaust by bullets' retrieved from: https://www.ushmm.org/information/exhibitions/ online-exhibitions/special-focus/desbois (accessed 26 April 2021)
31. Rubenstein, R.L. and Roth, J.K., *Approaches to Auschwitz: The Holocaust and its Legacy* (Atlanta: John Knox Press, 1987), p.137.
32. Hilberg, *The Destruction of the European Jews*, p.276.
33. Browning, *Ordinary Men*.
34. Goldhagen, D., *Hitler's Willing Executioners* (New York: Alfred Knopf, 1996).

9

After the War

'That I survived the Holocaust and went on to love…to talk, to write, to have toast and tea and live my life – that is what is abnormal.' Elie Wiesel[1]

My mother and grandfather returned to Kraków in May 1945, several months before my father. For them, Kraków exerted an emotional pull. For me too, tears come when the aeroplane touches the runway, so I can imagine their joy of seeing Kraków again after six years of such a harrowing absence.

To their surprise, they found the city unchanged and almost unscathed. One witness, returning there at the same time, wrote: 'A vibrant city! Shining windows, perfect pavements, untouched roofs…With people walking here and there in decent coats with leather collars.'[2] It is not clear how Kraków came to be spared the devastation that befell Warsaw and Poznań. The explanation I was given in my early history lessons was that Kraków was saved by the strategic genius of the Red Army, led by the heroic Marshal Ivan Konev. In post-Communist Poland, the more common view is that the Germans had no intention of destroying the city: 'the risk of being encircled was substantial', so they fled only blowing up a couple of bridges 'to secure a safe line of retreat'.[3] Another possibility is that the Nazis considered Kraków to be *urdeutsch*, essentially German, and they did not wish to bomb one of their own. Warsaw by contrast had not been part of the Austro-Hungarian Empire and anyway the Nazis considered it to be a nest of Polish resistance. Or maybe Kraków was spared because it provided an essential train and road link between Germany and the East, and its hospitals could be used to treat German casualties.

Of course, Kraków was 'home' to Jadwiga and Alfred, but where were they to live? Their flat in Mikołajska had been requisitioned, so my grandfather went on a recce to see which of his pre-war acquaintances were still alive. He found his old friend Hugo Haber on Florjanska 51, in the same flat which they had owned before the war. Hugo must have welcomed them because that is the address that my grandfather gave on one of his identity cards. Hugo Haber was a Jewish lawyer, married to an influential German lady (she always spoke Polish with a heavy German accent) and through her influence he must have escaped the worst of the atrocities. Before the war, the Habers had suffered a terrible tragedy, when their small son Kubuś died from a childhood illness. I used to visit them in the early 1950s in their elegant flat on one of the most beautiful of Kraków's streets and still carry an indelible memory of the bedroom in which little Kubuś used to sleep. They preserved it unchanged, sometimes with candles burning, as a shrine. My mother always marvelled how they managed to survive in such a time warp, given the traumas that had shaped her wartime. They were very kind to us when I was growing up. Since I know where little Kubuś is buried in the Rakowicki cemetery (now reunited with his parents), I sometimes leave him a flower and a stone.

My father returned to Kraków in July 1945. Unlike my mother, who at least had her beloved father, Artur had no-one. The writer and psychoanalyst, Dr Victor Frankl, himself an Auschwitz survivor, has a very thoughtful analysis of what prisoners felt after peace was declared on 8 May 1945.[4] The liberation which has been for so long a beautiful dream became to many a disillusionment, and even plunged some into what he calls 'an existentialist vacuum'. Like Frankl, my father would have 'travelled in his mind to the home which he had seen for years in his mind and pressed the bell...'. Yet he knew there was no such place anymore and no one there to await him. I am sure that the first thing he would have done on his return to Kraków would have been to look for surviving members of his extended family. He must have been relieved to find his uncle Aleksander alive, so it is probably to him that he would have turned for physical and emotional help.

Out of 68, 5000 Jewish inhabitants of pre-war Kraków (and surroundings) a mere 4,000 returned in 1945.[5] Slowly, throughout that summer, my father searched for his old peer group among the remnants of a once thriving community. Some emerged from hiding; a significant proportion owed their life to Schindler or other 'righteous gentiles'; some, having been imprisoned by the Soviets, returned from Siberia; only a handful, like my father, had survived multiple concentration camps. Survivors' names were posted on notice boards in the newly-resurrected Jewish Council offices, and my father scanned them eagerly. He now learned that his brother Ludwik was alive in London, living with a new girlfriend (who became my aunt Jasia). There were not many others. His cousins Edwin and Inka (Aleksander's adult children) survived, but they were not in Kraków at the time.

When Artek met Jaga, who was also searching among the ruins of her shattered past, it seemed inevitable that they must marry. What brought them together was not love, but the fact that they had made it and were alive. They did not then know yet how seriously scarred they both were, how difficult to live with. However, any misgivings that my mother might have had about the match were tempered by her mother's past approval of Artur when he had visited the Reiner family home in their student days. He was handsome, from a good family and hard-working.

I asked my mother much later when I was an adult why she restricted herself to finding a marriage partner from such a small band of damaged survivors. Her reply did not come as a surprise. 'The others were all antisemites', she said. For my mother it was antisemitism and not faith that defined her Jewishness. Even after the war, after all the Jews had been through, they were still subjected to random acts of brutality and organised mass pogroms. The most violent was the Kielce pogrom in which 42 returned survivors were murdered.[6] A pogrom also took place on their very doorstep in Kraków in August 1945. The *Kupa* synagogue in Kazimierz was stoned and then set on fire, and several simultaneous acts of violence against Jews took place by gangs of antisemitic hooligans. Later it was revealed that many of the attackers were Polish policemen and soldiers, and that Polish militiamen sanctioned the violence.[7] Obviously *Żydki* (Yids) despite their diminished numbers, were still thought of as unfinished business.

Artur and Jadwiga were married on 15 January 1946, in front of witnesses: Aleksander Bieberstein and Hugo Stefan Haber. On the beautiful photo taken that day, which I show on the front cover, they seem pleased to have found each other; yet my father's hand is clenched, not caressing, my mother's gaze steady but questioning. It is hard to believe that this photo was taken a mere 8 months after liberation. I can't but help feel proud of them both – for surviving.

Their married name to start with was Bieberstein. I was conceived within a few days of their marriage, and with this new responsibility to consider, they decided to ease my passage through life by taking on gentile sounding name, legally this time. They chose the name from a work of Polish literature. Henryk Sienkiewicz, the famous Polish author for whom their street was named, offered a good start. In the novel *Krzyżacy* (Crusaders) there is a noble warrior character, called Jurand, who fought against the Teutons. That seemed spot on. Jurand (pronounced Yurand) sounded good and international too. It is a pity that they did not consider how it would sound in English. The name change took place shortly before my birth, so sadly I never bore the family name of Bieberstein.

In 1946 my father testified at the trial of Amon Göth in front of the Highest Supreme National Tribunal of Poland 27 August to 5 September in Kraków, just two months before I was born. The HEART transcripts translated on the internet (Parts I, II and III)[8] made no mention of my father, so I started to doubt whether he might have been mistaken in his memories of the event, but I eventually found the full transcript of the trial (in Polish) in the Wiener library. After reading through over 300 harrowing pages, I found the testimony of Artur Bieberstein – on pages 321-327. I have translated it in the Appendix. Göth was sentenced to death by hanging for 'crimes against humanity' and 'genocide' (a word newly coined by Lemkin[9]). He was executed on 13 September 1946 in the Montelupich prison, aged 37. This was the very same prison where my grandfather, Marek, had been jailed six years earlier. When my father was interviewed by Thea Jourdan of the *Scotsman* in 1995, he said 'I went to see him hang.' My mother read of this with horror. 'What a heartless man', she said – and she did not mean Göth. I have often wondered why my father had wanted to witness this final act of vengeance. Was it to achieve closure? He knew my mother would not have approved, so he did not tell her.

I was born on 31 October 1946 and named Maria Kazimiera, but called Marzenka. Maria was a common Polish name, but it was also often given to Jewish girls. Furthermore, it paid homage to my mother's saviour, the Virgin Mary. Marzenka had at its root the word *marzenie* or dream, bringing to mind the child they had both dreamt of in their darkest moments. The first three letters of my name also honoured Marek, my paternal grandfather, while Kazimiera was my maternal grandmother's name. I was, of course, baptised. My mother, who had to buy a baptismal certificate to survive, was quick to ensure that I got one free.

When I was about two years old, we moved from Sienkiewicz Street, which was my first address, to the flat that I grew up in on Shopena 12. The flat was rented; you could not legally buy property in these early Communist days, but my parents paid a hefty *łapówka* (backhander) to get it from the corrupt officials who allocated housing. It had three rooms, a kitchen and a bathroom, and an alcove off the kitchen for the maid. The maid that my parents hired was called Anielcia or Nela. She was a country girl and was only 18 when she first came. What she might have lacked in education, she made up in innate practical intelligence, integrity and warmth. She was a wonderful companion and we adored and respected her. Now in her nineties, she lives in Nowa Huta, a suburb of Kraków, and faithfully tends my grandfather's and mother's grave. She is a truly exceptional human being.

The other person whom I worshiped and adored was my grandfather Alfred, my only grandparent to survive the Holocaust. He was a positive influence in all our lives – sunny of disposition, generous in both spirit and gifts. As a grandmother now, I am honoured to be an important person in the lives of three wonderful teenagers in London and two engaging little people in Edinburgh. The fact that I love them is understandable, but the fact that they love me back is a source of unexpected delight. Plenty of people have lost their grandparents to disease, but it was Hitler who stole three of mine.

My parents worked. My mother was a clinical chemist in Professor Tempka's laboratory on Kopernika Street, 15. She stayed there until 1958. My father initially took up his old profession as a pharmacist, first in the *Pod Złotym Tygrysem* Pharmacy (Under the Golden Tiger) for a year and then in the *Pod Słoncem* Pharmacy (Under the Sun), for another year. This second place of work was the very same one from which he had been summarily dismissed in February 1940, soon after the Germans occupied Kraków. It was staffed by some of the same people, and they were delighted to see that he had survived. Between 1946 and 1949, while still working at the pharmacy, he enrolled at the Jagiellonian University, to continue his interrupted doctoral studies in the Department of Biology and graduated with a PhD in 1949. From then on until 1957, when he left Kraków, he worked, first as an assistant lecturer, then a lecturer, then (from 1952) a reader (*docent*) in the University's Biology and Embryology Department. Like many professional people at the time, he joined the Communist Party. His swift progression in academia would not have been possible without it. (In pre-war Germany, academic advancement had also depended on membership of the party – in this case the Nazi Party).) In addition to his main job, he also fulfilled the role of Rector at the College of Physical Education (*Akademia Wychowania Fizycznegoim. Bronisława Czecha w Krakowie*). It was in that capacity that he and I accompanied his students on a water-sport holiday in the Polish Great Lakes in the summer of 1956.

The communist party membership offered other privileges too: special shops which stocked generally unavailable goods, special health service, access to good schools like the one I went to, and annual holidays. For several years running we went to Łeba on the Baltic coast where I browned on the beach, paddled in the sea, collected sea-shells and went on night-time walks lit by fire-flies. For the remaining period of my summer holidays my parents would book lodgings for Nela and me in the foothills of the Tatras. We went to Rabka, Wisła, Krynica and Myslenice, all near enough for my parents to join us for weekends. On one of these holidays, when I was about 8, we happened upon a staunchly antisemitic landlady. She told us that she 'saw with her own eyes' Jews murder a Christian child to make matzas. She thought that the death of 6 million innocent Jewish lives was just retribution; the only trouble was that Hitler did not finish the job. The landlady looked at me rather suspiciously and asked Nela if I was a Jewish child. 'No, of course not', she replied, but just to be sure, Nela taught me a few Catholic prayers. Then at night whenever the landlady was around, I would be made to recite them loudly kneeling by the open door. It must have worked because the rest of the holiday passed uneventfully. However, as I repeated the Hail Marys I debated silently with myself what this ritual murder was all about. After all blood was so red and matzas so white.

With my beloved Nela, 1950

On one of my holidays in the foothills of the Tatras, 1951

The other thing that Nela taught me on our walks in the woods was the joy of foraging for mushrooms. As a country girl she was an expert and knew not only which ones were good and which poisonous, but also the best ways to cook and preserve them. It was without a doubt this early experience with her that later inspired me to study fungi professionally, and to continue to consider foraging as one of my favourite pastimes. Kraków too offered all manner of adventures. In June there were *Wianki*, where candle-lit flower wreaths are floated down the river Wisła, colourfully re-enacting a pagan fairy tale. There were visits to the church with Nela to bless the eggs, ham and sugar sheep in my Easter basket and to the local market to have our milk churns filled. Nela always commanded respect and knew how to get the freshest, creamiest, unwatered-down milk. Street sellers offered *obwarzanki* (a cross between a bagel and a pretzel) and *oscypki* (salty, smoked sheep's cheese shaped like a spindle, made in the Tatras). I craved them terribly, but my mother usually forbade them because they had been touched by unwashed hands and might spread TB. My parents insisted that all food had to be washed and then boiled to death and yet Nela managed to cook wonderful meals without any recipes. And she sang Polish folk songs and the latest hits from the radio, enveloping my young childhood in song, love, and laughter.

While Nela was responsible for my love of foraging, it was my father who encouraged my love of the living world. He drew animals and plants to make play cards, and taught me their names in Polish and Latin. *Tussilago farfara*, he would chant, enunciating each letter clearly. In the autumn he and I would set out at dawn to pick shiny conkers from Park Krakowski. I knew those horse chestnut trees intimately and on a recent visit I re-found them; amazingly, they are still there. His favourite tree of all was *Ginkgo biloba*, the memory tree he called it, and rejoiced every time he found it. In the last few years of his life, he took extracts of it in pill form in the hope that it would enhance his memory. I doubt its efficacy in that respect, but admire its ancient place in plant evolution and human culture.

My school in Oleandry was a beautiful 1930s building. (During the war it had served as the Headquarters of the Gestapo.) It had steps leading up to wide entrance doors, spacious light-filled rooms and polished parquet floors. Every morning I stood to attention in the school hall in front of the eagle (divested of its crown) and the twin photos of Stalin and Bierut (Polish Communist leader and NKVD agent), lustily singing first the *Internationale*

With my parents in Łeba, 1954

and then the Polish anthem. When Stalin died in 1953, we all cried. The atrocities he had committed, which in terms of casualties were greater even than Hitler's, were not part of the curriculum. Nor was the Holocaust. Instead, we learned about the merits of collective ideology, the peasants' ownership of the land and the 5-year plans. My first ever school project (I always did love projects, my own and my children's) was to make a propaganda poster celebrating Lenin's triumphant overthrow of the Tsarist regime. I remember illustrating it with a waving red flag, hammer and sickle, and the word 'Revolution' written in Cyrillic. In retrospect, it is interesting to compare our lack of awareness to Stalin's atrocities to that of German citizens' ignorance of Hitler's evil deeds 10 years earlier.

In 1955 I became a member of the Young Communist League, a *harcerka*, proud of my red neckerchief. Since I started nursery as a 4-year-old, I had been indoctrinated daily in the ideals of communism, and swallowed it hook, line and sinker, too young to realise that idealist regimes

Newspaper article of the 'promise' day, 2 April 1955. In the foreground is my best-ever teacher, Pani Polo; I recited a poem, we sang songs; I glowed with patriotic zeal.

have a way of becoming totalitarian nightmares. As a daughter of a party member, I was expected to join the League, and my father seemed to accept this as a necessity. Yet 4 years later he was seriously reluctant to allow me to join the Girl Guides – probably because it offered no extra privileges, but also maybe he feared that I would talk to the others and disclose my Jewishness.

I want to tell you a little bit more about my wonderful teacher, Pani Polo. We had her for all 4 years of primary school. She taught us the basics, simply and clearly, she taught us to memorise and recite poetry, to take pride in our presentations, and above all to ask questions. Every week she would put up a poster on the board, and then she would say, 'Now, what questions would you like to ask about this picture?' I vividly remember a poster of a country scene with a river and sheep in the foreground and a skein of geese flying in a V formation in the sky. I said, 'that goose at the tip of the V, is it always the leader, or do they change over?' I still remember my pleasure and pride when she took out a notebook and registered a 5 (the top mark) in her jotter. It was a method of teaching which I adopted much later in my undergraduate classes. I would show students a data set

The 'promise day'; my father must have been there to photograph the occasion. I am third from the left. One of my best friends, Ania Bien, is furthest to the right. It is interesting that she is not wearing a necker. Her friends probably did not let her join the Communist League.

and say, 'What questions would you like to pose to the researchers that produced these data?' Asking questions is a fundamental skill, yet our examination system rewards answers, not questions. I once gave a lecture to the Higher Education Academy on this very topic, dedicating my lecture to Pani Polo.

Although Stalin died in 1953, his influence took a couple of years to wane. It received a body blow in February 1956 when Khrushchev exposed his abuses of power and publicly denounced him. From my perspective, one of the best things about the Polish regime in the Stalin period was the ban on state religion. Until 1956 no religion was taught at school, but then in October came what historians call the 'Gomułka's thaw'. It was not as dramatic as the Hungarian Revolution of 1956, but socially its effects were profound. One of Gomułka's liberalisation measures was the reinstatement of religious education in schools, and for me this had unhappy consequences As a Jewish child (how Jewish was I?) I was excluded from Catechism lessons, and prayers. I remember spring of 1957 as a particular turning point because the priests instructing my Catholic friends for their First Communion told the Easter story from the perspective of Matthew (27: 25), making no excuses for Christ's betrayal by the Jews. Other political issues were exacerbating the 'us versus them' divide. About the same time a Muscovite Jew called Jakub Berman was linked with Stalinist atrocities and removed from office, causing an antisemitic backlash.

From the foreign city of Edinburgh my mother wrote the following in her memoir:

> It was heart-breaking when a day came when I suddenly realised that my country does not want me anymore, that people look upon me as a foreigner. Ten years after the defeat of Hitler, ten years after six million Jews went into the gas chambers, a new wave of Nazi-ism was sweeping the country…Now most Poles even those who were not antisemites expected us to leave. Friends and colleagues watched me with sympathy, but their eyes asked, 'Why are you still here?'…Nobody ever said. 'Why should you go? You belong here with us.'

> More and more alarming events took place. My ten-year old daughter has experienced her first humiliation. While on a winter school course, the girls in the course passed a resolution that they did not want to sleep with Jewesses in the same room, so they transferred all the Jewish girls into a ghetto dormitory.

The incident is etched indelibly in my mind. My Jewish friend wet her bed. Some gentile girls started to tease her and a fight broke out. In the end this trivial incident became an 'us versus them' dispute. The teachers' response was to 'ghettoize' the dormitories, making us move our bedclothes and belongings. When my mother went to the school to complain about the incident, she noticed graffiti on the walls: 'Beat the Jews' and a 'terrifying feeling of homelessness' overcame her. It was soon after that on my way home across Park Krakowski I was followed by a gang of older children shouting in unison 'You killed Jesus Christ. You killed Jesus Christ. You killed Jesus Christ.' I fled home and wept. It was futile to want to belong.

It was about this time that another tragedy struck. My beloved grandfather died, aged only 66. One minute he was there, the life and soul of the party, and the next he was gone, felled by a massive heart attack on the street while walking back to us after a game of bridge. He was buried at Rakowicki Cemetery the day I turned 10 on 31 October 1956. His death, devastating though it was to all of us, meant that there was really nothing to hold us back. It was time to pull up the roots and leave.

'Where shall we go?' they asked. The choices were America, where my father's cousin Jurek Scheck had emigrated, Australia where my parent's best friends Irka and Julek Rutkowski had gone, Canada, where my father's death-march friend Bernard had settled, Israel where we already had many relatives or the UK where my father's brother Ludwik lived. Many of my Jewish friends were leaving or were soon intending to leave. Irenka Krieger had already left for Canada, Ania Bien was about to go to New York, and my cousin Krysia Korczak was going to Israel. I took out my school atlas and forlornly traced my finger round the outlines of these foreign lands.

In 1957 my father settled on the UK because that is where Ludwik was, the only other member of his family left alive. Immigration papers, what we now call visitor visas for the UK, were however, much more difficult to obtain, with no special circumstance exceptions made for Holocaust survivors. The only way in was through the academic route. By then Artur Jurand was a respected biologist, who had written a book and some papers both in Polish and English, so he tried his luck with the British Council. He filled in various forms and was astounded and delighted when the reply came: he was accepted. He packed his bags and leaving us behind, went off in the spring of 1957 to start his UK adventure.

He arrived in London, eager to meet Ludwik, whom he had not seen for 18 years. Ludwik and Jasia were welcoming, warm and generous, but they made it clear that they did not encourage reminiscences or mourning.

By then Ludwik was a Harley Street doctor, with extra private consultation rooms in his house in Earls Court, so my father was put up in a hotel.

A few days later my father presented himself at the offices of the British Council with a letter of introduction to Joseph Needham, a famous Cambridge geneticist with whom he had previously corresponded. 'Sorry', they said, 'Professor Needham is no longer working in this field; he has switched interests to Chinese', they said. 'Why don't you go to Edinburgh and work with Professor Conrad Waddington?'

So that is what brought him (and later us) here, to Edinburgh. My father's letters to my mother describe Edinburgh as a beautiful city, rather like Kraków, but they also tell of his isolation. 'There are only one or two Jewish/Polish families with whom I can talk freely. The Jewish Community is completely alien to me...they are devout to the point of tediousness.' The resident Jews were also completely uninterested in welcoming to their bosom a survivor. They did not understand what he had been through or they did not want to. Rather like his brother and sister-in-law, they reacted to any conversations about 'those dark times' with collective amnesia. Pankiewicz[10] recounts the same experience when visiting friends who had spent the Holocaust years in the US. They liked his book (the first edition published in 1947) but believed that he was simply exaggerating it all. With a faint smile they would say, 'let's forget about these sad matters and drink a toast to our past, our present and our future'.

In contrast to the people my father met socially, his work environment in the Edinburgh Institute of Animal Genetics was refreshingly open-minded. One friend and confidant, whom he valued, was Bill Taylor, who was seemingly never short of time. He and my father talked and talked, late into the night. Later Bill had a family of adorable little girls, who called my father Uncle Arthur, and we loved them. The Institute was a hub for refugees from Nazi Europe, where conversations on all topics flowed easily and freely. Professor Waddington (known as Wad to his colleagues) was not just a brilliant scientist, but a socialist in the old-fashioned sense, with profound sympathies for oppressed Jewish scientists. He offered sanctuary to several, including Charlotte Auerbach (who was my brilliant teacher later on), Henryk Kacser, Barney Woolf, Ruth Clayton and Ulrich Loening. My father was a good microscopist, and therefore indispensable in the expanding fields of embryology and protozoology. It was Wad who supported my father's application to extend his funding and encouraged him to bring his family over from Poland.

My father came back from the UK in February 1958 with the news that we would be winding down our affairs in Kraków and relocating forthwith.

I was devastated at the thought of leaving my home, my best friends, Ania Bień and Joanna Młynarska, my school and of course my Nela. Six decades later Ania Bień, who is my email and Facebook friend, reminded me of an incident that had burned itself on to her young mind. Apparently, my father on his return from the UK had brought with him some boxes of toilet paper. (There was no such luxury in Poland; we used cut-up bits of newspaper.) Ania was so amazed by this novel invention, of soft tissues nestling one inside another in the cardboard box, that she lined her knickers with some tissues and smuggled them home to show her parents.

In the event the toilet paper he had brought only lasted the couple of weeks that it took us to pack our portable belongings into suitcases, a few pieces of our favourite furniture into crates for shipping, and to sew the three diamonds, a legacy from my maternal grandfather, into the hems of my dress. Our prized landscape painting, a Fałat, was put up for sale and I remember gazing at it in the art shop window. I remember the tram ride to the station, waving goodbye to all my favourite sights while weeping silently all the way. My parents said we would return, but deep down I knew this was for good. On the train I clasped my hands around my knees to keep the jewels safe but feared that by doing this I would draw attention to them, that we would be searched, that they would be confiscated, and we would all be imprisoned. The train chugged slowly through Czechoslovakia, Germany, Holland; each border crossing was a nightmare as customs officials entered the train to check us and our papers.

On the Ferry from Hook of Holland to Dover I watched the churning water and thought of the turbulence of the present moment, of my relinquished past and uncertain future and to cheer myself up I thought about the things I was looking forward to in England. These were, in no set order, to meet my uncle and aunt, to eat a banana and to see a working television (black and white of course). I was impressed by my parents' seemingly fluent English as they chatted with the other passengers. In preparation for the UK, I had made my own picture vocabulary in an indexed notebook, but so far only one word proved appropriate. 'Rain', I said to a little old lady beside whom I was standing, and she replied with what I assumed was a volley of weather-related platitudes, but she smiled a lot, and it was a start.

In London I did indeed eat a banana, watch television, and meet my uncle and aunt. They were very kind to me, and I loved them both, even though they were never very keen on children. We also did a lot of sight-seeing. I walked about round the landmarks of London humming the

Internationale, just like I used to do in the streets of Kraków, before my mother shushed me and bid me never to do that again. 'Do you want to get us arrested?' she said. At Madame Tussaud's I experienced a sudden turning point in my conception of world politics when I saw my once revered hero, Stalin, standing opposite Hitler, both guarding the entrance to a room where British champions of peace like Churchill and the Royal Family stood assembled.

'You must never tell anyone you are Jewish. Finally, we are free' were words my mother repeated again and again. In a single rented room with my quarrelling parents, with no English to communicate with and no money to spend, I did not feel at all free. In Poland I had left a happy circle of friends and my beloved nanny. I was seriously homesick. My father, who had always been very strict, became even stricter. He pinned me down for hours each day to learn English by filling in missing words in boring workbooks meant for 7-year-olds.

At 11 I was at the educational crossroads between primary and secondary schools, and without English was unlikely to get into Gillespie's or Boroughmuir (the equivalent of grammar schools). The entrance exam for these, (the 11+), was very competitive, and in any case, it was too late to sit it by the time we arrived in the middle of May 1958. The only state school option available was one that my parents felt would offer poor educational prospects. My father could not afford the school fees for a private school, so he tried his luck with a Jewish charitable foundation. He was delighted to be awarded a small hand-out to pay for my fees, and as soon as he had the money he took me to sit the entrance exam for George Watson's Ladies College in George Square. I remember taking it with a roomful of others who all scribbled away. It was very hard, particularly the long division, which they seemed to do backwards. Somehow, I got in. In fact, they were so keen to have me that they offered me a place the very next day. So, dressed as I was, without a uniform, I was introduced to 30 solemn-looking girls clad in navy blue tunics and invited to eat a truly disgusting lunch of mince, mashed potatoes and processed peas. It was all so very different from my happy Polish school which I had left behind and I thought nostalgically of my best friends eating their crispy rolls filled with succulent Polish ham. However, my teacher, Miss Cowan, was wonderfully kind and patient; she sat me at the back of the class, gave me a magic painting book, and then spent an hour after each school day encouraging me to describe the pictures in words.

In the summer holidays I joined the public library and borrowed Enid Blytons until I had read them all. So, by the end of the holidays, I sort of knew English. When school started up again in September, I joined the first year of senior school, as one of the youngest girls in the class. French was a novelty, which the other girls had already started a year earlier, and then there was a choice of German or Latin. 'You cannot do German', said my father. 'Why not', I asked, though I already knew the answer. 'You can't do it because it is the language of the enemy', he replied. There was no answer to that one, so I did Latin, and I must say I have never regretted it. I cannot remember much vocabulary, but it taught me the rhythm of language and later I found it very useful in biology.

In the autumn of 1958 we moved into our very own house (owned by the bank of course) at 46 Ladysmith Road. It was a two-bedroomed bungalow with a large south-facing garden. The house was freezing and damp, and its small rooms were filled with a job lot of heavy Victorian furniture, acquired for a fiver. It was my parents' home, and they were proud of it. My father enjoyed growing vegetables in the garden, while my mother, who had always wanted to be an architect, drew plans on the backs of envelopes for alterations and extensions. None of her ideas came to fruition as we had no money for any improvements. A few weeks after our arrival in Edinburgh, a truckload of our Polish furniture arrived, including some of my childhood toys. I looked at them in disbelief; it was the beginning of a painful adolescence.

My parents still talked about their wartime experiences endlessly; it was a topic that bound them together, but outside the house the Holocaust was not talked about much, nor was it yet remembered nationally. Even my Jewish friends thought a 'camp' was a fun place where you spent summer holidays and countered my stories by telling me about their parents' rationing privations. The word 'Holocaust' came into common speech much later in the late 1970s and I was not yet familiar with the Hebrew word *Shoah*. Organised remembrance in the form of The National Holocaust Memorial Day on 27 January came in much later in 2001, too late for my father, who may have wanted to participate. My mother, however, was still in hiding as it were, and wanted no part of it. The Jews' equivalent Remembrance Day, Yom Hashoah (its date varies depending on the date of Passover), was instituted much earlier in 1953, but since it was mostly celebrated in synagogues, the few survivors who found themselves in Edinburgh were not invited.

My schooldays passed uneventfully. My father, who had high expectations for me, took charge of my studies, looking over my shoulder as I wrote out my homework. I vividly remember a holiday in an Oban guesthouse, where I was not allowed to read until I had done an hour of a boring Latin exercise. As usual we shared a family room, but it was my mother and I who occupied the double bed.

After 5 years in this country, we were finally eligible to apply for naturalisation. We filled in the necessary forms, supplied the necessary photographs, and became British citizens on 8 March 1964. In those days we did not have to prove our knowledge of English language or history to complete the naturalisation process. In the autumn of 1964, I started my tertiary education at Edinburgh University with fees paid and a small means-tested stipend to cover my subsistence. I still look back nostalgically on these golden years of British education.

I loved the university and that is where I really found my true sense of belonging. Who you were or where you came from was of no importance since all of us were united by the shared love of nature and the sense of wonder it inspired. My parents likewise found solace in their work as scientists. My father achieved a modest international eminence as biologist; he did some seminal research on the effects of thalidomide on limb development, wrote hundreds of well-received scientific papers, a book on Paramecium, and became an honorary professor in the US where he

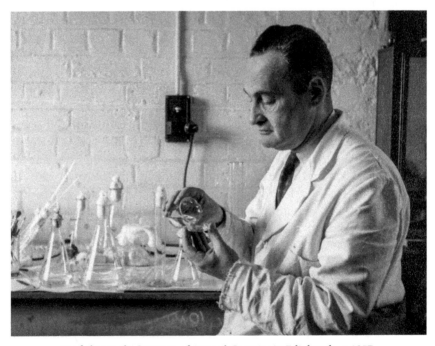

My father in the Institute of Animal Genetics in Edinburgh, c. 1957.

travelled on numerous sabbaticals. He was made an honorary citizen of the state of Tennessee by the governor of that state and was elected a Fellow of Royal Society of Edinburgh in 1970. My mother was known as the 'queen of HPLC' (High Performance Liquid Chromatography), at a time when medical applications of this analytical tool were being developed. Under the inspirational leadership of Professor John Knox, the Wolfson Unit cemented into a friendship group which endures even though its senior members have now died. Surviving members still meet for coffee once a month and include me in her memory.

I have not talked yet about the 'War After'[11]. My parents fought endlessly with each other and the atmosphere at Ladysmith Road was charged and unhappy. My father did not welcome people into his house. If anyone dropped in for tea unexpectedly, my mother and I would be terrified that he would tell them to leave or make a scene. Money was a big point of contention. My father had survived the war by being extremely parsimonious with his rations of bread, and now that he had a little bit of money, he wanted to save it. He once told me off for throwing away a length of redundant tacking thread. He salvaged it from the waste-paper basket and wound it round a piece of cardboard. 'Don't ever assume that you will always have enough', he said. My mother, on the other hand, was too generous in her spending. However, she had something that he completely lacked – a good business head. With their marriage deteriorating (they always, as long as I remember, slept in separate rooms), she invested her savings in a down-payment for a flat in the Marchmont area of Edinburgh. She initially rented it out to students, but in 1975, she moved in herself. I should say that my parents' separation was simply a practical arrangement; they still cared for each other and remained officially married until the end.

When David and I first announced our engagement, neither side of the family approved. My father thought I should buy him a razor; my in-laws said, 'David is marrying a Jewess.' I married David in 1972 and our children Martin and Tim were born in 1973 and 1976. As I described in another chapter, the boys were not circumcised, as neither of my parents were in favour of it, and my husband did not care either way. I decided to adopt my husband's (and my children's surname), rather than keep my maiden name. People said it was confusing that my scientific papers are published under two different names; however, for me Jurand was not my family name, and I did not feel any affinity to it. My married name was not mine either, but was at least real. My father was a stern, but respected Grandad to my sons. He would inspect their nails when he came and cut them with a pair of scissors he always carried. My mother became the adored and adoring Baba

(Polish for Grandmother). She played a large part in our lives, passing on her faith in the power of human love to all of us.

After retirement in 1982, my mother bought another flat, this time near us at 16 Saxe Coburg Street. It was a great help to have her so close. She picked my children up from school, she fed them their favourite snacks; later she taught them to drive (despite being a famously scary driver herself). She also took the children away on holiday to the Channel Islands, to Yugoslavia, skiing in Switzerland and to Poland. My mother was a huge support to Tim during his rebellious phase and became his champion and confidante. She also carefully vetted Martin's girlfriends, pronouncing an opinion on each. When Martin married Samantha and her great-grandchildren, Amy, Evie and Freddie (named after Alfred her father) were born in 2002, 2003 and 2006, she was beside herself with joy. The activity that gave her most pleasure in recent years was buying clothes for the children. She would sit regally in her wheelchair in John Lewis pointing delightedly at racks of old-fashioned dresses for little girls. The last outing was a week before she died, to buy a present for her grandson Freddie's fifth birthday, a T-shirt with a picture which glowed in the dark. If only she had lived to see Tim settled with his lovely wife Beth, and their two adorable small daughters Louise and Elinor, her cycle of life would have been complete.

My father never lived to see his great-grandchildren. How pleased he would have been to know that the family tree, which had been hacked so murderously, had sprouted five new shoots. If he could also have lived to see his grandson, Martin, receive a knighthood from the Queen, his pride would have known no bounds.

My father's heart, which had been failing for at least a decade, slowly ceased to beat in the early days of the new millennium. When he lay dying in the impersonal atmosphere of the Royal Infirmary, I pondered on his extraordinary, improbable life story, and remonstrated with the indifferent doctors that he was not just a number, to save him for another week, another day.

My mother also died of heart disease, but 11 years later. In the last 6 years of her life her condition necessitated almost full-time care. We were very lucky to find Grażyna Bielecka, who became my mother's weekday carer, friend and lifeline. I filled in at weekends. We also sometimes employed Milena Chmielewska to supplement some of the day-time care. Both Grażyna and Milena loved my mother, and my mother shared with them many of her survival stories. Some were new to me, and I have included them here. With their help she was able to live in her own home until 30 hours before she died.

These wonderful paper dresses were made by my granddaughter, Amy Chamberlain in 2018, for her GCSE Art Project. The theme was 'Fragments' and she explored how lots of fragments of stories are passed on through generations. As she explained, 'Baba would always welcome us with a big smile and a hug, as well as vast amounts of food, and she often bought me and my sister little dresses, which she took great pride in choosing.' [12] The hems hold valuables.

Both my parents had humanist cremations, facilitated by the celebrant James Russell (still my Facebook friend). The two funerals were slightly different. For my father, a Kaddish was recited by an observant friend and we requested that the cross above the coffin should be removed for the occasion. For my mother we were again asked whether the cross should be removed or retained. 'Retained', I replied without a trace of hesitation, for I could hear my mother's voice whispering in my ear, 'Why not? It's free.'

Notes

1. Elie Wiesel, Interview with Oprah Winfrey, 2000, retrieved from: https://www.oprah.com/omagazine/oprah-interviews-elie-wiesel (accessed 13 August 2021)
2. 'How Krakow made it unscathed', Culture, PL. Heritage, retrieved from: https://culture.pl/en/article/how-krakow-made-it-unscathed-through-wwii (accessed 20 April 2020)
3. Ibid.
4. Frankl, V.E., *Man's Search for Meaning* (New York: Simon and Schuster, 1997).
5. Pemper, M., trans. D. Dolenmyer, *The Road to Rescue* (New York: Other Press, 2008).

6. Engel, D., 'Patterns of Anti-Jewish Violence in Poland, 1944-1946', Yad Vashem Studies. Yad Vashem, Jerusalem. XXVI., 32, (1998), p..21, retrieved from: https://www. yadvashem.org/odot_pdf/Microsoft%20Word%20-%203128.pdf (accessed 18 April 2020)

7. Konopka, T., 'Śmierć na ulicach Krakowa w latach 1945–1947 w materiale archiwalnym Krakowskiego Zakładu Medycyny Sądowej', *Pamięć i sprawiedliwość*, IPN, nr 2 (2005), p.148.

8. 'The Trial of Amon Goeth' Holocaust Education and Archive Research Team.
Part 1: 'The indictment', retrieved from: http://www.holocaustresearchproject.org/trials/goeth1.html
Part 2: 'Initial Cross Examination and Witness Mr Mieczysław Pemper', retrieved from: http://www.holocaustresearchproject.org/trials/goeth2.html
Part 3: 'Selected extracts from the testimony (of Mr Mieczysław Pemper)', retrieved from: http://www.holocaustresearchproject.org/trials/goeth3.html
(accessed 3 August 2021)

9. Lemkin, R., *Axis Rule in Occupied Europe: Laws of Occupation: Analysis of Government - Proposals for Redress* (Washington, D.C.: Carnegie Endowment for International Peace, 1944), pp.79-95.

10. Pankiewicz, T., trans. G. Malloy, *The Krakow Ghetto Pharmacy* (Kraków: Wydawnictwo Literackie, 2013).

11. I apologise to Anne Karpf for borrowing her words.

12. Amy Chamberlain, 'Special Fragments', *AJR Journal*, 19 (January 2019), p.20.

10

Repercussions

'The years of terror, of barbed wire, of electric fences, they never leave you. You turn in on yourself, hiding in the only Hell you know.' Sam Pivnik[1]

Of course, psychoanalysis, cognitive brain therapy or just simple counselling was not something that concentration camp survivors were offered at the time of their liberation. Nowadays you only have to hear a mildly harrowing tale on radio or television before you are invited to phone an emotional support professional. The Red Cross repaired my father's body in the early summer of 1945, but offered little or no spiritual back-up. The term Post-Traumatic Stress Disorder (PTSD) had not yet been invented. Frankl[2] compares the release of prisoners from concentration camps to a diver's bends, saying, 'Just as the physical health of the caisson worker would be endangered if he left the diver's chamber suddenly…so the man who has suddenly been liberated from mental pressure can suffer damage to his moral and spiritual health'. He goes on to describe how some of the survivors turned to being the oppressor, becoming instigators, not objects, of wilful force and injustice. Many adopted the philosophy that they had the right to do wrong, because wrong had been done to them. I don't think my father ever thought that, but his uncontrollable rages, his recurrent nightmares and his (on occasion) bullying attitude to my mother and me were, I believe, the symptoms of unresolved and untreated damage from the camps.

It has been said that no survivor could have made it through the war without a series of miracles. My mother's war-time adventures can be divided roughly into three phases: the Soviet tenure of Lwów, the German tenure of Lwów, and her 'life as an Aryan on false papers'. My mother survived all three of these phases because she was daring, resourceful and street-wise; she had capacity for guile, deceit and an innate ability to read people's faces. She also survived because people appeared at opportune moments, willing to risk their lives to help another, unknown human being.

Looking back at her story I can enumerate several. There were the two kindly-looking Ukrainian guards who turned a blind eye while she slipped out before being herded onto a death train, the Polish waitress who hung the medallion on her neck, the German director of the glass factory, the director's Polish servant, and another Polish servant who hid her in Warsaw. There would have been numerous others that I never knew about. None of these are lauded as 'righteous gentiles', yet they risked their lives to help her. Their actions not only helped her to survive pivotal moments, but because 'a bit of humaneness in a world become inhuman had been achieved'.[3] Their selfless acts renewed her zest for life and offered what Nietsche called 'a why to live' allowing her to 'bear almost any how'.

My father survived in a different way. Whereas my mother's strategy was to read peoples' faces and to appeal to their emotions, my father's was to avoid eye contact. In his testimony at Göth's trial he describes how looking the man in the eye would almost certainly have cost him his life. Ten per cent of the Jews of Poland survived the war, but that statistic hides the fact that most of the survivors owed their life to their flight or deportation to the Soviet Union.[4] The odds for survival for concentration and extermination victims were much smaller. Statistics for survival of concentration camps vary. 'The statistics show that one in 28 camp inmates survived.'[5] The odds of living through the death march were about 15 per cent (according to my father), so when those two odds are multiplied I realise how awe-inspiringly improbable his survival was. He had experienced starvation, cold, violence, exhaustion and the death of his family and friends. He survived because he was strong and at an optimal age – not too young and not too old. He survived by making himself useful when he could and invisible when he could not. He worked hard and practised self-restraint, keeping his rations for later, conserving his energies when he could. But he also became adept at knowing which were the 'good *kapos*', and which were the ones to avoid. He also was at various stages capable of being what was called in camp parlance an *organizator*', a *kombinator*, and by virtue of being a chemist a bit of a *prominent*. However, to survive required him to build a stiff cocoon around himself to distance himself from the daily atrocities all around him. The cocoon persisted after the war and according to my mother got in the way of emotional closeness between them.

In his autobiographical memoir *The Lucky Child*, Thomas Buergenthal[6] writes 'moral resistance in the face of evil is no less courageous than physical resistance, a point that has frequently been lost in the debate over the lack of greater Jewish resistance during the holocaust'. I have to conclude from both my parents' narratives, that they both exhibited moral, if passive, resistance, and managed to survive without sacrificing their integrity or dignity. Neither was ever what survivors call *Typ po trupach* (the type who walks on corpses). My father was not a *kapo*, not an orderly, not an OD-man, or a block-keeper; he was in his own words, a 'grey prisoner'. At no time could he have been considered a boot-licker or a collaborator. He tried to help whenever he could. He helped Basia, the orphan child, and Dora who Pankiewicz[7] said would have died without his intervention. In the camps survival depended on the moral resources to remain human in the midst of hell. My mother's escape from the train showed an ability to make second-by-second decisions. Living on false papers required an ability to lie and wriggle out of difficult situations. She was not a natural actress, my mother, but she had to become one during her two and a half years of living on someone else's papers. People would ask her about her family and about her neighbourhood so she invented a whole new water-tight history for herself. After the war, this whole way of being, of telling fibs, of bribing, of hiding the truth was difficult to shed. There was, however, never any pretence in her warmth and generosity. She was always intuitively selfless, as for example when she offered her last sugar cube to a starving child.

Survivors' attachment to portable wealth is touched on in other memoirs. I described our exodus journey from Poland to the UK when, with my heart in my mouth, I carried the remaining family wealth in the form of diamond rings sewn into the hems of my dress. Thereafter, they were safely deposited in a bank and survived the various robberies we have had in my parents' home and our own. Jewels were prized, not so you could wear them, but so you could trade them when times are hard. My uncle, who had not really lived through the Holocaust, did it in London. My Israeli relatives did it in Tel Aviv. Statistics are not available on the users of bank safe deposit boxes, but I would not mind betting my bottom dollar that survivors and their descendants are represented disproportionately among them compared to the general population. In his wonderful graphic novel *Maus*, Art Spiegelman[8] illustrates a visit to a bank vault with his father. The conversation with the banker went like this, 'Yes, I have here my son Artie, I want to sign him a key, so he can go also to my safety box.' Then he said to Artie, 'In case anything bad happens to me you must run right away over here. Therefore I arranged for you this key.' I laughed out aloud when I read it in the 1980s because I had just visited the bank with my mother for exactly the same reason, and the words Spiegelman used mirrored my mother's both in content and sentence construction.

My parents read *Maus* too, and admired its artistic merit, but strangely did not appreciate its humour. They themselves would not have wanted to be thus ridiculed. The book touches on some very important issues concerning the effect that the Holocaust had on survivors' subsequent lives. Re-reading it now, 30 years on, I love it still, and am reminded of my mother's voice throughout, including the evocative interjections 'Pft, Pfhe, Hmf, Oy, Acch'.

As Art Spiegelman says, all survivors are 'whacked up in a different way'. His father, like my father, suffered from obsessive stinginess, which is probably an after-effect of the Holocaust. Spiegelman describes how he saw his father pick up pieces of wire in the street, (in case it should come useful), and how he saved matches by leaving the gas on (why not it's already paid for). My father would take his washing to his place of work (why not, as hot water there is free) and collect up the tiniest pieces of soap to boil up in a saucepan to make washing-up liquid for clothes or car washes. Waste management was never an issue because he incinerated everything in our open fireplace. On one memorable occasion he burnt a leaky old hot water bottle filling the house with the smell of burnt rubber. My mother and father disagreed on the subject of money, and conversations between my parents were verbatim just like those between Art Spiegelman's father and his stepmother. My mother, like Art Spiegelman's stepmother, did not save money, she spent it, but she also knew how to invest it – which she did wisely in property just before an economic upturn.

A legacy that the Holocaust drilled into both my parents, and now to me, is the total inability to waste food. If I have two brown bananas, I make a banana loaf (why do I need a banana loaf?). I freeze little bits of uneaten meals in small containers, and then one day lump them all together into a festive UFO (unidentified frozen object) pie. I boil up chicken bones to make stock, and am an obsessive maker of soups, especially from scraps of wilting vegetables or food for free, such as sorrel or nettle. Is this some left-over second generation baggage? I shall never know.

My parents often rowed and disagreed on all manner of subjects, but there was one philosophical issue on which they concurred absolutely. They both categorized people dichotomously: good or bad, us and them, Jew or Aryan, victim or survivor, the vanquished or the victor. This always elicited heated family discussion. I once upset them horribly by saying that I thought the Nazis were also victims, brought up in and by a brutal regime. I tried to see the situation through the Germans' eyes, but the very idea sent shivers down their spines. 'Any of us has the capacity for atrocity, just as we have capacity for heroism', I insisted. 'No', they said, 'They were baaaad'.

Anne Karpf[9] describes the same approach to life in her Holocaust survivor parents. 'Their world had been split into good and bad; if you were not one, you must be the other'. Nelken[10] interprets it a different way: 'the inhuman environment intensified character traits: a bad person tended to become evil, a good one – almost a saint'. Yet another example of this binary attitude is to be found in Victor Frankl's classic work *Man's Search for Meaning* written in 1946, soon after the war. Frankl, a psychotherapist and concentration camp survivor writes: 'From all this we may learn that there are two races of men in the world, but only these two – the race of the decent man and the race of the indecent man. Both are found everywhere; they penetrate into all groups of society.'

Simon Wiesenthal in his autobiographical novel *The Sunflower*[11], recorded the dichotomy poignantly, while at the bedside of a perpetrator: 'I looked around the room and glancing at the window, I saw a part of the sun-drenched courtyard, with the shadow of the roof crossing it obliquely – a boundary between light and dark, a defined boundary without any transition.'

It could be that this way of thinking is a consequence of survivors' experiences. Maybe after having to pass a selection process (left is death, right is life) a dichotomous way of thinking is inevitable. I, on the other hand, had never suffered first-hand, and so I adopted and also taught my children a 'shades of grey' philosophy. My argument went something like this. There were those who felt compassion, but did not act on it, giving you three, not two categories. The third category (the bad Germans) can also be sub-divided into those who simply unquestioningly followed orders and those that revelled in acts of sadism. That already gives you four categories. We can go on sub-dividing until you have a whole sliding scale from goodness to badness. I also insisted that good people can do bad things and vice versa, and that one should uncouple the act from the person. Thus one can act in a way that is good and bad, kind or unkind, thoughtful or thoughtless, but those adjectives describe the act and should not be used to define the person.

Another conversation I had with my father concerned Oskar Schindler, whom he would have met at the JSS, though he did not know him personally. 'What motivated Schindler'? I asked. My father's answer was interesting. 'When I came across him', he said, 'he had the reputation of a *cwaniak* (this best translates as a wide-boy). He thought he would make his fortune employing a cheap Jewish workforce, and he also benefited from all those *łapówki* (bribes) the richer Jews paid him to secure employment in his factory.[12] So when Schindler first confronted his workers, they were just an anonymous mass, but then he came to know them individually, his attitude changed. So, he was a 'Good German', I said. 'Yes', he replied, 'and Göth was a bad German, because he got to know people individually and still he shot them'. There was no getting away from the good and bad dichotomy.

My father, more so than my mother, spoke of the Germans as an undifferentiated malevolent entity. 'It is a nation capable of doing it again', he said in his interview to the *Scotsman* journalist.[13] 'Of course there were some good Germans', he would add to me, when I challenged his view, but they were the exceptions, each deserving to be flagged up with a special mention. So, to my father forgiveness was not a word that could be used in the context of the Holocaust. Until he died, he vetoed all things German. He would not allow me to buy a Volkswagen car, even if his own Ford was the brainchild of a man who wrote and sponsored antisemitic articles and is mentioned most favourably in *Mein Kampf*. When my husband served a fine Alsatian wine, he refused to drink it, claiming that Alsace was culturally German, whoever it belonged to now.

My mother approached modern-day Germans cautiously, using her special personality detection radar. About a year before her death, she refused to have a tooth extracted by a German dentist, and called her *Niemra*, a derogatory term for a German. I disliked that particular dentist too but because of her manner, not because she was a German. I admire Primo Levi's philosophy which remained so refreshingly unaffected by his experiences. He said, 'I cannot tolerate the fact that a man should be judged not for what he is but because of the group he happens to belong to.'[14]

The best exploration of the possibilities and limits of forgiveness is to be found in Simon Wiesenthal's heart-wrenching autobiographical story called *The Sunflower*[15], which I already mentioned throughout this narrative. While interned in Janowska camp (where my mother was brutally beaten while awaiting her deportation), Simon is taken to a makeshift hospital where he is confronted with a wounded member of an *Einsatzgruppe* death squad. The dying SS-man confesses his sins and pleads for Simon's forgiveness. His crime, like the crimes of every other SS-man, is the murder of countless Jews. Simon, chosen as the token Jew, listens patiently, but offers no absolution. As his friend says later, 'what would have given you the right to forgive in the name of the people who had not authorised you to do so?' Nevertheless, Simon is deeply shaken by the experience. Four years later he visits the SS-man's mother but chooses not to enlighten her of her son's guilt. Five decades later he still wonders if he was right not to offer forgiveness, and to this end he asks over 50 people for their opinion. I read this moving book cover to cover right through the night and now so wish that I could discuss it with my parents. Was Simon right not to forgive? Was the forgiveness not in his gift to offer? Or was he wrong not to grant a dying man his last request? Although my parents (to my knowledge) have never read *The Sunflower*, and I never discussed the issue of forgiveness with them directly, I can guess what they might have said. I think my father would have condoned Simon's action and not offered the desired absolution. In his *Scotsman* interview my father said, 'I will never forgive, and I will never forget'.[16] For him to forgive meant to condone. My mother, on the other hand, might well have had other ideas. She was always touched by warmth and might have responded to the dying SS-man's honest humanity.

In my family apologies were rarely demanded. What was important was that you consider your guilt or acts of thoughtlessness seriously and present them fairly and squarely in front of your own conscience. Go on, give yourself a hard time, spend a sleepless night, examine all the what-ifs. The important thing is to confess to yourself because if you don't then you will not have learned from the experience. To confess to a disinterested third party, like you do in the Catholic Church, to be granted pardon upon the recitation of some oft-repeated words, is considered to be a cheap cop-out. I now wonder whether this approach to morality in my family was a left-over of my parents' Holocaust past, or maybe its basis lay in the intrinsic difference between a Christian and Jew, however atavistic their beliefs have become. Interestingly one of Wiesenthal's distinguished guests asked for their opinion in *The Sunflower* (Eva Fleischner), who used Wiesenthal's dilemma in her teaching of students, found a significant discrepancy between the opinions of Christian and Jewish students. The former, almost without exception, were in favour of forgiveness, whereas the latter were not. A similar observation is made by a religious Jewish respondee, Dennis Prager, though he explains the discrepancy using the basic Judaic law that only the victim can forgive, and since the murdered have no voice, the matter of forgiveness does not come into it. The Christians believe that that however bad you act, God still loves you. That philosophy is alien to most Jewish people, and it is certainly complete anathema to me.

I want to relate a short vignette that touches on this subject from 40 years ago when my two sons were boisterous 6 and 4-year olds. Some of the neighbourhood children belonged to a worthy Christian organisation called the Crusaders (now known under the name of Urban Saints). I suffered one or two qualms of hypocrisy when I agreed to let my boys join them, but I have to confess that the promise of a quiet Sunday afternoon was my main incentive. The boys came home with prizes, a pencil each, and a magazine that looked like the Jehovah's Witnesses' *Watchtower*. It was in fact called by some other name, which I don't remember, but the grainy paper and the typeface were the same. On the back page were 4 cartoons. One showed a boy slitting a bus seat with a penknife, on another a boy was slitting a bicycle tyre, on the third a girl was pick-pocketing, and in the fourth a boy was scratching a car with a key. Underneath each and every one of them was a big caption 'And Jesus Still Loves Me.' I can't help wondering if modern-day Urban Saints still produce pamphlets with messages which condone such anti-social urban activities and crime. A Christian theologian with whom I recently discussed this topic said that I was being inconsistent, for if I believe, as I say I do, that it is the act that is wrong, not the person, then obviously Jesus can still love an evil-doer. He may be right philosophically, but at the time I did not consider the finer points of theology, and simply withdrew my children from the organisation.

Much has been written about the second generation's symbiotic ties with their parents. Without a doubt my parents were overprotective, overambitious and over-controlling. I could not leave them to go away to university somewhere else, because for them the umbilical cord was still short, and separation would have seemed like a loss. Once, on an undergraduate expedition to the Spanish Pyrenees, I found a Spanish policeman peering into the tent, sent by my parents to check on me. They had reported me missing because I had not phoned for three days. This very much fits in with the psychologist's, Joan Freyberg's, view that survivor parents regard their children's individuation as another familial loss.[17] I regret to say that I have inflicted the same intrusive parenting approach to my own children, until both rebelled in their different ways.

Anne Karpf in her lovely book *The War After*[18] also ascribes the symbiotic relationship which she had with her parents (also from Kraków) to the Holocaust. However, she includes in the syndrome a couple of other characteristics, which I believe have nothing to do with survivor trauma. One is the fear of draughts, and another is the 'blame culture'. I shall describe what we mean by these, because both she and I suffered from them (through our parents), but I have to disagree with Anne Karpf that they have anything to do with the Holocaust. The fear of draughts is at its worst when applied to small children, who are molly-coddled way beyond their years and have to be kept warm at all times. My children will testify how my mother repeatedly bemoaned the lack of '*vool*', especially on her great-grandchildren. The blame culture is best characterised by the words *bo ty...* ('because you...'). Whenever I admitted to a personal failing, my mother's reaction was to blame and criticise, rather than to sympathise or console.

However, both these characteristics are purely Eastern European and are not limited to survivors or Jews.

Another 'second generation' memoir which I read with great interest was Eva Hoffman's *Lost in Translation*[19] when it was published in the 1990s. Eva and I were contemporaries and neighbours in Kraków and even went to the same school, though a year apart. We also left Poland (she for Canada, I for the UK) at approximately the same time in 1958. It seems strange that we did not know each other as children, but without a doubt our early lives were shaped by the same experiences: the dark cloud of the Holocaust, the communist ethos, and the love of the same books (*W Pustyni in W Puszcy* and *Anne of Green Gables* – in Polish). We played separately in Park Krakowski, yet the shared memory of the weeping willow still moves us both to tears. Eva Hoffman later reflects on the effects of the Holocaust on survivors, their descendants and subsequent world events in an incisive series of essays *After Such Knowledge*[20], written after her parents' death. This 'Knowledge', which was dripped 'intravenously' throughout our early childhood and adolescence, has left us both with a heavy 'sense of responsibility for the past'. Of course, she has discharged her sense of responsibility for the past admirably in all her many writings, but for me it has remained as an unresolved burden which I knew I had to set down publicly on paper before I could let it go.

I loved Eva Hoffman's and Anne Karpf's books (I even imposed them on my reading group), and I remember feeling at the time that they had absolved me from writing my own second generation narrative, mirroring as they did, many of my own feelings and experiences. My parents, who were still alive when they were published, read them too but were not as impressed as I was. They thought that the authors of both these books indulged in too much navel gazing. Like Anne Karpf's and Eva Hoffman's parents, my parents never thought of themselves as psychologically damaged, and would have been outraged at the idea that I was blaming them for my neuroses. How could I, who had not been through it, complain about second generation effects; to blame my maladjustment on their past experiences seemed a bit like accusing them of bad parenting.

Neither of my parents read about trans-generational transmission of trauma (TTT), which has been the topic of numerous scientific studies – most published after my parents' deaths. As a geneticist, my father would have understood the epigenetic effects of methylation, a sort of chemical coating on the chromosomes, brought about by environmental stress or major emotional trauma, and passed down through the generations.[21] Am I thus marked epigenetically? Does this explain my vulnerability?

My father would probably have been less impressed by the theory of 'trans-generational haunting', formulated by the Hungarian psychoanalysts Abraham and Torok,[22] who claim that traumas that have not received a proper burial can be passed down the generations. Gabriele Schwab similarly explores echoes that reverberate through the generations in her book *Haunting Legacies*[23] drawing on evidence of both Holocaust victims and perpetrators.

Most survivors have dealt with their traumas stoically. Now for all the good reasons enumerated above, it is their children and grandchildren, who have to address their Holocaust ghosts. They write newsletters (e.g. *Voices*), organise a Facebook group,[24] arrange international conferences and outings to Holocaust museums and concentration camps. All of us second generation 'victims', for that is what we feel we are, appear to be in need of some resolution. I am now seeking it by writing it all down. Some do it by holding out her hands in forgiveness to present day Germans by taking up German citizenship.

My parents did not really do organised religion, but perhaps they might have done had it not been for the Holocaust. For both of them the idea of a redemptive God was killed stone dead by their experiences, but then I don't think either of them had what Dawkins' followers call a strong 'gene for God'. (There is of course no single gene, for religiosity is inherited in a multi-factorial way, rather like height or skin colour.) The effect of the Holocaust on peoples' attitude to their faith is one that fascinates me, so I scoured different survivor memoirs and testimonies. Survivor Elie Wiesel, who started off as a devout practising orthodox Jew, lost his faith completely, as he describes in his beautiful Nobel prize-winning memoir *Night*: 'Never shall I forget those flames that consumed my faith forever. Never shall I forget the nocturnal silence that deprived me for all eternity of the desire to live. Never shall I forget those moments that murdered my God and my soul and turned my dreams to ashes...'[25]

On one occasion, when witnessing a public hanging, someone asked 'Where is God?' A voice from within Elie Wiesel answered, 'This is where – hanging here from the gallows.' Elie later describes how when the other inmates celebrated Rosh Hashanah in the autumn of 1944, he felt a void. 'In the midst of all these men assembled for prayer. I felt like an observer, a stranger.' Rita Goldberg in her second generation memoir *Motherland*[26] describes her mother's loss of faith movingly: 'For her God had died long ago, and was buried with the innocent ashes of her parents and of so many others in some tainted corner of the earth where evil had finally won.'

A similar reaction was experienced by the survivor Ernest Levy. He remembers sitting half-dead on a camp latrine asking God to act: 'Surely if there is a time to act, God, now is the time.' His pleas remained unanswered. He finishes his memoir[27] with some very wise words in a chapter called 'Challenging God'. His camp experiences caused him to abandon his blinkered religious dogma of the orthodox faith and replace it with a much more refreshing, almost humanist approach. When asked 'What is God?' he replied, 'God is part of us. He is the imperceptible in our existence, the spiritual dimension in us.' With this view he continued to practise as a reverend and a cantor in his new Scottish homeland of Glasgow.

Simon Wiesenthal reports cynically that 'God was on leave' in the Holocaust, not just for the victims, but also the perpetrators. He believes that National Socialism had robbed people of their God and replaced him with the Führer. But what did they think the words *Gott mit uns* meant? There it was holding up their trousers, engraved on their belt buckles as they went on to commit their unspeakably sadistic crimes.

Some survivors still retained their fundamentalist views of God as a meter out of punishments and rewards. A view that makes me shudder in horror is that the Holocaust was God's punishment. Apparently, the Torah says (so I am told) that Jews, having been expelled from the Holy Land for blaspheming God, could only redeem themselves if God punished them for their transgressions. All I can say is that the fact that people can think that way is the best evidence there is for Dawkins' genetically hard-wired religiosity. I have tried to engage with the more enlightened religious Jews on this topic, but they mostly decline to discuss it. A few substantiate their innate religious feelings with the logic that to deny their God after all they had suffered is to confer upon Hitler the ultimate victory. I take their point. To many any talk of God in the context of the Holocaust makes a mockery of both their God and what happened because Shoah was the fault of Man, not God.

Nevertheless, a few orthodox survivors retained their faith, despite their experiences. Pearl Benisch[28] describes how she derived comfort during the horrendous days of the camps from memorised passages of the Torah, particularly King David's sufferings, while pleading her case before the Almighty. She sees her own survival as an affirmation that God exists because her prayers were after all answered.

In post-war Kraków there was really no religious Jewish life to speak of – though there must have been some, because someone made matzos, which my father produced secretly every Pesach, wrapped in plain paper, so that no-one would see what they were. I loved them, and the fairy-tale story of redemption and freedom which they symbolised. Although we never celebrated Pesach or read the Haggadah, my parents were both partial to gefilte fish, made from carp that swam in our bath. I thought of it as a pet and cried when it met its end on the kitchen table.

We never went to a synagogue, and I do believe that my mother had never set foot in one before the war or since. When we came to the UK, my father did go once a year on Yom Kippur and fasted, not because he believed in God, but to venerate his lost family. To my mother the Jewish God and the Catholic God were the same, as indeed he is, but he had failed her. The Virgin Mary, however, was something else. She had returned the medallion which had saved her to the kind waitress but bought another which she regularly wore round her neck. This one, like the original, had both the Virgin Mary and Baby Jesus, a beautiful, empathetic symbol of mother love. She did not care so much for the cross. 'Why would you want to wear an instrument of torture round your neck', she would say. On the odd occasion when my mother went to Jewish gatherings, such as the Association of Jewish Refugees, she would slip the medallion neatly to the back of her neck, to avoid having to explain its significance.

I grew up confused about God, Jesus, and the Holy Ghost (who he?), and Mary's virginity, once I understood what that meant, left me a bit puzzled. I knew nothing at all about Judaism. Even now my grandchildren know more than I do from their comparative religion lessons. When at the age of 12 I joined the Girl Guides, which I did despite my father's protestations (all those insignia gave him the creeps), you had to swear allegiance to God and the Queen and declare a religious affiliation. Jews were not something that the guiders or the guides had heard of, except in a negative way from the New Testament, so the choice had to be Catholic or Protestant. The highlight of the year for me was the summer camp, where we sang songs round a camp-fire and slept in tightly regimented tents. I loved it. Recently I found this little memoir written by my 13-year-old self:

> On Sunday we had to go to church. 'You are Polish, so you must be Catholic. You will go to church with the other girls,' said the guider. I said nothing. All the other Catholic girls have had their First Communion and went to confession each week. They discussed their experiences in the tent at night. Crikey, that meant they would be taking communion. I spent a sleepless night. We cycled to the church on bicycles specially hired for the day, and as I cycled, I agonised about what I should do. If I followed meekly and took it too, would I ever be found out? Found out that I am a fraud, an interloper; that again I did not belong? In the end I sat at the back of the church, and

nobody commented that I did not go with the others. Maybe they knew? Had they had found me out?

I was so desperate to belong somewhere that I tried out both the Polish and the Jewish communities. I joined a Polish youth club and learned Polish dances and performed in Polish shows which we staged for the benefit of our Polish parents until I once overheard some Polish children describing a shopkeeper as a *Parszywa Żydówka* (a scabby Jewess), and another time someone was said to have hooked nose 'like a hundred Jews'. But it was in the Jewish community that I really stood out like sore thumb. Not speaking Yiddish, yet from Europe, I was a suspect Jew anyway. 'You are Jewish?' they would say with the typical Yiddish intonation. 'Not very, but Hitler would have thought so', I would answer. 'But Maria is not a Jewish name', they would needle. 'She was you know', I would retort.

I recently attended a liberal Jewish community Seder, and although or perhaps because Jewish rituals have never been part of my upbringing, I felt incredulous that these people keep on celebrating the allegorical narrative of a flight from Egypt four millennia ago with bread that had no time to be leavened, while our Holocaust survivor forebears, who were lucky if they got any kind of food at all, get no mention. Nevertheless, as the words of the Haggadah ring in my ears, I feel closer to my devout grandfather Marek, imagining his beautiful Hebrew pronunciation and my father's young voice asking the four questions before being let loose on a boisterous hunt for the *Afikomen*.

What would my grandfather have thought while mouthing the words *L'Shana Haba'ah B'Yerushalayim* (Next Year in Jerusalem) during the annual family Seders of the 1920s and 1930s? If only he had taken these words literally, they would have been safe and sound, all of them. My mother's family would never have gone to Palestine, but they might have managed to defect to the West. I can't help these thoughts: If only, if only. They have always plagued me, but it's a useless way to think. There could have been many, I dare say, happier endings in which my parents would have found different partners, had different descendants, but then I would not have been here to tell their entirely different stories.

Notes

1. Pivnik, S., *Survivor* (London: Hodder Paperbacks, 2013).
2. Frankl, V.E., *Man's Search for Meaning* (Boston: Beacon Press, 2006), originally published 1946.

3. Sereny, G., *Into That Darkness: From Mercy Killing to Mass Murder* (New York: Random House, 1974).
4. Jockusch, L. and Lewinsky, T., 'Paradise Lost? Postwar memory of Polish Jewish Survival in the Soviet Union', *Holocaust and Genocide Studies*, 24, Issue 3, (2010), pp.373-399.
5. Frankl, *Man's Search for Meaning*.
6. Buergenthal, T., *A Lucky Child* (London: Profile Books, 2009).
7. Pankiewicz, T., *The Kraków Ghetto Pharmacy* (Kraków: Wydawnictwo Literackie, 2013). This was first published in Polish in 1947.
8. Spiegelman, A., *Maus I and II* (London: Penguin, 1987).
9. Karpf, A., *The War After* (London: Minerva, 1996).
10. Nelken, H., *And Yet, I am Here* (Amherst: University of Massachusetts Press, 1999).
11. Wiesenthal, S., *The Sunflower: On the Possibilities and Limits of Forgiveness* (New York: Schocken Books, 1998).
12. Bieberstein, A., *Zagłada Żydów w Krakowie* (Kraków: Wydawnictwo Literackie 1985), p.149.
13. Thea Jourdan, 'Arthur Jurand's List', *The Scotsman Magazine*, 26 January 1995.
14. Levi, P., *The Drowned and the Saved* (London: Abacus Books, 1989).
15. Wiesenthal, *The Sunflower*.
16. Thea Jourdan, 'Arthur Jurand's List'.
17. Freyberg, J. 1980. 'Difficulties in separation individuation as experienced by offspring of Nazi Holocaust survivors', *American Journal of Orthopsychiatry* 50 (1980), pp.87-95.
18. Karpf, *The War After*.
19. Hoffman, E., *Lost in Translation* (London: Vintage, 1998).
20. Hoffman, E., *After Such Knowledge* (London: Vintage, 2004).
21. Yehuda, R. *et al*, 'Holocaust exposure induced intergenerational effects', *Biological Psychiatry* 80 (2016), pp.372-380; Kellerman, N.P.F., 'Epigenetic transmission of Holocaust Trauma: Can nightmares be inherited?' *Epigenetic transmission,* (2011), retrieved from: https://peterfelix.tripod.com/home/Epigenetic_TTT2.pdf (accessed 5 August 2021)
22. Abraham, N. and Torok. M., *The Shell and the Kernel* (Chicago: Chicago UP, 1994).
23. Abraham, N. and Torok, M., 'Secrets and Posterity: The Theory of the Transgenerational Phantom' in N. Rand (ed.), *The Shell and the Kernel* (Chicago: University of Chicago Press, 1994), pp.165-171.
24. 'Children of Jewish Holocaust Survivors': retrieved from: https://www.facebook.com/cjhsla/ (accessed 6 August 2021)
25. Wiesel, E., *Night* (New York: Hill and Wang, 1956).
26. Goldberg, R., *Motherland* (London: Peter Halban, 2014).
27. Levy, E., *Just One More Dance* (Edinburgh: Mainstream Publishing, 1998).
28. Benisch, P., *To Vanquish the Dragon* (New York: Feldheim Publishers, 1991).

Appendices

1. My father's witness statement at Amon Göth's trial

Translation of the trial proceedings of Amon Göth, made from the original Polish edition of the trial proceedings: *Proces Ludobójcy Amona Leopolda Goetha* published by Centralna Zydowska Komisja Historyczna (The Central Jewish Historical Committee), 1947, pp.321-327.

27 August - 5 September 1946

Witness: Artur Bieberstein, 32, Master of Pharmacy.

I have been in 11 concentration camps, and I had the opportunity to come up against more than 20 'lagerführers', more than 100 various kinds and calibres of SS officers, NCOs, hundreds and thousands of SS-men, but I have never met such a German, with such murderous instincts, as that in the person of Amon Göth. I have never been a Kapo, or an OD-man. I have never been a block keeper or held any other position that required responsibility for other prisoners. My statements are the statements of a 'grey prisoner', in the most part of a concentration camp worker. I first heard the surname Göth, when he arrived in Kraków in order to take over the leadership of the Płaszów camp. It was in February 1943. I also found out at the time that he used to be in Lublin. In the previous period of time, that is, in the years 1940, 1941 and 1942, I worked for the JSS (Jewish Self-Help Association), which had a branch in Lublin until the end of 1942. From this source, in the middle of 1942, we received detailed information concerning the extermination of Jews in the camp there. We continued to receive information from them until the Jews there were cut off from the outside world in Majdanek, on the outskirts of Lublin (called Majdan Tatarski). The news that Göth was coming to Kraków did not fill us with confidence. The first time I came across the accused indirectly was through Dr Schwarz, who was the director of the radiology unit of the hospital, where I worked from December 1942 to March 1943. This doctor, together with my uncle, attended 2 meetings with the accused. From one of these meetings, he brought a list, entitled *Liste der Häftlingsernährung* (List of food for Detention Prisoners), which included the daily rations. I am not going to go into the matter of daily calorie intake, rather I was concerned about something else. I recall a pivotal psychological moment. We got this list from Dr Schwarz, in order to carry out the calculations, but we were more concerned about the title of the list. Why *Häftlingsernährung*, why should we be prisoners; of what were we guilty?

The first time I saw the accused with my own eyes was on the 13 March 1943, on the day that the rest of the Jews which until that day had survived in the Kraków ghetto were transferred to the Płaszów camp. I saw him at the junction of Węgierski and Limanowski Streets through which everyone had to pass – as the end of these streets were the collection points for the ranks of prisoners. Jews were transferred to the camp in columns. He personally conducted the selections. Whoever he did not like, whoever was too young or too old, whoever walked crookedly, or weakly, would be withdrawn and instructed to go to ghetto B. It was later revealed that this B section was destined for extermination. I personally experienced this selection as I went with my elderly parents, who miraculously passed the selection by Göth, either because he did not notice them or because he let them through.

A fact which I can cite here, which I witnessed with my own eyes, took place in May 1943 on the *Appellplatz* in Płaszów. It was early in the morning, before 6am, that's when we formed into groups so as to leave the camp at 6am to walk into town to work [a distance of about 3 km)]. The day before 2 prisoners had escaped, and the previous night several Ukrainians, reputedly carrying a machine gun from the tower had also escaped. The accused arrived at the *Appellplatz* just at the very moment when they were counting us, and when the kapos were endeavouring to find the passes for individual groups of workers. These passes were given out at a desk on the *Appellplatz*. The accused arrived on the *Appellplatz* and first entered the Ukrainian barracks, where the Ukrainian policemen lived. He stayed there for a short while and then left. He was dressed in his ominous 'rogatywka' hat [this must be the infamous Tyrolean hat mentioned by others]. His appearance in this hat signalled death.

He came, stopped by one group of workers, slowly approached the group in which I stood – this was a column of cleansers. This column went daily to the [by then] empty ghetto in order to segregate the furniture and objects of everyday use. This lasted between March and May. The camp was at the time being actively expanded. The accused approached from the right, I stood at the end in the last four of that column. Although I did not work in the cleansing column, I used to leave the camp with them, probably to save on guard man power. I worked in the ghetto in the JUS [Jewish Aid Centre]. That's when the accused came near from the right of the column, came right to the front of the column and there started to talk with the kapo of the cleansing column, and beat him with a whip asking – these are the accounts of the people who stood near-by, mainly women, because the women stood at the front of the column – 'how long will these trips to the ghetto go on for? I need people to build the camp'. Next, he walked round the column from the left side, missing out the women. At one moment he saw one prisoner and asked him, 'Why are you smiling? Is there something you don't like?' and summoned him by beckoning with his finger. And he started to whip him. The Highest Tribunal may not be familiar with the style that the accused used to beat prisoners. It was an individual, characteristic style that he perfected. He beat, in a different way from anyone else for with every stroke he beat twice once on the left and once on the right side. All the strokes fell on the head. In this way he beat the prisoner more than 50 times. Then he stopped, turned the whip over and used the club-end to beat him only in the face, because the club is short. When the victim started to bleed heavily, which I could see very clearly, because I stood maybe 30 metres from the scene, he put his whip under his arm, took out his revolver and shot the victim in the head from a distance of less than 2 meters. I saw this so accurately that I even saw the bullet scale which sprang out of the pistol, rolling while it fell. Next, he walked two or three steps and summoned another prisoner. Without asking him anything, and without beating him, he shot him. He then walked along the column, nearing our foursome. We stood at the very end. When he came near, I heard clearly what he said. That's how it went: 'If anyone does not like what he sees, maybe they should step forward. I am a fair person. I can talk with him. Please.' Saying this he was approaching our four, at last he stood in front of the left wing. I stood third in line from his side. He asked: 'Maybe you don't like something'. He asked this of my colleague who worked with me at the JUS, who by profession had been a sergeant in the Polish Army, and who found enough will-power not to turn his head to look the accused in the eye. Because that would probably have been sufficient for him too to be shot, and also all of us in our line of four. We stood like we were changed into pillars of salt, so as not to move, so as not to give any reason to be noticed.

From this scene, which I have here described, I got the impression then that the accused was in an inebriated state, or maybe even drunk, because how can you imagine that a man who had just murdered two innocent people can call himself a fair and decent man. It has to be someone who is intoxicated, or Amon Göth! In any case I got the impression that he was somehow intoxicated.

The next few facts come either from accounts from the most reliable sources, or (they were scenes) which I witnessed myself. The first one relates to abuses committed by Göth in the camp. I don't know what sort of abuses they were because I was never in the administration or the camp office, but I know for sure that one day an inspection visit took place in the camp. The inspector with his entourage visited the camp bakery along with the accused. He asked in the bakery how many loaves of bread per week each prisoner receives. At that moment the accused put up two fingers behind the back of the inspector, suggesting the answer to the person who was asking the question. We then only got one loaf of bread per week.

I will also talk about the perfidious murder of 6 people from the office of the camp, as a result of a report by one of the camp officers to the accused that he found one woman prisoner working in the administrative office, with some food. For this 'crime' six people were murdered, and this was done instantaneously without any hearing, without him telling anyone for what and why. The perfidy was further documented by the death two days later of the families of these six people.

Finally there was a personal, direct encounter with the accused, which took place once and ended as you can see happily for me. It took place in 1944 when the Płaszów camp was already a concentration camp. Namely, one day at noon I went – admittedly during work hours – to an unfamiliar bespoke tailoring workshop intending to hand in my jacket for mending. When I was in the workshop I found out from fellow prisoners who worked there that Göth on his horse was on his way to the camp. The Highest Tribunal will surely know what that meant. At that moment prisoners would gladly have hidden in a mouse hole, because everyone wanted to avoid danger. One of the directors of the workshop said to me 'please leave, Göth is on his way'. At that point I could have sat down and pretended to sew, but I realised that the bespoke tailoring workshop would have been one of the favourite places of the accused, and he might know the staff personally. I therefore decided to leave. It turned out that indeed the accused got there on his white horse, rode round the workshop, and at the very moment when I was leaving I met him vis-à-vis, on his horse. He stopped the horse, beckoned to me with his finger and asked *was macht du denn hier?* (What are you doing here?) I had no answer; in fact, I said that I was visiting a relative, though this was untrue, because I had no relatives there. *Komm näher* he said (come closer). I stood near him. My eyes were level with his boots. He took out his whip. It will be just like the cleansing column, I thought, as I felt the first strike. I think I was beaten several dozen times, I did not count them. Affected by the beating I involuntarily moved back. 'Come nearer, I say' he said, and then another series of lashes. At last, I look up to see him putting the whip away in his boot and he says, 'now run, because I will shoot you like a dog'. During this period [as it was now a concentration camp], he would have been warned not to shoot without a hearing. Subconsciously, I counted on this. However, I am one of the few whom Göth beat, but did not shoot. As a result of these beatings, I had cuts and wounds on my shoulders, on my head and under my eyes. Nevertheless, as I said, it all finished well.

Defense Counsel Pokorny: When the incident with the cleansing column took place, do you by any chance remember the names of the two victims who were shot?

Witness: Yes, if I remember rightly they were Spielmann and Sonnanscheln.

The Accused: The witness said about the incident in the cleansing column and claimed that it took place after the night when the Ukrainian branch deserted with the machine gun.

Witness: Yes.

Accused: If the Highest Tribunal has at its disposal police reports, it would be easy to convince them that that night there was a great skirmish. I chased these deserters to the area of Kielce and was absent from camp for 4 days.

Witness: It is possible that it was not after that very night, and that the incident happened after the return of the accused from his trip.

2. Table of Chemist Commando prisoners

I am supplying this table of chemists about whom information is available in case someone, maybe a Master's Student, might take up the challenge of researching the role of prisoner chemists under Nazi rule.

Name	Information	Source of information
Dr Louis Broder	This witness was part of the group of chemists who with my father was deported to Flossenbürg, and then sent back to Płaszów. In Płaszów he (and presumably my father too) worked in the Berg-und Hüttenacademie (*Akademia Górniczo-Hutnicza* – which I passed daily on my way to school) but lived in the camp. When Płaszów was evacuated on 14 January 1945, they were sent on foot to Auschwitz. Broder escaped from the transport between Auschwitz and Gleiwitz. My father never mentioned him.	'Plaszow KL/KZ "Schindler's List" Part 3' retrieved from: http://dachaukz.blogspot.com/2012/08/plaszow-klkz-schindlers-list-part-3.html (accessed 16 August 2021)
Felek Orenstein	He went to Flossenbürg at the same time as my father but was not sent back to Płaszów. He told his brother that he had been engaged on a project to invent an immobilising gas for motorised vehicles. He died in the last few days before liberation.	Orenstein, H., *I Shall Live: Surviving Against All Odds 1939-1945* (New York: Beaufort Books, 1987).
Sam Orenstein	Survived the war.	Orenstein, H., *I Shall Live: Surviving Against All Odds 1939-1945* (New York: Beaufort Books, 1987)
Fred Orenstein	Doctor, survived the war and emigrated to the US.	Orenstein, H., *I Shall Live: Surviving Against All Odds 1939-1945* (New York: Beaufort Books, 1987)
Heniek Orenstein	Became a famous toy manufacturer (he invented Transformers) in the US, and a multi-millionaire.	Orenstein, H., *I Shall Live: Surviving Against All Odds 1939-1945* (New York: Beaufort Books, 1987)
Bernard Arończyk	Settled in Canada. Was a successful industrial chemist. He sent us a	Various letters from my father to Bernard Arończyk

	generous gift of £50 in 1958 (a lot in those days), which my father used to buy me some new clothes.	
Julek Hofman (Wysocki)	Settled as a chemist in France; his one-time address was 15 Rue Cordier, St Rambert, l'ille Barbe, Rhone. He died a few weeks after my father.	My father's letter to Bernard Arończyk 19 December 1958
Leszek (Lolek) Hupert	Deported to Flossenbürg, and from there back to Płaszów, 'from where I had to walk on foot to Auschwitz, and within a few days to Gleiwitz – where there was a rigorous segregation'. He escaped from Gleiwitz. After the war he settled in Offenbach (near Frankfurt). He worked as a chemist manufacturing synthetic resin, then set up a PVC plastics company, which produced napkins, collars and other articles.	Letter from Leszek to Bernard Arończyk 26 May 1963
Adam Folman	Survived and lived in Tel Aviv	My father's letter to Bernard Arończyk 12 January 1988
Abram Finkelstein	Survived to hold a diplomatic post in Sweden.	My father's letter to Bernard Arończyk 19 December 1958

Index

Lightning Source UK Ltd.
Milton Keynes UK
UKHW021420110522
402821UK00002B/2

9 781803 710143